THE
VICTORIAN
HOME

*A Dinner Party at Haddo, 1884, with Mr. Gladstone
on the Hostess's (The Marchioness of Aberdeen's) right
and the Earl of Rosebery on her left*

Detail of a painting by A. E. Emslie

The Victorian Home

SOME ASPECTS OF NINETEENTH-CENTURY TASTE AND MANNERS

By

Ralph Dutton

LONDON
B. T. BATSFORD LTD.

First Published 1954

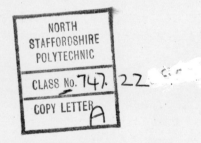
MADE AND PRINTED IN GREAT BRITAIN BY
WILLIAM CLOWES AND SONS LTD, LONDON AND BECCLES
FOR THE PUBLISHERS
B. T. BATSFORD, LTD.
4 FITZHARDINGE STREET, LONDON, W.1.

CONTENTS

		Page
THE ILLUSTRATIONS		vii
INTRODUCTION		1

Chapter

I	EIGHTEENTH-CENTURY TWILIGHT: 1837–1840	12
II	AN AGE OF CONTRASTS: 1840–1850	33
III	GOTHIC TRIUMPHANT: 1850–1860	59
IV	MATERIAL PROGRESS: 1860–1870	91
V	COMMERCE ENTERS SOCIETY: 1870–1880	118
VI	EMANCIPATION AND CULTURE: 1880–1890	146
VII	THE END OF AN EPOCH: 1890–1901	173
INDEX		201

THE ILLUSTRATIONS

Page

A DINNER PARTY AT HADDO. *From a painting by A. E. Emslie: The National Portrait Gallery*   *Frontispiece*

ENDSLEIGH COTTAGE, DEVONSHIRE. *From "Devonshire and Cornwall Illustrated", 1832*   2

"THE TOILET". *From "Beeton's Housewife's Treasury"*   5

PRIE-DIEU CHAIR AND WHAT-NOT. *From "Beeton's Housewife's Treasury"*   7

LIBRARY TABLE. *From "The Art Journal Catalogue of the Industry of All Nations" (Great Exhibition), 1851*   8

A VASE OF WAX FLOWERS. *From "The Art Journal Catalogue of the Industry of All Nations" (Great Exhibition), 1851*   11

"A SWISS COTTAGE AS AN INDEPENDENT LODGE". *From J. C. Loudon, "An Encyclopaedia of Cottage, Farm and Villa Architecture", 1835*   12

BELGRAVIA. *From Richard Doyle, "Bird's-eye Views of Modern Society", 1864*   16

SCOTNEY CASTLE, KENT. *From C. L. Eastlake, "The Gothic Revival", 1872*   19

"FANCY CHAIRS FOR DRAWING-ROOMS". *From Loudon, "Encyclopaedia . . .", 1835*   23

"A COTTAGE LODGE IN THE OLD ENGLISH STYLE". *From Loudon, "Encyclopaedia . . .", 1835*   32

"A DOUBLE LODGE IN THE DORIC STYLE". *From Loudon, "Encyclopaedia . . .", 1835*   33

"A GENTLEMAN'S RESIDENCE IN THE COTTAGE STYLE". *From P. F. Robinson, "Rural Architecture", 1826*   38

"A DESIGN IN THE ELIZABETHAN STYLE". *From S. H. Brooks, "Designs for Cottage and Villa Architecture", 1839*   39

VILLA "IN THE IONIC STYLE". *From Brooks, "Designs . . .", 1839*   40

THE SERVANTS AT LACOCK ABBEY. *Victoria and Albert Museum. Photograph: W. H. Fox Talbot*   41

A MID-CENTURY CONVERSATION PIECE. *From a painting: Messrs. R. Frank*   43

"A CHIMNEY-PIECE IN THE STYLE OF LOUIS XIV". *From Loudon, "Encyclopaedia . . .", 1835*   45

THOMAS AND JANE CARLYLE IN THEIR DRAWING-ROOM. *From a painting by Robert Tait: The Marquess of Northampton*   46

"CONVENTIONAL MEDIÆVAL GASELIER". *From "Beeton's Housewife's Treasury"*   47

"GOTHIC CORONA LUCIS". *From "Beeton's Housewife's Treasury"*   48

CONSERVATORY AT ALTON TOWERS. *From Loudon, "Encyclopaedia . . .", 1835*   49

A GARDEN FOUNTAIN. *From Loudon, "Encyclopaedia . . .", 1835*   51

vii

THE ILLUSTRATIONS

THE ROYAL RAILWAY CARRIAGE. *From "The Illustrated London News",* 1849   54

CAST-IRON DOOR PORTER. *From The James Foundry Co.'s Catalogue*   58

"BERLIN BLACK INKSTAND". *From the James Foundry Co.'s Catalogue*   59

CAST-IRON UMBRELLA STAND. *From The James Foundry Co.'s Catalogue*   60

"FOR SALE". *From the painting by James Collinson: Messrs. M. Bernard*   61

VISITING THE GREAT EXHIBITION. *From a painting. Photograph: Messrs. A. C. Cooper Ltd.*   64

SOCIABLE SEAT. *From "The Art Journal Catalogue . . .",* 1851   65

"WANSTEAD SOFA". *From "The Art Journal Catalogue . . .",* 1851   66

A GROUP OF ECCLESIASTICAL OBJECTS. *From "The Art Journal Catalogue . . .",* 1851   67

THE GLASS FOUNTAIN AT THE GREAT EXHIBITION. *From "The Art Journal Catalogue . . .",* 1851   68

A CABINET OF OAK. *From "The Art Journal Catalogue . . .",* 1851   69

PRINCE ALBERT'S MODEL DWELLINGS. *From a contemporary engraving*   70

THE PRINCE CONSORT IN "HIS" STUDY. *From a painting: Messrs. Cavendish Hood & Co.*   71

FAMILY PRAYERS. *From a painting by Samuel Butler: St. John's College, Cambridge*   73

"CHILDREN AT PLAY". *From a painting by W. M. Egley. Collection: Mrs. William King*   75

"DESIGN FOR A VILLA—ENGLISH DOMESTIC GOTHIC". *From E. L. Blackburne, "Suburban and Rural Architecture . . ." (no date)*   79

ORCHARDLEIGH PARK, SOMERSET. *From Eastlake, "The Gothic Revival",* 1872   80

QUAR WOOD, GLOUCESTERSHIRE. *From Eastlake, "The Gothic Revival",* 1872   81

A "COMIC" PHOTOGRAPH OF 1855. *"Picture Post" Library*   84

"THROUGH THE LOOKING GLASS". *From the illustration by Sir John Tenniel,* 1872   85

PRINCESS BEATRICE'S SITTING-ROOM AT OSBORNE. *"Picture Post" Library*   86

OSBORNE: THE DRAWING-ROOM. *Gernsheim Collection*   87

GRAND SALOON OF THE STEAMSHIP *Atlantic. From "The Illustrated London News",* 1850   89

CHANDELIER FOR A SUMMER-HOUSE. *From "The Art Journal Catalogue . . .",* 1851   90

A HOUSE IN THE "COTTAGE STYLE". *From Robert Kerr, "The Gentleman's House",* 1865   91

BALMORAL: THE QUEEN'S DRESSING-ROOM. *Gernsheim Collection*   92

BALMORAL: THE PRINCE CONSORT'S SITTING-ROOM. *"Picture Post" Library*   93

BALMORAL: THE QUEEN'S BEDROOM. *Gernsheim Collection*   94

MORRIS'S OAK SETTLE. *Photograph: "Country Life"*   97

CLOVERLEY HALL, SHROPSHIRE. *From Eastlake, "The Gothic Revival",* 1872   100

THE ILLUSTRATIONS

KNIGHTSHAYES COURT, DEVONSHIRE. *From Eastlake, "The Gothic Revival", 1872*   101

WILLIAM BURGES'S HOUSE. *From Maurice B. Adams, "Artists' Houses", 1873*   102

RESIDENCE AT MOORLAND NEAR YORK. *From G. A. Dean, "Selected Designs for Country Residences ...", 1867*   107

A FAMILY GROUP OF THE LATE 'SIXTIES. *Photograph: Author's Collection*   111

"ENGAGING THE NEW PAGE". *Gernsheim Collection*   113

A CONVERSATION PIECE OF THE 'SIXTIES. *"Picture Post" Library*   114

"PARIS FASHIONS FOR MARCH". *From "The Illustrated London News", 1869*   115

A "SCENT FOUNTAIN". *From "The Art Journal Catalogue ...", 1851*   117

"A STATE PARTY". *From Doyle, "Bird's-Eye Views ...", 1864*   118

"AN IMP OF MISCHIEF". *From a painting by C. Hunt. Collection: Mrs. F. L. Evans*   126

EATON HALL: THE ANTE-DRAWING-ROOM. *Photograph: the Author's Collection*   127

"DINING-ROOM SIDEBOARD". *From C. L. Eastlake, "Hints on Household Taste", 1878*   129

"IRON BEDSTEAD WITH CANOPY". *From Eastlake, " ... Household Taste", 1878*   130

A CAMBRIDGE UNDERGRADUATE'S ROOM. *Photograph: the Author's Collection*   131

ARRANGEMENT OF A ROOM, BY LEWIS F. DAY. *From "The Magazine of Art", 1881*   132

"THE DINING-ROOM". *From "Beeton's Housewife's Treasury"*   134

AN OXFORD UNDERGRADUATE'S ROOM. *Gernsheim Collection*   135

LAWN-TENNIS PLAYERS. *From "Punch", 1878*   139

THE PICNIC. *From a painting by Richard Doyle*   140

49, PRINCE'S GATE, LONDON. *From a contemporary photograph*   143

BASKET FOR REELS OF SILK. *From "Beeton's Housewife's Treasury"*   145

A DIAPER OF DAISIES, BY LEWIS F. DAY. *From Lewis F. Day, "Everyday Art", 1882*   146

"AN ESCRITOIRE, A CHAIR AND A SIDE-BOARD". *From R. W. Edis, "Decoration and Furniture of Town Houses", 1881*   149

"OCTAGON BOUDOIR: ADAMS STYLE". *From Edis, "Decoration and Furniture ...", 1881*   152

"A DINING-ROOM CHIMNEY-PIECE". *From Edis, "Decoration and Furniture ...", 1881*   154

MIDDLE-CLASS COTTAGE RESIDENCES. *From R. Norman Shaw, "Sketches for Cottages and Other Buildings", 1878*   156

IN BEDFORD PARK. *From a lithograph in "Bedford Park", 1882, by H. M. Paget*   157

OLD SWAN HOUSE, CHELSEA. *From Hermann Muthesius, "Die Englische Baukunst der Gegenwart", 1900*   159

MARCUS STONE IN HIS STUDIO. *"Picture Post" Library*   160

"THE DRAWING-ROOM AND CONSERVATORY". *From an illustration by Randolph Caldecott in "The Graphic", 1883*   161

THE ILLUSTRATIONS

EDWIN LONG'S HOUSE IN HAMPSTEAD. *From Adams, "Artists' Houses",*
1883   163

"MR. ALMA TADEMA'S DRAWING-ROOM". *From "The Magazine of
Art",* 1882   164

IN A PARK. *From a painting by Val Prinsep: The City Museum and Art
Gallery, Birmingham*   166

AESTHETES OF 1880. *From an engraving after George Du Maurier in
"Punch",* 1880   171

CAST-IRON DOOR PORTER. *From The James Foundry Co.'s Catalogue*   172

COLLEGE TUTOR'S HOUSE, OXFORD. *From H. Heathcote Statham,
"Modern Architecture",* 1897   173

A BEDROOM OF 1892. *From E. Knight, "Taste and Economy in Furniture
and Decoration",* 1893   177

CYCLISTS OF 1896. *From "The Graphic",* 1896   178

"A FASHIONABLE PASTIME: THE MORNING RIDE IN HYDE PARK".
From "The Graphic", 1896   180

"THE EVENING PARADE OF AUTO-CARS". *From "The Graphic",* 1896   182

A SMALL COUNTRY RECTORY. *From C. J. Richardson, "The Englishman's
House",* 1898   184

"AN END VIEW OF A MORNING-ROOM". *From Mrs. J. E. Panton, "A
Gentlewoman's Home",* 1896   185

"A CORNER OF A DRAWING-ROOM". *From Mrs. J. E. Panton, "A Gentlewoman's Home",* 1896   186

"THE CORNER OF A COSY SITTING-ROOM". *From Mrs. Waldemar Leverton, "Small Homes and How to Furnish Them",* 1903   187

LILY LANGTRY'S BEDROOM. *"Picture Post" Library*   188

A DRAWING-ROOM OF THE 'NINETIES. *"Picture Post" Library*   189

"AN IDEA FOR A BEDROOM". *From Mrs. C. S. Peel, "The New Home",*
1898   190

"MODERN DINING-ROOM PANELLED WITH PLAIN OAK", BY C. F.
A. VOYSEY. *From "The British Home of To-day", ed. W. Shaw Sparrow,*
1904   196

"CORNER OF A MODERN BEDROOM", BY GEORGE WALTON. *From
"The British Home of To-day",* 1904   197

THE DRAWING-ROOM OF C. R. MACKINTOSH'S HOUSE IN GLASGOW.
*From Dr. Thomas Howarth, "Charles Rennie Mackintosh and the Modern
Movement",* 1952   198

The Authors and Publishers are most grateful to the owners of paintings and photographs mentioned above for permitting their reproduction in this book. In addition,
they would like to thank Lord Stanmore for allowing his painting, An Early
Victorian Interior by P. C. Wonder, to be reproduced on the jacket, and Lady Pentland for loaning the colour blocks of the Frontispiece, which was originally illustrated
in *A Bonnie Fechter,* 1952, her biography of her mother, the Countess of Aberdeen.
The author would also like to record his gratitude to Mr. Francis Needham for his
great kindness in checking the proofs.

INTRODUCTION

THERE has been no epoch in English history when the home played a more important rôle in the life of the country than during the Victorian era. The family circle and the home which contained it were the corner-stone of the structure of society, and the community were at one in bolstering up the system and in allowing no crack or flaw in the fabric of their lives to appear to the outer world. However despicable a character the paterfamilias might be, however evident his shortcomings to his wife and children, the family would unite before the world to adulate dear papa and to present him publicly as a noble, Olympian figure. There was a strong sense of family patriotism, not fully shared by the rather disillusioned generations living before and after this period.

Just as it was essential to have an imposing figure-head, so it was also important to live in a house of a size which enhanced the status of the family. In the eighteenth century the very rich had vied with each other in building vast palaces, and now in the following century the same principle, reduced to appropriate proportions, had descended the social scale to those of more modest means. Thus all, from the moderately rich landowner to the man who had made a large fortune in commerce, would expand their dwellings to the furthest limits of their incomes. For in the nineteenth century social position depended more on the size of a man's house than on any other factor; and since it was an age of blatant snobbery when wealth, at least during the later years of the century, was as acceptable as blue blood, the home and all that pertained to it took on a special significance.

In the first years of the century a man and his family could be content and socially well placed in a stucco villa of chaste Grecian aspect. The house might be quite small, but its elegance would compensate for any lack of size. A decade or two later they could live in a *cottage orné* and still not expect to be snubbed by the county families of the neighbourhood. After all, did not the Duke of Bedford condescend to live occasionally in his glorified cottage at Endsleigh in Devon? As the Victorian era advanced, however, it became socially essential to live in more substantial surroundings. Grecian elegance was anyhow out of fashion, and a wistaria-clad cottage was thought to savour a little of the serf.

Size, then, was the first requirement for the Victorian home, and with this went the necessity for a handsome drawing-room and

1

Endsleigh Cottage, Devonshire (c. 1812). Sir Jeffry Wyatville, Architect

dining-room in which to receive the afternoon calls of neighbours and to hold an occasional reception. Beyond the confines of the reception rooms the standard of furnishing could decline, and this was often found in upper middle-class houses: great trouble would be taken in buying or building a house as large as, or a little larger than, means would allow, the drawing-room would be filled in random style with furniture and bric-à-brac so as to produce a lavish, luxurious air, and the remainder of the house would be left largely to chance.

But apart from the question of size and importance, mid-Victorians were not greatly interested in the appearance of their domestic surroundings. That a man of that period should hold any decided opinions about decoration or furniture was considered almost improper, and with women it was not looked on as a particularly commendable quality. In the eighteenth century it was generally the owner who at great trouble and expense embellished his house with splendour, while the wife accepted what her lord and master had provided with little criticism. It was a subject beyond the mental capacity of a woman. Before the middle of the nineteenth century

2

this position was entirely reversed, and it was the wives who bought the furniture and chose the curtains and carpets. Could this be one reason for the decay of taste?

In any case the decoration of the home was, like the mention of money or food, not a general subject for conversation except in the form of a passing compliment; and there was none of that exchange of ideas by both sexes on this subject which is such a promising feature of the present day. As the century advanced this reticence died away, as is evidenced by the number of books published to assist the anxious housewife in making her house attractive and fashionable. "Artistic homes" and "the home beautiful" were phrases freely bandied about as the 'eighties passed into the 'nineties.

As early as 1865 Kerr had produced his comprehensive work entitled *The English Gentleman's House*, but it dwelt rather on planning and general arrangement than on decoration. Charles Eastlake's *Hints on Household Taste* of a decade later embarked boldly on the shifting sands of decorative fashions. On furniture, wall coverings, materials for curtains and carpets he was happy to advise, and even entered into such details as table glass and bedroom china. In the early 'eighties appeared *Beeton's Housewife's Treasury*, a massive compilation from various contributors which was designed as a companion to *Mrs. Beeton's Book of Household Management*. The introduction to the former optimistically states that the fortunate and prudent possessors of these two works will "have a library by whose aid everything will go well, and family life be happier and more prosperous every day".

Possibly the *Housewife's Treasury* failed fully to achieve the bold purpose for which it was designed, though it contained much sensible advice; but in any case during the 'nineties a spate of authors rushed in to sustain the good work. Robert Edis, Mrs. Panton, Mrs. Peel were a few of those who provided the latest news on taste and decoration, and the flood of books was to increase after the turn of the century.

These works are naturally extremely revealing, not only about the swiftly changing vogues, but also about the modifications in the way of life. Although Kerr's book claimed to throw light on houses ranging in importance from "the parsonage to the palace" it was the upper section of the range which came in for the greater part of attention. Thirty years later a social change had clearly come over the scene, and it was principally the houses of a moderate size for which advice was given. This did not indicate that there were fewer large houses in commission—far from it, for huge country houses were being built all through this period—but rather that there were families living in small houses who took an interest in their homes and were anxious to make them attractive.

3

This surge of enthusiasm, though some of it may seem to us rather ill directed, was an exceedingly healthy sign. The torpor on this subject which was manifest in the average home during the 'forties and 'fifties had lifted, and a more critical spirit was abroad. No longer were people convinced that their possessions and the decoration of their rooms must be beautiful merely because they were their own: they now viewed them with less partial eyes, and took trouble to present an agreeable effect. Illustrations and photographs of these rooms, created with much thought and advice, do not seem to us to have been very successful; but, equally, could anyone from the 'nineties be shown the rooms of today, without passing through the experience of fifty years, they would no doubt think them barren and cheerless.

The problem of changing taste has never been satisfactorily solved, and there is no pretence that the following pages supply the elusive key. There seems no alternative to accepting that the standards of taste change like the seasons. The high summer of the eighteenth century passed into gentle autumn during the first decades of the next century and was followed by an early and rigorous winter which lasted, with an occasional interlude which falsely promised the coming of spring, for the greater part of Queen Victoria's reign.

The dark days did not materially brighten until towards the end of the century; but how singularly dull it would be if taste remained at a constant elevated standard, like an endless, unvarying tropical summer. For even during the sombre winter months there is much to charm and to interest, though the pleasant incidents are less obvious. So it was during the Victorian era; and it is necessary to search carefully amidst much that offends and dazes to find the scattered features which are rewarding.

Although beauty can be found only after close sifting, the interest of the period is immense, and thus it must be accepted that the charms of the Victorian age are mental rather than visual. The interest is becoming ever more apparent as we withdraw from it, and no longer can the whole era be written off as one of miasmal taste, and be left at that. It is far too complex, too full of impulses—often contradictory—thrusting this way and that, but generally inspired by the highest artistic principles.

Architecture and furniture are perhaps the two arts by which we now judge the Victorian home: decoration was a less permanent, a more superficial affair, which could be altered to a mood, and so was primarily the product of individual feeling. And yet, taking a general view, the basic principles of decoration moved majestically forward through the decades in a similar way to the other visual arts.

4

"*The Toilet*". As illustrated in *Beeton's Housewife's Treasury*

Scholarship, integrity, craftsmanship were tenets to which the fore-most designers earnestly subscribed, and none can doubt the sincerity of their intentions and feelings; but there was also the vast quantity of productions made for the popular market in which this high moral tone was entirely lacking. This became particularly pronounced when new processes and inventions, appearing about the middle of the century, made the manufacture of machine-made goods both easy and cheap.

Domestic architecture, for it is only this aspect of the art with which we are here concerned, was on the whole more formidable in design than the contemporary furniture which accompanied it. There are few people nowadays who would deliberately choose to inhabit a house built in what may be called the rectory style of the middle decades of the century, the style of which Waterhouse was the outstanding exponent, though he was usually employed on buildings of far greater size and magnificence than humble parsonages. And yet contemporary houses designed in the bleak classical style then favoured, and found in great numbers in the new quarters of London such as Bayswater, South Kensington and Pimlico, have distinct merits, though beauty is not amongst them. Solid, spacious and well windowed, there are many people who prefer to live in flats made in these tall, gaunt structures than in the pinched and complicated surroundings of a steel and concrete block.

Many Victorian London houses have been given a new career by conversion into flats, but the country houses of the same age have fared less well. Whether designed in the Gothic or the classical style there are now few of these huge, ambitious houses, raised with such gusto during the century, which still serve the purpose for which they were created. A few, a very few, continue as private houses, where the owner has sufficient sentimental attachment for the place to maintain the struggle for existence, in spite of the domestic difficulties and inconveniences which mid-Victorian architects usually provided; some serve as institutions, to which their robust construction is well suited; others remain empty awaiting the hand of decay to obliterate them from the earth.

The singularly unsuccessful careers of these houses is not of course entirely the fault of their architecture: the change in economic conditions has also taken a dominant part in the eclipse of Victorian country houses, as it has, but to a lesser degree, in those of earlier periods. But whereas Georgian buildings are often well adapted to conversion or reduction, nineteenth-century houses, with their complex planning and style, usually defy any attempt at modification. They bear the resolute, uncompromising character which we also detect in the stalwart personalities for whom they were generally

6

"Modern Prie-dieu Chair" and "Louis XV What-not"

designed. The same cause has excluded much of the best Victorian furniture from the average home of today; for the finest examples were apt to be also the largest, and those cubic feet of well-seasoned oak are not easily accommodated in houses of the size to which we are now accustomed. Where it still exists in large houses, this type of furniture has usually spent many years of banishment in unused servants' halls or lumber-rooms, where it awaits a similar glorious resurrection to that which took place fifty or sixty years ago, when the finest work of eighteenth-century cabinet-makers was discovered in attics and cellars, and was brought to places of honour in drawing-rooms and dining-rooms.

It seems probable that the majority of nineteenth-century objects will await this trump in vain, for it is the furniture of the strongest character which is now the least popular. On the other hand the conventional objects, those in fact against which the foremost designers and craftsmen were reacting so strongly, find considerable favour today. The vast mahogany sideboards now give an air of dignified welcome to hotel dining-rooms, solid occasional tables make adequate dinner tables for present-day houses; pretty, if generally rather ill-constructed, papier mâché what-nots, which must have

7

been anathema to William Morris and his school, are prized ornaments in many sitting-rooms; while bedrooms furnished with Victorian mahogany have that pleasant air of peace and security with which we now endow the whole of that varied age.

The fault of so much Victorian furniture, which was designed by craftsmen of standing, was that it was unduly forceful: it seems to have been fabricated with the express purpose, not of fitting into but of dominating a room. There is a lack of sensibility about it, as there was about most of the visual arts of the period. This was clearly exemplified in the exhibition of Victorian furniture held in the Victoria and Albert Museum during the winter of 1952. Almost everything at first sight seemed bold, crude and assertive. Furniture and other objects were slightly above life-size, and seemed determined to proclaim the excellence of their materials and craftsmanship. Every point was ruthlessly hammered home; and the beholder, little accustomed to these offensive tactics from furniture, felt stunned and oppressed. The works of the Pre-Raphaelite school provided a distinctly soothing note. The furniture produced by Morris and Company is less formidable than that of Pugin, while the needlework, tapestries and textiles of the school have charm as long as flowers and foliage, and not the human figure, provide the principal theme.

In the following pages I have endeavoured to trace the course through the reign of Queen Victoria of the various styles, tastes, fashions, vogues, whatever one may call them, as they affected the average home of the day; and with a description of the decorative arts I have included incidents which had a bearing on domestic life. At first sight there may seem little reason for including in a modest survey of this sort apparently unconnected facts such as drawing-room wall-papers, farm labourers' wages and the emancipation of women. But all these, and many other phases and events, were factors in the fabric of the average home and in the lives of average people. Labourers' wages may not have directly affected a family living in

Library Table (1851). Exhibited by Messrs. Gillow

London or in one of the big cities; but it was a point of importance to their country cousins, and in any case had repercussions far beyond the tumble-down cottages where the rise or fall was primarily felt.

It has been necessary to be selective in choosing matter for remark, and numerous features of the life of the period have had to be omitted. Many sources have been drawn upon in an endeavour to portray the multitudinous facets of domestic life of the period, and facts have been gathered from reference books, memoirs, illustrated papers and so forth, but not from contemporary fiction. A line had somewhere to be drawn, and it seemed on the whole better to elim- inate fiction as a source for facts. Probably, if the reverse plan had been adopted, the resultant overall picture would not have been very different. The architectural side has been stressed more than any other, but this, as it formed the background to the lives of every family, though many may not have been particularly conscious of it, seems an aspect of primary importance.

There is always an inclination to look back at a period less than a century away with a slightly patronizing air, the air of someone who has outgrown the rather childish manners and pleasures of a benighted age; also it is irresistible sometimes to poke a little fun at anything which seems, after a lapse of time, to have been particularly absurd. We shall naturally suffer the same fate from writers in the twenty-first century, and it is more than probable that they will see much that is absurd in the life of the middle decades of this century and little which is commendable.

As an illustration of this attitude to the immediate past one thinks of Lady Charlotte Schreiber, a highly intelligent woman, writing in her journal in 1876 that she had been "studiously reading" four of Miss Austen's novels. She was not enthusiastic, but added graciously: "For the epoch at which they appeared, some sixty years ago, they are very remarkable". It is impossible to say exactly what she had in mind when writing this phrase, but it would seem that she was voicing the view that the period two generations before her time was one of little cultivation, and one when both taste and artistic accom- plishments were not of a very high order.

This, it must be admitted, is the view generally held today of the long period when Queen Victoria was on the throne. A darkness seems to hang over England during some of these decades. The rooms of the average family, with their heavily curtained windows and sombre crowded furniture, one visualizes as constantly in twilight, and the sun seems to have shone less brilliantly than it did during the eighteenth century. One has a feeling of hushed voices, of laughter sternly repressed, and thoughts and actions directed austerely

towards what was right, and away from what was gay and amusing. There was inevitably much hypocrisy, for human nature and human impulses must have been as wayward and uncontrollable then, beneath the veneer, as they have always been. Who, for example, could have borne an air of more terrifying rectitude than the majority of Victorian murderers and their female assistants?

The picture one now has of sublime respectability is doubtless an exaggeration, but it is one which the mid-Victorians united in creating. It was not only the great middle classes who produced an effect which excelled the truth. One might suppose, for example, that the Pre-Raphaelite Brotherhood were a melancholy band of bearded misogynists, whose lives were seldom warmed by mundane pleasures. The truth was far different: at least during their early years. Many of their tragic and emotional pictures were painted against a background of robust high spirits, practical jokes and terrible puns. The aesthetic movement of the 'eighties demanded that its supporters should appear cerebral and defeatist in their attitude towards life, but here again the part was rather overplayed, and they were certainly not as invertebrate and disconsolate as the caricaturists would have us believe.

We have, then, on the one hand the somewhat repressive atmosphere of the prosaic middle-class home, and on the other the pseudo-melancholy of the artistic section of the community. Both were in some measure the outcome of the great wave of commercial prosperity which touched the lives of many people. The former class felt it reprehensible to give way too freely to the pleasures which were for the first time available to them; the latter were impelled to revolt against the atmosphere of materialism which was widespread. Both perhaps wished to blind themselves to the unhealthy squalor which was rampant in the poorer parts of London during the greater part of the era. Outbreaks of typhoid and cholera swept through overcrowded slum dwellings, drunkenness and under-nourishment went hand in hand, and the lives of many feckless members of the ever-increasing working classes were as miserable and contaminated in the middle years of the century as they had been at the time of the Great Plague. The brightest feature of many of these lives was their brevity. Improvement, however, was at hand and some of the measures directed towards ameliorating the living conditions of the poor are described in the following pages.

The Victorian approach to life, as we now use the adjective, faded away before the Jubilee of 1887, and a new spirit awakened, which was to lead to the drastic changes in the social structure accomplished during this century. In the up-to-date Victorian house fumed oak and pitch-pine were cast out and replaced by hygienic white paint, and this new lightness in the home was evidence of a general lifting of the fog-impregnated atmosphere, and of the revival of a fresher and more tolerant mental outlook.

The merits of the many-sided Victorian era have not yet fallen into their proper perspective, and will not do so for many decades to come. It is probable that those living at the end of this century will view it in a very different light to that in which we do today, and what that light will be it is impossible to foretell. A survey such as this, then, must be looked on as no more than an interim report; but though aiming only at this limited objective an attempt has been made to present fairly the various elements, both good and bad, which affected the domestic scene.

A vase of wax flowers

"A Swiss Cottage as an Independent Lodge" (c. 1835)

CHAPTER I

EIGHTEENTH-CENTURY TWILIGHT

1837—1840

WE look back at the eighteenth century as at a panorama of all that was finest in the visual arts of this country. In architecture, in decoration, in painting, in the designing of furniture, in the moulding of landscapes; indeed in all that contributed to the pleasure and grace of living, the century seems to stand out as an era of consummate achievement. The whole of the hundred years seems bathed in golden sunlight, while the nineteenth century, like that part of the globe turned away from the sun, is overcast by a sombre grey shadow. But in the same way that the globe turns and the light gradually passes across the world's surface, so the taste of the nineteenth century is emerging from the darkness in which it has rested for the past half-century, and salient features are beginning to stand out. Not yet does the whole period seem suffused with an equal, approbatory radiance, but this may come, though only to those who can appreciate the arts as manifested during the reign of Queen Victoria without considering them against the standards of the eighteenth century. There must be no backward glances: the slate of preconceived taste must be wiped clean, and Victorian art must be judged solely on its own intrinsic merits.

The violent alterations in taste which have taken place throughout history make it clear that standards are largely ephemeral: there is not only the individual, to whom that which gives pleasure to the eye may vary as much as that which gives pleasure to the palate: but there is also the overwhelming influence of fashion. It is given to few to lead fashion; few for example can achieve the position of Horace Walpole who, owing to his unusual interest in, but not profound knowledge of, mediaeval art, was largely responsible for the Gothic wave which engulfed the architecture, and to some degree the kindred arts, in England for the greater part of a century. All *cognoscenti* and collectors would like to believe themselves in a similar position to Mr. Walpole, at the head of a fashion; but how constantly and how cruelly it is brought home to them that they are panting expensively behind it.

Taste, then, it must be conceded, can only be appraised through eyes at least partially obscured by contemporary fashion. Thus in the biased view of the middle years of the twentieth century it would seem that the graph of taste during the eighteenth century followed a wide, even curve. Starting high, it progressed gently upwards, the smoothness of the arc being disturbed here and there by some of the extreme extravagances of Vanbrugh, Hawksmoor and their school, until the middle of the century when, with the introduction of Strawberry Hill Gothic and several exotic styles, the level begins to drop a little. Taking a maximum of ten, one might say the line began at just over seven, reached eight or nine, and passed out into the nineteenth century at a little over six. The graph for this period, therefore, presents a convex form; during the nineteenth century it is distinctly concave and ends the era at a point lower than that at which it began. The first thirty years are fairly level, showing no more than a slight decline; during the next ten years the drop is more marked, and reaches the mathematical mean. It then plunges downward, drawn on the lavish and elaborate taste of the Great Exhibition, makes a hesitant turn upwards on the support of William Morris and his associates, and keeps fitfully in this direction until the end of the century. The further tendency of the graph of taste we need not here pursue: indeed though we have already passed the meridian of the twentieth century it would be difficult to say in what direction the line is moving.

This is a highly simplified picture, but the interesting feature emerges of the comparatively constant level of taste during the first three decades of the nineteenth century. This led on to the gradual decline during the short reign of William IV and the early years of Queen Victoria's reign. The spirit of the eighteenth century was too vigorous and profound to die easily and quickly, and George IV, both as Regent and King, did much to sustain it, while his brother did little to extinguish it. The accession of a young queen, enthusiastic and fresh, seemed to portend a return to those happy years before the Napoleonic wars had cast a cloud of anxiety over the country, and the dissolute sons of George III had darkened the social scene with their quarrels and their scandals.

This clearly was Victoria's own view of the situation, and young though she was she introduced a simple gaiety to the life of the Court which had been lacking during the reigns of her two uncles.

Momentarily the Duchess of Kent's fervent intention to bring up her daughter above all things as a "Christian Queen" seemed to have failed in its primary object, and the rigid control which she had exercised for seventeen years was rather rudely broken on her daughter's accession. The Duchess was in many respects a product of the eighteenth century, but in the upbringing of her daughter she evinced the austere principles more usually connected with the Spartan, sermon-reading curricula prevalent during the middle years of the nineteenth century. From this harsh childhood Victoria passed into the genial sunshine of Lord Melbourne's deferential influence, an influence founded entirely on the easy style of the past century, and free from the thwarting restrictions which were to become a feature of behaviour later in the reign. Her friendship with this sophisticated and disillusioned man, this autumn rose of the eighteenth century, as Lytton Strachey called him, was the dominating feature of the Queen's life until her marriage.

Within a month of her accession, the Court moved from the constricted and inhibiting surroundings of Kensington Palace to Buckingham Palace, the splendid and graceful creation of the taste of her wicked uncle, George IV, and of the genius of John Nash. This splendid composition of pillars, pediments and far-flung wings, later solidified and given a portentous dignity by the addition of a massive new front, was in spirit as much a product of the eighteenth century as Lord Melbourne himself, though it had not been created until about 1825, and no monarch had as yet inhabited it. Perhaps it was a little too closely related to the work of the Palladians to find general favour in the 1830's. Certainly Creevey, who visited it in the summer of 1835 when William IV and his queen were considering moving in, thought it a "specimen of wicked, vulgar profusion" and suggested that its name should be changed to Brunswick Hotel. And yet it seems curious that Creevey, who was at the time a man of sixty-seven, should have found fault with it architecturally. That he might have thought the million pounds he believed it had cost, and the forty thousand pounds for the Marble Arch which stood before it, a waste of public money is understandable, but one wonders why the architecture, the decorations, the "raspberry coloured pillars" turned him "sick to look at them". Creevey was far too deeply interested in people to consider architecture as anything but a background to the figures he studied with such minute and sustained interest. But undoubtedly he was influenced by fashion, as well as by his dislike of its originator. He must have been veering, in company with his contemporaries, towards the rather bleak, indeterminate manner which found favour during William IV's reign and the young Queen's first years.

If the Palace seemed wicked and vulgar to old Creevey, to its new mistress it epitomised all the gaiety and pleasure which she was now determined to introduce into her life. The Duchess of Kent was firmly relegated to a suite of apartments far from her own, and the Queen's day revolved round her intimate, informative talks with her beloved Prime Minister, while Baroness Lehzen remained discreetly at hand in an adjoining room.

The spirit which emanated from the Palace infected London and to a considerable degree the whole country. It was not due simply to the high spirits of a girl of seventeen, but to a general sense of relief that the turgid days of royal scandals, intrigues and extravagances were at last at an end. William had not been particularly unpopular: the upper classes looked on him as something of a buffoon, but the working classes had a friendly feeling for the simple-minded old man. It was a feeling which was shared by his niece, and by his Fitz-Clarence grandchildren who, according to Lady Munster, were fascinated by his bright, pink face and snow-white hair smelling strongly of rosewater. In general, however, a new régime was warmly welcomed; and, as it happened, it inaugurated a new era of prosperity for the middle and upper classes and, in a lesser degree, for the workers on whom this prosperity depended.

The land-owning classes had seldom been more wealthy than they were at the opening of the new reign. The great country houses and large houses in London were maintained with the lavishness and splendour of the eighteenth century, with the additional amenity of the many comforts and conveniences which were then coming into vogue. Furthermore, great areas of London were being laid out with houses designed not for the aristocracy, but for the swiftly expanding upper middle class, for families of substance and position who were making fortunes in commerce and the professions; for those who went down to the City in their carriages every morning and returned as richer men almost every evening. With expanding trade, acumen and industry were swiftly rewarded with a sound fortune.

The more affluent country squires, or those ruled by mundane spouses, found it was pleasanter and more convenient to own a moderate-sized house in London than to lodge in hired rooms for a month or two during the winter or summer season. Their parents may have been in the habit of migrating into the neighbouring county town for the coldest months of the winter, but with improved roads and so swifter transport the metropolis became from the social aspect a far more desirable objective.

The great squares laid out on the marshy fields lying to the west of the garden of Buckingham Palace had been begun sixteen years before Victoria came to the throne, but work continued on much

15

of what is now known as Belgravia for many years after her accession. Simultaneously extensive areas in Bayswater, north of Hyde Park, were being developed on similar lines and with somewhat similar architecture; but whereas in the former the architect George Basevi, under the critical eye of his employer Mr. Cubitt, was maintaining the eighteenth-century tradition in the spaciousness of his lay-out and in the good proportions of his façades, the latter, starting some years later, shows little of the grace of the previous century. Bayswater was begun in the first years of the queen's reign, and like much architecture of those indecisive years seems devoid of all style. The general layout of the estate must have appeared quite impressive on plan, but in practice was vitiated by the extreme height of the austere stucco façades of the houses. Where Belgravia is light and cheerful, Bayswater, even in its prime, must have seemed rather gloomy and forbidding: its streets are stucco-sided gorges, its squares desperate valleys of monotony. The exteriors of the houses were faithful mirrors of their interiors, and it is hardly surprising that after barely a century of existence a number of these sad, high blocks of upper middle-class homes have been replaced by buildings better adapted to the life of today.

Though the architectural style of Queen Victoria's first years was so indeterminate, there was no lack of architects, some very capable, available to design and build in the style which was in effect no style. The classical manner which had been used with purpose and vigour by Nash and to some degree by Basevi had now passed into a

16

vacuum—the tranquillity of the centre of a vortex—which it had reached through the various splendid developments of the eighteenth century, and from which it was very shortly to pass out to the heavy-handed classicism of much of the nineteenth century. Of Gothic much the same could be said, though the process was in many respects the reverse. Unlike the classical, the Gothic style had not reached these years of pause and uncertainty through more than a century of high achievement. On the contrary, Gothic Revival architecture of the latter half of the eighteenth and early years of the nineteenth century had in general few solid virtues to recommend it, but it had the more endearing quality of charm, an immense charm which disarms the criticism of all except those who are inherently hostile to it. From the quiet centre of the vortex it swept forward in a greatly chastened form to become the mainstay, the worthy buttress of domestic and, unfortunately, civic architecture for upwards of half a century.

If one searches for the cause for this short hiatus in the development of architectural style, and historically a pause is unusual, for development has generally been evenly continuous, one might attribute it to a mortality amongst famous architects round the year of the Queen's accession. Sir John Soane died in 1837, John Nash two years earlier, William Wilkins, the capable architect of the National Gallery, two years later. Jeffry Wyatville, a practitioner of rather dubious attainments, had only three years still to live. All these were men famous in their profession, though now we rate their achievements by very differing standards. Soane seems to us an outstanding figure of his period: at the time of his death he was probably no more highly regarded than the other three.

The names of many of those who contributed to the spate of building in these prosperous years—for building was active though style was stationary—have faded into obscurity, but a number stand out. There was Robert Smirke, designer of the British Museum and a number of other dignified if uninspired buildings; there was Charles Robert Cockerell, one of the most scholarly architects of the period, and Charles Barry whose work at Westminster will, whether the credit is justified or not, always keep his name fresh in the public mind; there was the rather pedestrian Basevi, already mentioned, and Edward Blore to whom the same adjective can properly be applied. All these were essentially capable in their profession and have left good, sound work to posterity; but, with the possible exception of Barry, they were not initiators and were content to carry on in styles which their predecessors had formed. All these were men in their maturity in 1837 and well established in their careers, but there were also several younger men who were making their way towards

17

the centre of the stage and were soon to drive domestic architecture out of the pleasant pastures in which it was gently browsing. There was Anthony Salvin, for example, a sound practitioner of the Gothic style, who was born in 1799 and so was twelve years younger than Blore, who was the junior of the first group; and Decimus Burton, whose name seems indicative of the light classical manner he favoured. He was one year younger than Salvin and so was separated by only a decade from Gilbert Scott and eleven years from Augustus Welby Northmore Pugin. Though the space of time was so short, a century would seem to separate the work of Burton from that of the two last.

The great "Battle of the Styles" was about to open, but at this point the balance still seemed to be weighted on the side of classicism. The prestige of the Houses of Parliament, in which Barry had the enthusiastic assistance of the young Pugin, lies majestically in the Gothic scale, but against this must be set Smirke's British Museum, Barry's Reform Club, Basevi's Fitzwilliam Museum, Cockerell's Taylorian Institute at Oxford, and the most impressive of all, Elmes's St. George's Hall at Liverpool, to mention only a few important public buildings erected in the classical style. In domestic architecture, in the field that is to say of large country houses, Smirke, Cockerell and Burton favoured classical, Salvin and Pugin a rather specialized version of vernacular, while Barry and Blore were prepared to oblige in whichever style their clients desired, though both were more successful with their classical productions. The rather rare Gothic country houses of this exact period are an interesting study, since they form a bridge between the light-hearted structures founded on the elaborate plagiarism of Strawberry Hill, which developed into James Wyatt's soaring, clustering abbeys, and the rigidly correct manner employed later in the century. Both Anthony Salvin and Augustus Pugin each designed a large country house to which the date 1837 is generally assigned, though both must have taken several years to construct. Scotney Castle in Kent was the work of the former, and Scarisbrick Hall in Lancashire (to which Edward Pugin made large additions thirty years later) that of the latter. In neither of these buildings is there to be found a trace of that insouciant convention of the eighteenth century by which the Gothic style was treated merely as a superficial trimming or decoration applied to a classical base. The pattern books, which were published by many of the less successful architects of the early decades of the nineteenth century in the hope of attracting custom, often displayed "elegant villas" which, without change of plan or general form, could be erected in the Grecian or the Gothic manner. Such turn-coat architecture would have been absolutely abhorrent to Salvin or Pugin, and certainly neither Scotney nor Scarisbrick, with

Scotney Castle, Kent (1837). Anthony Salvin, Architect

their carefully arranged but asymmetrical grouping, could possibly have been altered into classical buildings by the mere alteration of superficial detail.

Thus amateurism in the treatment of Gothic was largely at an end, and a growing sense that the style should not be used unless it was fully understood may have deterred the less accomplished architects from adopting this manner for buildings of moderate size. It was far easier to design a small house on plain classical lines than in the Gothic manner, and there was no risk of getting into trouble with the masters of the profession who had now become so censoriously inclined. This may account for the comparative rarity of small Gothic houses dating from these years: they had been common earlier, they were to become common again a little later.

Meanwhile, a safe and unadorned classicism generally prevailed, not only in the new streets and squares of London, but also in market towns and in the countryside. Houses were designed as simple cubes with yellow brick or stuccoed walls, and shallow slate roofs rather deeply projecting over a meagrely contrived cornice. These rigid little houses can seldom be called beautiful, but they can be entirely satisfactory to the eye: sensible, practical, with no unnecessary ornament, they are the descendants of the handsome works of Henry Holland, Thomas Leverton, John Plaw and other architects of the pre-Regency school.

The interiors, behind these bland façades, were generally soundly planned. The houses of Bayswater, as has already been said, suffered from having too much above ground and also too much below: excessive accommodation was compressed on to too small a ground area, and this made them inconvenient. But in more spacious settings both in London and in the country the arrangement of rooms and staircases in early Victorian houses was entirely straightforward and quite free from the convulsions of planning which became usual some years later. Occasionally too a dash of eighteenth-century taste would appear: a pair of columns, an elliptical arch, an elegantly moulded architrave to a doorway or window opening. Rooms were light for windows were large, too large in many cases when filled with an unbroken expanse of the plate-glass which was just coming into vogue. The Georgians had contentedly viewed the landscape through windows divided by glazing-bars without, it seems, suffering any inconvenience or any sense that the beauty of the prospect was marred. Now suddenly, when a method of making large sheets of glass was invented, these first Victorians felt a great advance in amenities had been made. Their predecessors had been living in bird-cages or, still worse, prisons, from which the outside world could only be viewed through a grill. Could one properly enjoy the beauty of a picture, it was asked, if it were criss-crossed with wooden bars? Of course not; and the same principle applied to a view.

With a zeal far in excess of that of a century and a half earlier when sash windows were inserted in place of wooden transoms and lead lights, Stuart and Georgian glazing-bars were replaced by the shining, unbroken surface of plate-glass; and whatever the effect from within, the façades punctuated with black cavernous openings were seriously damaged. Where the structure was designed for plate-glass windows the effect was less disastrous, indeed it was sometimes one of comfort and opulence. One thinks of some of the club houses of St. James's erected in the austere but determined classical style of the 'forties and 'fifties. Here, an added lustre is given by the plate-glass to the rich folds of heavy curtains which admit a discreet glimpse of solid mahogany furniture, golden picture frames, and elaborate chandeliers casting a subdued glow over the comfortable but unimaginative scene. Thus the unbroken window-area may provide as pleasant a spectacle for the pedestrian as for the clubman within.

This scene, however, was still a pleasure in the future, for in 1837 the furnishing and decoration of rooms had not yet assumed the opulent but sombre appearance which was to be in vogue later in the century. The age of velvet, rep, chenille, and kindred heavy materials was not yet, and furniture and draperies had still the same lightness as women's fashions. These are years one connects with muslins, silks and rosewood furniture. Curtains were hung in graceful folds from gilded pelmets, but being generally made of thin materials they had little of the light-reducing quality of the heavy draperies which became popular later in the century. Between the windows would be a gilt pier-glass with a console table below it, following a tradition which had existed almost since the Restoration. At first glance the effect will be very similar to that in a mid-eighteenth-century room, but inspection will reveal some essential differences: the unbroken area of mirror will be larger, the tone of the glass will be brighter, while the surrounding frame and the console table will have a coarseness and an indecisive rococo flavour, which one would not find in the work of the previous century.

However, it will not be gilt but rosewood furniture which will predominate in the room. This beautifully marked wood, which gains its name from the scent of the timber when the tree is first felled, had been imported for some years from Brazil and India and had found an ever-increasing favour. It had not perhaps quite the distinction of amboyna or coromandel, which had been used so effectively in the furniture of the Regency, but it was thought to present a more lively and interesting surface than mahogany. It was well suited, too, for veneering on the simplified forms which were beginning to be adopted for furniture. These were the years of transition from Regency into Victorian, and the elements of both styles can be seen in furniture made at this period. Chairs had the backs and arms of the 'twenties together with the turned legs—the unlovely turned legs—which were soon to become general; and tables were often equally hybrid with Regency tops but with supports and stretchers which were closely allied with the furniture of the 'fifties.

With the gilt and the rosewood there would also be a few pieces of papier mâché furniture, a small table or two, a few chairs, perhaps the equipment of the writing-table and a box for needlework. In this medium were produced for the next two decades objects in which the pleasantest fancy was allowed a free run. While furniture in mahogany and rosewood became every year more pompous in design, papier mâché, owing to the method of its manufacture, retained a frailty, if not always an elegance, of form; and the decoration of flowers, birds or landscapes brightly painted on the black ground demanded no very high degree of technique to present a gay and pretty effect.

There was little affinity between these three types of furniture—the rococo gilt, the rosewood, and the papier mâché, except that they were all products of the early years of Queen Victoria's reign; and yet rooms of the period must have been attractive, cheerful and comfortable, with their floors close-fitted with a patterned carpet

21

probably of Brussels manufacture, rather lightly-flowered wall-papers, and simple, white marble chimney-pieces on which shell flowers beneath a glass dome might be making their up-to-date appearance.

As usual, decoration of rooms and the style of women's clothes were in harmony; it would be difficult to find any period of history when they were not closely related. Materials for dresses, at least dresses for social occasions, were little different from those in vogue during the Regency, but the line had greatly altered. The high waists, jutting breasts, and short wind-blown hair had disappeared, and the female figure had miraculously adapted itself to a style demanding a different emphasis.

With Regency fashions the figure, below the protuberant bust, had been allowed almost complete freedom, but now the waist, which once again had returned to the position where nature had placed it, was closely confined by whalebone and webbing. The smaller the waist, the greater the elegance, and the wasp-like effect devised was enhanced by puffed sleeves and billowing skirts. Shoulders now became the most admired feature, and a sloping, drooping line was particularly favoured, so that in *costume de gala* the effect would be as of Clite emerging from her sunflower. Hair styles naturally changed as well, and the short crop of the Regency had been allowed to grow long so that the hair could be braided into the strange "teapot handles" which decorated the heads of the more fashionable of William IV's female subjects. Before the death of the old King these curious and unbecoming erections had begun to give way to the gentle ringlets which flanked the faces of early-Victorian women like the ears of well-bred spaniels. The essential femininity of this style contributed in a large degree to the reputation for submissiveness, which was so carefully nurtured by women of the period; but those soft swinging curls concealed many an iron will, and, it may be added, partially concealed many an iron face.

Men's clothes, too, had altered and sobered since the Regency; but mellow-coloured cloths and embroidered waistcoats were still widely worn, and it was considered no reflection whatever on a man's masculinity that he should wave his hair and put scent on his hand-kerchief. However, it was a custom fast dying, and there were few who, like Disraeli with his pomades, brocades and elaborate clothes, maintained the tradition a decade later. The brilliance of male costume had indeed vanished with the Regency, and during the ten years of George IV's reign the dandies assumed a duller plumage. The tail coats of cerulean blue or viridian green, the pale lemon or saffron trousers which gave such a pleasing elegance to the legs, and the tall top hats of sweeping line and narrow brim had given

"Fancy Chairs for Drawing-rooms" (1835)

23

way to a more subdued style before the Sailor King mounted the throne.

Hair which, except for moustaches, had been largely banished from the male countenance since the Restoration, was allowed once again to make a tentative appearance. It took the form of a neat fringe round the face, giving the look of a chinstrap tethering the curls, which were encouraged to luxuriate on the head. At the same time a narrow moustache was tolerated on the upper lip. Decorated with embellishments such as these the young Prince Albert of Saxe-Coburg-Gotha came to visit his cousin, the Queen, at Windsor in the autumn of 1839. To Victoria the proposed visit gave no pleasure, indeed it seemed to her "a disagreeable thing". But once she had seen Albert again her sentiments were drastically altered. The blue eyes, the exquisite nose, the beautiful figure, and above all "the delicate moustachios and slight but very slight whiskers", left her in no doubt at all about her feelings.

Fashion soon allowed moustaches and the fringe of whiskers to become more pronounced, but the middle of the century was passed before "aggravators" in which the moustache joined bushy whiskers came into vogue. The bust of Whyte-Melville by Boehm in the National Portrait Gallery provides an admirable example of this hirsute fashion. About the same time beards attained the popularity which they held for several decades.

Hair on the face was a small indication of the break-away from the modes of the eighteenth century: there were many others. Drunkenness, for example, was no longer regarded with the easy tolerance it had earlier enjoyed. During the previous century, that golden age of grace and elegance, a convivial dinner party was hardly considered a success unless the male members of the gathering had spent the latter part of the evening in an advanced state of intoxication. The distressing scenes which must have taken place in the exquisite dining-rooms designed by William Kent and the Adam brothers, and amidst the fine furniture of Chippendale and Sheraton, would seem nowadays highly incongruous. Until the death of William IV this weakness appears to have been as prevalent in royal circles as elsewhere, in spite of Queen Adelaide's efforts to introduce a more sober tone; but it would seem from this distance that the confirmed drunkard, a character with which we have now become reluctantly familiar, was not a very usual figure. Amongst the upper classes it was principally wine of good quality which was consumed on these festive occasions, burgundy, claret and port; the more insidious and more destructive spirits were considered the drink of the lower orders.

Queen Adelaide's modest efforts at introducing reforms had not been conspicuously successful, but the young Victoria, though in general sympathetically inclined towards the somewhat unrefined gaiety of the period, viewed with grave disfavour the habit of the gentlemen of sitting over their wine at the end of dinner. The results were so obviously painful. It was on this subject, so it was rumoured, that one of the very rare disputes arose between the Queen and her Prime Minister. The Queen at the time was only eighteen, Lord Melbourne was a man of sixty: it must have been galling for this great man, nurtured in the habits of the eighteenth century, to be lectured by his usually submissive pupil. On this point, however, she was adamant; though it is possible that it was less an antipathy to excessive drinking than a reluctance to be bereft of the company of her beloved "Lord M." which gave her the determination to enforce her wishes. The example of the royal household came slowly to be followed in less august circles, and inebriation on social occasions was soon looked on as a regrettable lapse in taste.

The conduct approved at Windsor and Buckingham Palace affected only the upper strata of society, but some years earlier regulations had come into force designed to induce some degree of temperance amongst the masses. By the Beer Act of 1834, which was the amended form of a previous act, public houses were allowed the very generous hours of opening from five in the morning until midnight, unless they served a district where the population was under 2,500, in which case they had to close at ten o'clock. On Sundays, however, houses were not to open until one o'clock. These hours did not at first apply in all parts of England, and it was not until 1848 that Sunday morning closing was enforced all over the country. Concurrently with these measures several Temperance Societies were formed, the first being in Bradford in 1830, while another soon followed in London. At their inception these societies were designed only to combat the drinking of spirits, a habit which was causing havoc amongst workers in the rapidly developing industrial towns. At Preston, however, the society was under the ardent leadership of one Richard Turner, himself a reformed drunkard, who advocated complete abstinence from alcohol and in support of his campaign coined the catchword "Tee-tee-totalism". Whatever his success in his endeavours, he has the distinction of having added a word to the English language.

Thus both from above and below a spirit was moving towards a moderation which was in time to pervade all classes. But hand in hand with these estimable reforms there persisted amongst the young men of the richer classes a highly disedifying element of rowdyism. To some degree this has always prevailed, until late years when excessive high spirits have been partially extinguished by the necessity of directing all energy to earning a living; but during the first years of Queen Victoria's reign the violence of these escapades was phenomenal. In a sense, perhaps, they could be looked on as practical jokes, but they were often carried to a pitch where all joke was eliminated, except presumably in the mind of the perpetrator; while the fact that they were often directed by the rich against the poor gives one a singularly uncomfortable feeling as one reads contemporary newspaper reports of the appearance of these rowdy young gentlemen at Bow Street and other police courts. Lord Waterford and his two brothers James and William Beresford, Lord Waldegrave, and many others, were continually paying small fines for a variety of offences: brawling and attacking inoffensive men in public houses, overturning the stalls of street traders, driving a cab along a pavement to the danger of pedestrians, and the particularly popular pastime of tearing knockers off front doors. There was so much of this style of rowdyism amongst the gilded youth that a name was given to it: it became known as "Tom and Jerryism".

The rhythm of life in 1837 had remained almost unaltered for a century, but already an invention was being developed which was soon to speed the tempo. This was, of course, the construction of railways. A mobile steam engine had been constructed a quarter of a century before the Queen's accession: William Hedley's "Puffing Billy", with its elaborate superstructure of cranks and pistons, had been brought into use at Wylam Colliery near Newcastle upon Tyne to carry coal away from the pithead. This was the first attempt to run a smooth-wheeled engine on a smooth line. To the astonishment of all the engine not only proceeded forward but was also able to draw a heavy load. For sixty years this redoubtable veteran continued in constant use, until it eventually went into honourable retirement in a museum.

The fact that this antiquated machine remained so long in service is an indication of the unexpectedly slow progress of the development of railroads. In 1825 the first public line was opened between Stockton and Darlington, and on this 8¾-mile run the engine achieved a speed of sixteen miles an hour. But this line was merely for goods traffic; passengers were still not trusted on these dangerous machines. Five years later, however, amidst national excitement, the first passenger line was opened to connect the great towns of Liverpool and Manchester; and Stephenson's "Rocket", its lofty, frilled funnel emitting clouds of black smoke, skimmed along the course at the rate of thirty miles an hour, about three times the speed of a fast horse-drawn vehicle.

The pace of life was beginning to quicken; but so far the centre of railroad development remained in the north, where fuel was readily available. In September, 1836, Creevey, while staying with Lord

Sefton at Stoke, walked over to view progress on the construction of the Grand Junction railway which was to join Liverpool and Birmingham. "Four miles there and back . . . has made me dead lame" he wrote to Miss Ord, and it was probably the last expedition of this sort he attempted, for seventeen months later this most industrious letter-writer died. Thus by 1837 the principal industrial towns of the north were connected by railroads, but London was far less well served: there was still only one railway running out of the metropolis. The Greenwich railway it was proudly but optimistically named, for in fact it deposited its passengers amidst the attractive pastoral surroundings of the market gardens round Deptford, whence it was a considerable walk to the domes and colonnades of royal Greenwich. But from this time forward the construction of railways proceeded with ever-increasing speed, though unfortunately no attempt was made to devise an overall plan to serve the country to the best advantage. A large number of small companies were formed which issued their shares for public subscription. As will be seen in the following chapter, the "Railway Mania" which seized a public in pursuit of easy money rivalled in its effects the South Sea Bubble of a century and a quarter earlier.

The nineteenth century, it seemed, was moving forward with some reluctance into the mechanical age. The growing network of railways, with the attendant electric telegraph, without which they could not have functioned, represented a step into the future, but at the same time there was evidence that the romantic movement as exemplified by the Gothic Revival was by no means entirely extinct. The building of vast rambling, mock-mediaeval houses was a thing of the past: the spreading wings and soaring tower of Fonthill, the far-flung cloistral buildings of Ashridge, belonged to the previous century, and even at Alton Towers, which was a purely nineteenth-century conceit, a halt had been called to the crazy spate of construction, to the keeps and towers, galleries, and gloomy baptisteries, in 1823. A temporary halt, it should perhaps be added, for alterations were later made by A. W. N. Pugin, but these were on a more sober note and were largely directed towards exemplifying the noble birth and piety of the owner: earl's coronets and religious emblems competing in hot rivalry for first place in the scheme of decoration.

Though a degree of staidness and common sense was entering into architecture and the kindred arts, a last noble gesture was made in 1839 to show that the age of romance was still just alive in the humdrum days of "Puffing Billys" and buzzing telegraph wires. This gesture was the Eglinton Tournament, which, though conceived as a stupendous entertainment, brought the romantic movement to an end on a tragic scene of bathos, on a scene of rusting armour, of dripping tresses, of warriors and damosels crouching beneath umbrellas. The Tournament might be dismissed as having had no deeper significance, even in the event of its having been successful, than one of Louis Napoleon Parker's mammoth historical pageants which were so successfully produced in the years before the first World War, but this would be to underrate its importance. The attempt to revive the days of Froissart, to re-create a stupendous tournament of the Age of Chivalry, was entered into with an enthusiasm which may well have proved alarming to the instigator, Lord Eglinton. His lordship's first intention, so it was said, was to exercise his mediaeval leanings to the tune of two thousand pounds, for which sum a splendid spectacle could have been produced. Such, however, was the zeal of the upper ranks of society, so strong their determination to take part in the enterprise which was awakening national interest, that the final sum expended on the melancholy fiasco was no less than forty thousand pounds.

The story of so much wasted effort is too painful to recount in detail, but at least it can be said that the dress rehearsal, which took place at Kilburn on 13th July, was a success and gave pleasure to more than six thousand spectators. The whole paraphernalia, including a great quantity of fine mediaeval armour, was then conveyed to Scotland where a much elaborated version was to open on 28th August and continue for three days. A huge number of performers, headed by the Queen of Beauty, Lady Seymour, with all the complicated panoply of a grandiose tournament, was assembled at Eglinton Castle: all was prepared for a display which would recall one of the most romantic periods in English history. But one thing was amiss—the weather. Deluges of rain and a tearing wind, which continued almost without intermission for the three days, reduced the whole brave display to a squalid, gloomy embarrassing fiasco.

Thus the last flicker of the romantic spirit, which had burnt in England for the last seventy or eighty years, was temporarily extinguished. It had become a faint flame which would anyhow have soon been quenched without the adverse attentions of nature; but it was to be brilliantly lit again later in the century by William Morris and the school of Pre-Raphaelites. Perhaps it would be more correct to say that the spirit was never entirely suppressed but managed to carry on an underground existence, for it would occasionally and unexpectedly surge to the surface, through layers of materialism, in lively, but narrowly based, manifestations.

Meanwhile, wealth became the general fetish, and this desirable commodity was fast coming to many families which had not previously possessed it. One of the first ambitions of these new rich was to surround themselves with all the appurtenances of affluence and security, which would form an unsurmountable barrier against the penury they had known in their early lives. Thus began the decline, as we now see it, in the standard of taste. The fashion was for the sumptuous and ornate, and these characteristics gradually crept into many aspects of domestic life: into its architecture and planning, into decoration and furnishing of interiors, into the style of women's clothes, so that before the middle of the century was reached the female form was almost obliterated beneath complex upholstery in a manner which had never previously occurred, not even in the days of the farthingale. How disconcerting, one would suppose, it must have been for a woman who as a girl had come out into society in the high waist and clinging dress of the "Grecian" style, to find herself at middle age enveloped in the billowing folds of a crinoline. What drastic adjustment of both mind and deportment must have been necessary to carry off such opposing styles with grace. A manner lively, impetuous and sensual was becoming to the first: a demure dignity to the latter. Superficially, at least, the drastic change in temperament was generally achieved.

The new prosperity came to some classes, but by no means to all. Factory workers in London and in the great industrial towns, whose efforts brought wealth to their employers, were still living, at the opening of Queen Victoria's reign, in conditions of extreme squalor. No Local Government Board, no Ministry of Health, existed to supervise sanitary conditions in urban areas. The Municipal Reform Act had been passed in 1835, but its primary purpose was to bring to fruition in towns what the abolition of "Rotten Boroughs" had achieved in the country; and the great benefits which derived from it during the following hundred years were largely fortuitous. As Professor Trevelyan wrote in *English Social History*: "No one in 1835 foresaw the day when the 'New municipalities' would not only light and pave the streets, but control the building of houses and the sanitation and health of the borough; convey the workmen to and from their work; provide public libraries; carry on great municipal trades and industries; and finally educate the people".

In the year before the passing of the Act, Sydney Smirke, a younger brother of Robert and his assistant in the later stages in the building of the British Museum, had published his *Suggestions for the Architectural Improvement of the Western Part of London*. This serene title concealed a terrible description of the districts known as the Rookery and the Holy Land which lay in the parish of St. Giles-in-the-Fields: "The unutterable abominations of it can only be conceived by those who, in the exercise of charity or in quest of crime, have been forced to become familiar with its recesses". He goes on to

29

describe conditions of life in the tenement houses, in one of which consisting of nine small rooms he found fifty-four human beings, men, women and children living. Drainage was everywhere almost non-existent, and the sanitary conditions were such as could not be described. It was in this district, he recalled, that the Great Plague broke out in 1665, but whereas it was then a plague district, it was in 1834 a fever district. The remedy he suggested was demolition and the building of lodging-houses—hostels we should now call them—at various points a mile or two away in what were then suburban areas. These buildings he reckoned could be raised on a sound financial basis, and no doubt something on these lines would have been feasible had these poor people not preferred to live in independent squalor rather than under supervision in hygienic institutions.

The immediate effect of Smirke's paper was apparently slight, but that it stirred uncomfortably the complacency of prosperous Londoners there was no doubt. However, in a period busy with the development of fine new squares and streets this unpleasant subject was allowed to fade into the background until 1838, when a renewed and severe jolt was provided by the issue of a report on the sanitary conditions in Whitechapel and Bethnal Green.

The appalling disclosures caused consternation to all who took any interest in the living conditions of the poor. As a result two bills were introduced in Parliament in 1840 designed to control building and sanitation in congested areas. The proposals were not very drastic and included regulations to prevent houses being built back to back without an intervening space between them, or being constructed below ground level. These innocuous suggestions caused an outcry amongst those who saw here a threat to cheap and remunerative speculative building. It was an attitude which, one regrets to say, was supported by *The Times*: "A reckless and wanton invasion of property and liberty", thundered the national newspaper, crimson with virtuous anger. The protests were effective, and only emasculated versions of the bills were passed by the House.

Consciences, however, were not entirely easy behind the stucco façades of Belgravia and Bayswater, and it soon became the general opinion, in which *The Times* shared, that reforms were essential. During the following twenty years distinct advances were made in urban conditions, one of which was the proper paving and draining of streets. Oxford Street was chosen as a suitable site for experiment, and in the first days of 1839 a long stretch was completed with twelve different specimens of surface; there were forty feet of Robinson's Parisian bitumen; a length of parish stone paving set in Claridge's asphalt; another of Bastenne and Gautac bitumen; one of dressed Aberdeen granite laid diagonally on a concrete bottom; and several others. But the specimen which excited the greatest enthusiasm from the large number of people who came to view the experiments, was Mr. Stead's pavement of wooden blocks. The carriages and carts passed over this section as silently as if they were rolling over a carpet, and the metallic sound of horses' hooves was soothingly muffled. This, as it has transpired, is the surface to be found in the majority of London streets to this day.

Another amenity of urban life which was beginning to attract notice was the provision of open spaces in the more congested areas. In March, 1839, some prominent inhabitants of Whitechapel, where the housing conditions were so deplorable, started a scheme for the forming of a park in their area. Their efforts were crowned with success, for two years later an Act was passed which enabled the Commissioners of Works to dispose of the Crown lease of the great house at the corner of the Green Park which had been barely finished by the Duke of York at the time of his death, and to use the money thus obtained for the buying of land in the Whitechapel district. The transaction was highly successful: the house was sold to the Duke of Sutherland and renamed Stafford House, and two hundred and ninety acres of land were purchased and formed into a public park. As the Victoria Park it was opened for the enjoyment of all in 1845.

Thus in urban areas, councils and commissions were turning their endeavours towards a modest amelioration in the living conditions of workers; but in the countryside, where the air may have been fresher but standards were otherwise little better, improvement was left to individual enterprise. In general landowners showed consideration towards those living in their cottages; but standards remained very low, and there was much penury and hardship with the agricultural wage at under seven shillings a week. Anxiety was felt in the country as in the cities, and charity to the poor and sick became a regular feature of country house life. Little comforts would be prepared in the big house for distribution to the deserving cottagers on the estate; soups were concocted according to the most austere recipes; flannel petticoats, coarse in material and flamboyant in colour, were cut out and stitched; blankets of a suitably utilitarian texture and tone were obtained. Piling this depressing collection of commodities into her carriage, the lady bountiful would drive down to the humble dwellings beyond the confines of her park. On each threshold she would be received by smiles and curtsies, and an assiduous dusting of chairs should she condescend to enter a cottage. Her errand of mercy completed she would bowl home again with humble words of gratitude still sounding pleasantly in her ears.

The motives which inspired these charitable acts were undoubtedly of the best. There was no conscious desire to adopt a patronizing attitude towards the poor, but there seems to have been little realization that these well-intentioned palliatives barely touched the fringe of a great social question, which could be solved only by higher wages, better housing conditions, and old-age pensions. It is often said that the agricultural worker was as happy in the early part of the last century, when conditions were apparently so adverse, as he is now when so much has been achieved in his interest. It is possible: for human nature has that resilient quality which makes happiness feasible under almost any conditions; but that he has now greater cause for happiness, so far as amenities are concerned, there can be little question.

This, then, sketches in very lightly some of the conditions during the rather indeterminate years between the Queen's accession and her marriage: the short space of three years in which there seemed little indication of the direction in which the social structure would develop, whither the arts would move, in what manner the varied aspects of home life, the subject with which this book is concerned, would alter and improve. All seem to have been poised in an attitude of uncertainty. It was finally the material prosperity which the country was enjoying, rather than any impulse derived from the practitioners of the arts, which determined the sombre course during the Victorian Age.

"A Cottage Lodge in the Old English Style"
(*c.* 1835)

"A Double Lodge in the Doric Style"

CHAPTER II

AN AGE OF CONTRASTS
1840—1850

THE first three years of Queen Victoria's reign saw the last flickers of the flame which had burned so brightly through the eighteenth century and had seemed undimmed during the Regency, though the wick was growing short. The sentiments, the fashions, the taste of the past were slowly and fairly gracefully dying. It was in general a period of decline. The following ten years in contrast was an age permeated with new impulses: new discoveries and inventions, new laws and reforms, a new attitude towards the arts, and above all new families bursting into the sacred circles which had previously been reserved for those of aristocratic birth. It was not that the newly rich were yet able to penetrate into the world of fashion—that was to come rather later—but the rising middle classes were swiftly becoming an influence, almost a paramount influence in the government of the country.

The social order was changing, the way of life was slowly but distinctly altering, while taste was undergoing a radical transformation. But in spite of this gentle, almost imperceptible revolution which was quietly in progress, there was no very decided trend in the development of the arts, as they affected the Victorian home, until the latter part of the decade. It was as if many small streams were winding through adjacent valleys, apparently without aim, but were in fact moving towards the point where they would unite into a single river and sweep forward along a well-defined, if somewhat turgid, course.

On the 10th of February, 1840, the marriage of the Queen took place at the Chapel Royal, St. James's; and this event, though it aroused far less excitement and enthusiasm than would a parallel royal festivity in these days, was destined to have a marked influence on English home life. The tepid quality of public rejoicing is exemplified by a leading article which appeared in *The Times* on the morning of the wedding. The intention was probably to adopt an avuncular attitude towards the young couple, but now, as one reads these astringent sentences, the approach would seem rather that of a governess than a benevolent relative; while the nuptial morning seems hardly a felicitously chosen date for publication.

It was desirable, wrote *The Times*, that the Queen should marry a member of a family without political importance in Europe, and in this direction the "weakness and insignificance" of the bridegroom's background made him a suitable candidate for the royal alliance; but, the article continued, it was an "undoubted fact that the name of Saxe-Coburg is not popular in this country". *The Times* was thus shaking a warning finger at "Uncle Leopold" in case he should endeavour to interfere in matters which were no longer his concern. Maintaining this cheering note, the writer then devoted a number of paragraphs to several unsatisfactory features in the manner in which the Queen conducted her life and duty, "the petty artificial world" in which she lived, "the evil influences" which surrounded her, and the ill-chosen guests invited to the "Royal table". It was to be hoped, though by inference it was deemed unlikely, that Prince Albert would be able to effect some improvement in this unfortunate state of affairs.

The article must have made discouraging reading for the earnest young man on his marriage morning, but it is to be hoped that he was cheered later in the day by the stimulating scene surmounting the wedding cake. On this mountain of sugar, three yards in circumference, stood a noble figure of Britannia in the act of blessing the royal couple, who were depicted in Roman costume, while bevies of Amorini capered and postured round them.

The royal wedding, with its muted splendours, formed a fitting opening for a decade which was to become known as "The Hungry 'Forties", a decade in which riches and poverty were to advance, not perhaps hand in hand, but at least in close alliance. If in the great cities the effects of the Reform Bill were beginning to be felt in the increasing power of the middle classes, in the countryside the old aristocracy was still dominant. During the Napoleonic wars, which were little more than a quarter of a century in the past, the small landowner, the "cultivating freeholder", had known prosperous days; but since that time the vicissitudes had been great, and the bad years had far exceeded the good, so that many had been compelled to put their farms and properties into the market, where the large landowners were always ready to acquire them. Many of the latter had both the resources and the initiative to improve their properties, and they thus greatly benefited not only themselves but also the State by raising the productivity of the land. Coke of Norfolk, for example, in the course of a long life which ended in 1842, increased the annual value of the sterile East Anglian acres he had inherited by no less than ten times.

Thus there was great prosperity not only for the great landowners but also for the professional classes and the industrialists, while, with income tax at the modest figure of sevenpence in the pound, there was plenty of money available for indulging the Englishman's favourite hobby—launching out, that is to say, into bricks and mortar. There were great works of public and semi-public building in progress to give the private individual a lead, had he required one. Robert Smirke's dignified composition of colonnades and pediments, with decorative sculpture by Westmacott, was sweeping like a remorseless tide over the continental elegance of Montagu House, which had contained the British Museum since its inception in the middle years of the eighteenth century; in the university cities, Charles Robert Cockerell was occupied with the Soane-like Taylorian building at Oxford; and at Cambridge, Basevi was engaged on the monumental classicism of the Fitzwilliam Museum. In Pall Mall and St. James's Street noble club-houses were converting these modest Stuart promenades into thoroughfares of stupendous dignity; and, in spite of much good architecture, were entirely ruining the original genial proportions of house height to street width. Charles Barry had completed the Travellers Club in 1831; the even more majestic building of the Reform was begun in the year of the Queen's accession; Sydney Smirke, with Basevi, began the Conservative Club-house in 1843; a year or two later Barry began a house, larger perhaps than any of his club buildings, for the fabulously wealthy Lord Ellesmere on the borders of the Green Park within the purlieus of St. James's. Further east, the Gresham Committee were considering in May, 1840, the rival plans submitted by Mr. Cockerell and Mr. Tite for the rebuilding of the Royal Exchange, which had been burnt to the ground two years earlier. The decision went to the latter, then President of the Architectural Society, whose name, in spite of this commission, is now little remembered.

Another useful building, and one which was less exclusive and more capacious than the clubs of St. James's, was Pentonville Prison which, fulfilling what was considered a long-felt want, arose in the Caledonian Road in 1840. Seven years later a great construction, almost equally forbidding in aspect but designed for a very different purpose, was begun from the designs of Edward Blore. This was the formidable block which joined Nash's wings at Buckingham Palace, and presented an unrelenting façade to the Mall. Sir Ahton Webb's refacing improved the situation, but the massive block effectually destroyed the grace and movement of Nash's design and was a heavy price to pay for added accommodation and convenience.

These, then, were a few of the great works of construction which were in progress during the 'forties; but there was one which transcended all those here mentioned both in scale and importance. This was the fabulous new Palace of Westminster which was raising its delicate lace-like fabric from a great new terrace formed on the bank of the river. Would it be insular presumption to assert that this building shares equally with the Colosseum in Rome and the Eiffel Tower in Paris the place of the best-known building in the world? To all Englishmen, at least, it is so familiar as to be beyond criticism: whether it is good architecture or no seems of minor importance in comparison to the infinite pleasure derived from a sight of its soaring lines softened by a river mist, as Monet painted it, or its fretted outline silhouetted against a winter sunset.

Charles Barry's design was finally accepted in February, 1836, and building continued for the whole of the decade now under review. Had the fire and choice of designs taken place ten years later, it is probable that only the blindest patriot would have been able to view the Houses of Parliament with pride and pleasure. As it is the building represents the final, splendid flourish of the early Gothic Revival: in spirit it is nearer akin to James Wyatt's Fonthill than it is to George Street's Law Courts, and it possesses to the full that dash of bravado which makes the earlier buildings so sympathetic.

These encomiums are confined to the exterior. In the interior, where the hand of A. W. N. Pugin is everywhere to the fore, we see the beginnings of the style which was to have so profound an effect on the architecture and decoration of Victorian houses during the second half of the century. The superabundance of ornamentation, the dim lighting, the colours which were intended to be rich and glowing but which soon, in the London atmosphere, became sombre and fuliginous, the repetitive stencilled patterns: these were the ingredients so lavishly used within the grey, romantic fabric. Now much of Pugin's careful, scholarly but entirely unpractical decoration has disappeared beneath coats of light paint, and so shares the fate of similar, if less elaborate, work which found its way into many nineteenth-century homes.

Horace Walpole's method of creating a Gothic building was to gather details from a variety of ecclesiastical sources and adapt them to domestic use. Thus canopies of tombs lent themselves rather happily to reproduction on a smaller scale as chimney-pieces,

Decorated Gothic tracery could be introduced, with tactful alteration, into bookcases; and there was much other ingenious conversion of the same sort. In the early nineteenth century the approach to the subject had become a little more serious, but Walpole's attitude was not entirely lost, and even Barry's great conception sprang largely from this background. Pugin terminated this phase, and what had until then been a game suddenly became deadly serious. It came to be believed that Gothic architecture, to be worthy of the name, must be the outcome of deep spiritual feeling, the fruit of a burning faith, like the great cathedrals of the Middle Ages. All this made Walpole's fantasies and James Wyatt's sublimities seem very mundane indeed; but Pugin's intransigence and his sense of urgency achieved its objective. His followers in the latter half of the century may not have shared his ardour to the full, but once Pugin had blazed across the architectural path there was no question of returning to the attitude of the early Revival.

The change which Pugin achieved by his works and writings came slowly. Until the middle 'forties the style of architecture which P. F. Robinson, for example, advocated persisted both in the countryside and in suburban areas. Robinson's *Rural Architecture and Designs for Ornamental Villas* and his sequel on the same subject had a great vogue since its publication in the 'twenties, and there is no doubt that his rustic architecture, some of which was adapted for quite large houses, had considerable charm. His components, which could be endlessly varied, consisted of an apparently casual grouping, a broken roof-line from which tall, slim chimneys sprouted in a haphazard and uneconomic manner, while the gables, of which there were many, were decorated with wooden barge-boards as luxuriant and pendulous as Elizabeth Barrett's ringlets. These houses achieved their object, which was to present a picturesque appearance and to fit pleasantly into the English landscape. But to live in they must have had many unfortunate shortcomings: the latticed windows were seldom adequate in size, the planning was confused, and their broken and straggling form must have made them very inconvenient, while the cottages for estate workers, which formed romantic objects at the entrance to a drive or on the edge of a wood, provided very inadequate accommodation for any but the smallest family.

Many architectural pattern-books were published during the years on either side of 1840, and their principal interest lies in the fact that they were compiled to attract and please the public taste. Thus, though they seldom led in the way that Pugin was leading, they are indicative of the current approach to domestic architecture, and also domestic comfort. A representative example is *Designs for Cottage and Villa Architecture* by S. H. Brooks. The author by his own account had a

"A Gentleman's Residence in the Cottage Style" (c. 1820). P. F. Robinson, Architect

considerable practice as an architect, but neither his name nor many of his houses apparently have endured. He offers buildings in a variety of styles without, it would seem, any personal preference. This one would expect in a book designed to entrap clients, but it is startling that some of his designs seem now so attractive, while others are painfully ugly. His villas "in the Ionic style" for example, with their simple lines and well-arranged windows, could be placed amongst Nash's terraces in Regent's Park without creating disharmony; but his proposal for a villa in the Elizabethan style seems as nauseating to us as it would undoubtedly have seemed to sixteenth-century builders. "The decorations are both numerous and rich, and would therefore be expensive if they were carved in stone . . . but it will be sufficient if they are executed in some hard wood, such as chestnut." Thus the finials and mullions, the cupolas and strap work, were only to simulate stone, and the whole crazy structure both in materials and design could hardly have been further removed from the principles so forcefully advocated by Pugin.

Brooks's views on aspect were unexpectedly sound: he fully realized the necessity for the principal rooms to face the meagre English sunshine. He also proposed two systems of heating a house which were important innovations. One was the principle to which we have now grown accustomed of a hot-water boiler feeding pipes, those massive, echoing coils which were usually contained within a solid cast-iron casing topped by a slab of marble; while the other, which was doubtless highly unsuccessful, was distantly reminiscent of the Roman system. It was suggested that houses should be built with a five-inch space between the inner and outer skins of bricks; into this cavity warm air would be introduced by means of an inlet set in the outer walls behind and just below the fireplaces. When the fire was lit the cold air would be sucked in, heated and dispersed by some scientific means which is not very clear into the hollow walls, whence gratings would admit a gentle warmth, and probably also a great quantity of dust and grit, into all rooms. It must be presumed that in practice the system was a failure, for it was the pipe installation which was to become the standard.

An early example of heating in a more conventional manner by hot air was that at the new House of Lords. The Rev. Richard

"A Design in the Elizabethan Style of Architecture" (1839). S. H. Brooks, Architect

39

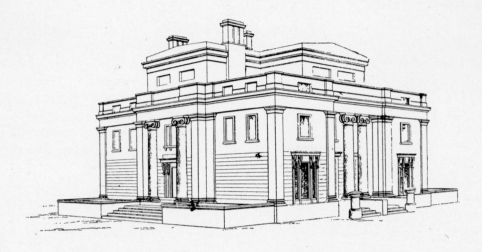

Villa "In the Ionic Style" (1839). S. H. Brooks, Architect

Barham, author of *The Ingoldsby Legends*, accompanied the Bishop of London on a tour of inspection in October, 1839. He was introduced to Dr. Reid, who was in charge of these operations and who explained the process:

"The walls of the rooms were of thick gauze, painted to represent oak panelling, and were perfectly porous. Below in Guy Fawkes's cellar, was an hydraulic apparatus, which being put in motion, all the air introduced was forced to pass through the purifying medium of a heavy shower of artificial rain. This detached all the dusty and sooty particles. The air was subsequently warmed by furnaces above."

One can picture poor Pugin shying at the sight of the sham oak, much as one shies today at the sounds of the wireless drifting through canvas screens disguised as panelling.

The aspect of a drawing-room in the house of an average well-to-do family at the time when Victoria ascended the throne has been briefly sketched in the previous chapter, but the general disposition of the furniture remains rather nebulous. Before very long, however, the invention of photography was to provide authentic records. In the early 'forties William Fox Talbot had produced admirable photographs of life at Lacock Abbey, and these were soon followed by Octavius Hill's and Mrs. Cameron's remarkable portraits. But the successful production of studies of interiors was a more complicated procedure, and it was not until the turn of the century that improvements in photographic plates made indoor photography generally feasible.

At the beginning of 1854 the Royal Photographic Society was formed under the presidency of Charles Eastlake, and with the Queen and Prince Albert as patrons. The society was able to make available for use by the public the various photographic processes invented by Fox Talbot, Scott Archer and others; and thus the interest in this new science spread to an ever-widening circle. A decade later, photography presented no difficulties to the great number of amateurs who took up the hobby with enthusiasm, and there are accomplished photographs of Victorian rooms to be found dating from that time forward; indeed they are even more numerous during the 'sixties and 'seventies than they became later, for with the invention of rolled films and instantaneous exposures, the enthusiast found the "snapping" of moving scenes more interesting than still life.

To obtain, then, a correct image of rooms of the 'forties one must still rely on contemporary paintings and drawings, and hope that these render a true picture of domestic surroundings before the taste of the Great Exhibition had crept into the furnishings of the average room. But even pictures of interiors of this period are unfortunately rather rare. The artists of these years favoured historical scenes with figures in Tudor, Elizabethan, or eighteenth-century dress, and seldom portrayed contemporary rooms containing people in the fashions of the day. The former, unless of great artistic merit, are now of no

The servants at Lacock Abbey about 1840. From a Calotype by W. H. Fox Talbot

41

interest, while the latter are much prized even when the quality of painting is poor.

The appearance of the average Regency room was generally one of considerable lightness, but the Regent himself, in the decoration and furnishing of Carlton House, had introduced a more lavish, a more opulent, a more generous style than was to be found in contemporary houses. At Carlton House the floors were close covered with carpet, generally of a brilliant blue scattered with golden fleurs-de-lis—a reference perhaps to the lilies of France which the Regent's father had dropped from the royal coat of arms; the windows were draped with curtains and pelmets arranged in the richest and most luxuriant folds, while along the walls stretched sofas, their deeply buttoned surfaces giving a welcoming air of comfort.

The short, brilliant flowering of Carlton House had lasted barely forty years, for in 1828 it was demolished; but the magnificence gathered within its sober-looking walls had an influence on taste which endured for more than a decade after the disappearance of the palace. It was an echo, a distant rarefied echo, of this style which formed the basis for rooms of the 'forties, though few people had the wealth to attempt the standard of Carlton House, nor, if they had the money, the ability to employ it with so much taste. In the desire to fill their rooms, they began to lose that sense of quality which had given distinction to the varied styles of the past century and a half, and from now forward quantity was to be the aim. Colours darkened, crimson and bottle-green came into fashion, and heavy materials such as velvet and rep were found to lend themselves happily to the pendulous draperies which were festooned round the windows.

Solid mahogany furniture was the typical product of the period and was gaining a lead in the race with rosewood. The straight turned leg had now finally superseded the curved reeded leg of the earlier period and had greatly diminished the grace of line which was general in Regency chairs. Large round tables carried on a single central support—monopodium is the proper name—which were introduced with the Regency style, became a feature of almost every sitting-room. They showed little fantasy: no longer would the support be formed as the curving, scaled body of a dolphin, or as a group of gambolling *putti*, no longer would the feet be winged as those of Perseus, though the form would be that of the paw of a lion. Instead, a solid, bulbous leg would carry out the duty, and lack of elegance would be compensated by an increase in stability. There was a general coarsening in style. Like a slim young woman growing into maturity, the figure was thickening, the delicate line was lost, and a rather ponderous dignity was taking the place of the former gaiety

A Mid-century Conversation Piece. By an unknown artist

and lightness. Furniture, indeed, was becoming distinctly *grande dame*. There were, of course, exceptions. For example, all through this period the pretty, gimcrack papier mâché furniture remained in vogue, contrasting strangely, with its gay painting and inconsequent form, with the robust and sensible mahogany productions.

If rooms became crowded, so also did walls. The age when Robert Adam had introduced a few romantic landscapes into the theme of the plaster decorations of his rooms, or roundels representing scenes from Greek mythology into the elaborate schemes of his ceilings, was long past. Now walls would be covered from below eye level to cornice with a multitude of paintings. It was a great age for water-colourists: on the walls might be found the delicate landscapes of Cotman or

43

Varley, both of whom died in 1842, or the gentle rivers and ruins lying beneath a wide, soft sky of De Wint or Copley Fielding but more probably there would be examples of the vast and popular output of the great company of second-class painters in water-colour at work during the first half of the nineteenth century. Their names are now forgotten, but their work conformed so closely to a settled style that it is difficult to differentiate one hand from another.

In oil-painting there was perhaps greater individuality. Etty's luscious canvases would be seen on many walls, for his output was enormous; there might be, though it would be unlikely, a Turner landscape, or one of G. F. Watts's early scenes; possibly poor Benjamin Haydon would have contributed a vast canvas of a brooding Napoleon at St. Helena or a victorious Wellington on the field of Waterloo. A narrative picture—some heart-rending occasion in English life—might have come from Martineau's brush, or an animated scene from Frith's. One of David Wilkie's *genre* paintings, or a Lawrence portrait, for Lawrence did not die until 1830, might give special distinction to the collection; but in any case good and bad would be almost as closely crowded in a fashionable private house as they were at the exhibitions at the Royal Academy, then held in the National Gallery building in Trafalgar Square. The walls of Walter Savage Landor's rooms at Bath, for instance, were covered in this indiscriminate manner, with the frames of the pictures fitting so closely to each other that no space was visible between them. Only a very few of these paintings were of any merit: the remainder, importantly labelled Titian, Giorgione, Vandyke and so forth, came from the junk-shops of the town.

Since a galaxy of pictures was so greatly admired it was fortunate that the structural decoration of houses of this period was usually severely plain. This was the case whether the exterior conformed to the classical or the Gothic manner, and the only indication from inside of the style of the exterior would be in the shape of the windows. Cornices and architraves to doorways and windows were simple, unenriched mouldings, and four-panelled doors, of which Soane was the principal pioneer, were coming into favour in place of the more graceful six-panel design which had been usual until a few years earlier. Chimney-pieces still showed Regency feeling, but, as with furniture, the style was coarsened. The marbles also, of which they were usually made, were chosen with less sense of colour: the whitest and shiniest products of the Carrara mines, or dark, mud-coloured marbles from Cornwall, were very popular. Short, stout columns on either side of the fire-opening would support a deep shelf which provided ample space for a catholic assortment of ornamental objects: clocks and vases, bronze figures and shell flowers would

jostle in neighbourly confusion, and so form a
strange contrast to the
austere *garnitures de
cheminée* of the previous
century.

Fitted grates made of
steel or iron became more
general than baskets and
were often extremely
attractive, showing much
fantasy in design and in
the moulding of the brass
ornamentation. Almost
invariably they were cast
out at a later date, when
grates at once more

*"A Chimney-piece in the style of Louis XIV,
fitted up with one of Sylvester's open grates"*
(c. 1835)

efficient and more economical were devised, so that comparatively
few still exist.

This cursory description applies only to the conventional sitting-
rooms of the 'forties, of those rooms indeed of which no exact
descriptions have survived, and which seldom formed the subject
of pictures for the excellent reason that there was little to remark in
them. When we consider the rare details that have come down to
us of the rooms of the famous, we find that they often diverge from
the commonplace. Lady Blessington's rooms at Gore House, Kensington, for example, to which rural situation she moved from Seamore
Place in 1836, had more in common with the style of the Regency
than with that of the new reign which was about to open.

Camilla Toulmin, in *Landmarks of a Literary Life*, seems to have
been the only one of the many who thronged these rooms who left
any account of them. The fabric of the house was late eighteenth
century, but the interior decoration was entirely Marguerite Blessington. The library, which ran right through the house with windows at
either end and pillars at a point where a partition-wall had been
removed, was the principal room. Here the bookshelves lining the
walls were given lightness by strips of mirror set perpendicularly
between the tiers of shelves, while mirror also panelled the doors.
Green damask was used for the curtains, which were embellished with
deep fringes, and material of the same colour was on the chairs: a
dark green carpet covered the floor. Lady Blessington was a keen
collector of *objets d'art*, and the room contained a great number of
her purchases. It was generally accepted that she, with the assistance
of Count d'Orsay, was a leader of taste in such matters as interior

Thomas and Jane Carlyle in their drawing-room about 1858

From the painting by Robert S. Tait

decoration: it seems to us now, knowing what the future of taste was to be, that the attractive rooms in Gore House were essentially reactionary.

Lady Blessington's move from Seamore Place had been enforced by two factors, one social, the other financial. Since she was generally cut by every woman of fashion she met in the streets of Mayfair, it seemed wiser to move to a house with a large garden in which she could wander without experiencing these galling encounters. At the same time she expected to be able to live with much greater economy at Gore House. But Lady Blessington's poverty was poverty in the grand manner, and in no way precluded the decoration of her new home from cellar to attic.

A very different establishment was the little house of Thomas and Jane Carlyle at No. 5 Cheyne Row in Chelsea. They had come there in 1834, and were paying the modest rent of £35 a year. In the summer of 1843, Mrs. Carlyle took advantage of her husband's absence to have the house redecorated. "It will be a clean pretty house for you to come home to", she wrote to her husband, and warned him that the small sum of money he had given her for the purpose would be slightly exceeded. Meanwhile woodwork was rubbed down for repainting, ceilings were whitewashed and flowered papers were pasted on the walls; and poor Mrs. Carlyle suffered from more headaches than usual owing to the noise and confusion in which she

46

was living. Carlyle, who from the domestic aspect, as well as many others, was an exceedingly difficult man, seems to have taken little interest in the transformation which met his eyes on return, and on which his poor Jane had spent so much time and trouble. About 1858 the Carlyles were painted in their sitting-room by Robert Tait, and no doubt the scene is substantially as created by the redecoration of fifteen years earlier. There is the flowered paper, which in the meantime Mrs. Carlyle had industriously cleaned with bread-crumbs, the cream-painted woodwork, and the whitewashed ceiling somewhat blackened by lamp fumes and the London air. Unexpectedly the blossoming wall-paper was not concealed by crowded pictures, indeed there were only two or three in the room, while over the plain marble chimney-piece was a large rectangular mirror.

One would have expected that long before 1858 the Carlyle's house would have been lit by gas, but this does not appear to have been the case. The only visible means of illumination was a candle-stick placed rather conspicuously on a central table, which was draped with a richly patterned crimson cloth. In general, houses in towns were lit by this useful invention before the opening of the 'forties, for it had been introduced by William Murdoch as early as 1805. There had been serious teething troubles before the domestic use of gas was accepted as a welcome appurtenance to the average home, but by 1840 the Gas Light and Coke Company had been formed and was eager to supply carburetted hydrogen to almost any district of the metropolis. The gas-pipes were usually brought to brackets on either side of the chimney breast, and to an ornate brass chandelier suspended from a plaster rosette in the centre of the ceiling. Circular frosted globes, perhaps starred like the firmament, would shield and diffuse the light of the flame, and cast a pleasant and intimate radiance over the room. The sense of quiet comfort was increased by the gentle purring sound made by the gas as it emerged from the flame holder.

This modern amenity was naturally not available to those living in the country or in suburban areas, though a few of the larger country

"Conventional Mediæval Gaselier"

47

"Gothic Corona Lucis"

houses had their own gas-producing plants. In 1849 an enterprising Mr. Mansfield devised a "New Domestic Gas-Light Apparatus" which could be situated in the cellar of a house—if the occupier was of a confident nature. It was operated by a pair of bellows, worked by hand, which drove air into a gas-holder whence it passed into an airtight container filled with benzole. After various other adventures the air, now converted into gas, passed out of the cellar through pipes to the upper floors. A domestic was no doubt intended to spend long winter evenings in the cellar providing motive power for the bellows.

Where gas was unobtainable, camphine lamps were the most modern introduction. They provided a clear white light, more brilliant than gas, but distinctly more dangerous, for the spirit when mixed with air became extremely volatile. Loud explosions, breaking the calm of the cosy, crowded rooms of the period, were by no means unusual; but they were fortunately seldom on a major scale. Not until the invention of the incandescent burner in 1879, as is described in Chapter VII, was electricity put to domestic use for lighting, but as early as the summer of 1849 "electric rays" were used to illuminate Vauxhall Gardens. Many improvements had been made by the new "*Entrepreneurs*" for this season: the dreary "Hermit's cave" and the "tinkling tin waterfall" had been swept away, and a splendid Italian Walk, decorated with statues and urns, had been laid out in one part of the gardens, and elsewhere romantic Gothic ruins had been erected amongst the trees, "the real appearance" of which earned much favourable comment. Both these fine features were thrown at night into effective relief by the new method of lighting, while the Neptune Fountain, if not quite on the magnificent scale of the *Bassin de Neptune* at Versailles, presented a dramatic aspect, with its gambolling sea-horses and many jets of shimmering water, when irradiated by the dazzling beams.

The innovation was turned to practical uses as well in lighting Mr. Green's balloon, the "Victoria", which ascended from the gardens at eleven o'clock at night. The dazzling ray was emitted from a wooden construction fixed above the stands of spectators, and it was remarked that "its effulgence upon the balloon was very striking".

An attractive feature of country houses and suburban villas at this early-Victorian period was the conservatory, which was attached to the house and opened, if this could be devised, out of the drawing-room. In the eighteenth century many large houses had orangeries, designed in a simple classical style, set a little way from the main building so as to form an agreeable feature of the romantic lay-out and also a pleasant objective for a short walk. Early in the nineteenth century, however, Humphry Repton advocated attaching a conservatory to a house in such a position that it became a feature from within; ". . . an enfilade, or visto, through a modern house, is occasionally increased by a conservatory at one end, and repeated by a large mirror at the opposite end", he wrote in *Fragments* published in 1816. He then proceeded to give some elaborate examples, one of which was designated as a "flower tunnel" which, long though it was, would appear double its real length owing to the cunning placing of a mirror at the end of the leafy bower.

Victorians adopted Repton's innovation with enthusiasm, but, whereas conservatories of this style had at first been conceived only for large houses, during the 'forties they were being attached to small villas which could not boast a "visto" of any sort. Repton had advocated there being a lobby between house and conservatory "to prevent the damp smell of earth". The Victorians happily threw this careful advice to the winds, and in many of the smaller houses the only window of the drawing-room would open direct into the sub-tropical atmosphere of a greenhouse—a singularly unsatisfactory arrangement, which would ensure an airless room in summer and a dark one in winter.

The simple lines of these early Victorian conservatories were often charming, and retained the lightness and grace of the early Regency to a very considerable degree. It was from these structures that Joseph Paxton elaborated his design for the great conservatory at Chatsworth which was in process of building between 1836 and 1840. It was a huge building three hundred feet in length, and to some degree it formed the basis for the design for the great glass palace of 1851, which we shall visit in the next chapter.

Conservatory at Alton Towers. Designed by Robert Abraham

If the style of conservatories was changing more slowly than that of architecture, so also was that of gardens. The simple gardens of the 'forties must obviously have had great charm, in an ingenuous, artless way. There were, of course, the impressive formal lay-outs created by Sir Charles Barry with great success, such as those at Trentham, Shrublands, Harewood and others. These were schemes in which architecture played a large part, with balustraded terraces, flights of stone steps, stone rimmed pools and impressive vistas, with many formal beds to lend colour to the parterres: gardens, indeed, which required an army of workers if they were to be retained in the way the designer intended. But the typical gardens, those surrounding the average-sized country houses and the rustic villas which were creeping into the landscape, were very different in spirit. Here all was informal and bosky, and the principal aim was to make a garden look as if designed by nature and not by man. A few small flower-beds would certainly be allowed in the close neighbourhood of the house, but further afield, beyond an irregular stretch of lawn, narrow gravel paths would wind away amongst dull, evergreen shrubberies, and by ingenious twists and turns would provide the maximum length of path in a minimum area. Indeed Pope's lines, written a little over a century earlier and designed for the spacious landscape lay-outs which were then being created round the great Palladian country houses, were adapted with success to the crowded gardens of the 'forties:

> Let not each beauty ev'ry where be spy'd,
> Where half the skill is decently to hide;
> He gains all points, who pleasingly confounds,
> Surprizes, varies, and conceals the Bounds.

The surprises may not have been very striking, but at least the meandering paths were designed to conceal the restrictions of the site. Pope's advice has never been bettered, and perhaps in cycles of a century it will continue to be accepted as the best basis for garden design. Now, once again after a long interval, gardens are devised with these important principles in mind.

Until a few years ago the gardens of some of the larger squares of Belgravia survived as very fair examples of the style of the 'forties: here were to be found narrow gravel paths wandering rather aimlessly round thickets of privet and lilac, while the central lawn, concealed from the road within these barriers, would be decorated with a few flower-beds and a weeping tree or two. They were not unattractive. A number of them were laid out by John Loudon, who died in 1843, and who in the course of his extremely active life not only worked on these new square gardens, and planned a number of

A Garden Fountain (c. 1835)

large public cemeteries, but also edited several horticultural magazines. The style which he advocated influenced garden design for several decades.

The lines on which garden paths were designed were applied with even greater force to the drive of approach. "The drive up to the house should curve gracefully", wrote Mr. Brooks, whose book on cottages and villas has already been quoted. And not only should it curve, but it should also be as long as possible. The house might stand only fifty yards from the high road, but that the drive should approach it direct would be unthinkable. Once through the entrance gate it would strike out in a purposeful way in any direction except that of the house; after a short expedition into the landscape it would circumvent a group of evergreens or a grove of trees, and turn back to the forecourt of the house. If the house were in the classical style, surroundings in a slightly more formal manner might be countenanced, but in general winding paths and thickly planted shrubberies, such as those that the Ladies of Llangollen allowed

51

favoured visitors to their house to inspect, were essential features of gardens of the period.

A gentleman's house, even of no great size, would not be complete without a suitable lodge at the entrance to the drive. In appearance it would generally echo the style of the house to which it formed an outpost, classical, Gothic or castellated. It was particularly in this type of cottage that contemporary architects excelled: the accommodation was generally exiguous, but these little buildings designed with considerable fantasy and panache have great charm. Where the main house, whatever its style, became rather laboured, with the restricted repertoire of the architect stretched to the utmost, the lodges were often full of happy invention and fitted very pleasantly into their surroundings.

It was a prudent measure of aspiring architects to turn their attention to the designing of villas and houses of moderate size, but of supreme "gentility and elegance", two words which were much to the fore in books of designs, for there was a large class of people coming forward requiring houses with these two attributes, but who did not come into the big-house class. If London was to be their place of residence they would move, as we have seen, into one of the houses in the genteel new quarter of Bayswater or, a few years later, into the equally class-conscious area of South Kensington. If they decided to live in one of the many pleasant rural villages which still surrounded the metropolis, though only a few miles distant from the money-making centre, then something on a moderate scale, but modelled on the mansions of the very rich, was clearly indicated. The lodge and drive, the gravel sweep before the handsome flight of steps, these were essential features to create a correct first impression; while within the house, the reception rooms, which were often on a *piano nobile* so that the offices could be relegated to a basement, were planned with considerable pomp. The bedrooms, which would be seen only by the family and intimate friends, were of secondary importance.

The 'forties were a boom period for architects and contractors. The majority of the newly affluent were entirely ignorant of the rudiments of architecture, and their principal demand was for a new-built house which would testify to their sound financial status. To purchase a reserved Georgian house would hardly fulfil this requirement: something new, something discreetly showy was essential, for there is no doubt that the vulgarity of taste which pervades so much of the Victorian epoch was beginning to creep in.

There were many means of making a fortune at this time: in addition to respectable industry and commerce, there was also speculation, for 1845 marked the peak of the Railway Mania. In

November of that year Greville wrote on the subject: "It is incredible how people have been tempted to speculate: half the fine ladies have been dabbling in stocks, and men most unlikely have not been able to refrain from gambling in shares". It was not only Greville's acquaintances who were speculating: the excitement of easy money pervaded all classes. Up to 31st October, 1845, no less than three hundred and fifty-seven new railroad schemes were announced in the Press, inviting subscription for three hundred and thirty-two million pounds' worth of shares.

Many of these companies were entirely bona fide, even some of those which were formed to construct a very short length of line, and which could never, as it transpired, have been run at a profit. There was, for example, the Enfield and Edmonton Railway which was only three miles in length and adapted a fine Stuart house as a station at Enfield. There were many others on this scale, where the cost of construction and maintenance would never have allowed an economic return. These were examples of miscalculation and not of dishonesty. But there were a large number of companies floated merely for the purpose of extracting money from the public, where there was no intention of building any railroad at all. Shares in genuine and in bogus companies soared equally, irrespective of merits, and a number reached premiums of over two thousand per cent. with no more solid backing than optimistic statements and promises. Substantial profits were made by those who were prudent enough to unload their holdings before collapse came.

The ephemeral prosperity which the railway bubble created was widespread. Daily newspapers were deluged with applications for advertising space; in the City it was almost impossible to find sufficient accommodation for all the new Companies, and rents rose to extraordinary heights. Often the offices of a company offering a million pounds' worth of shares to the public consisted of no more than a garret into which two or three directors and a secretary would be crowded. High and low, rich and poor, joined in the rush for shares, and many who had never envisaged possessing wealth found themselves able to buy estates, build houses, and generally to adorn their lives with all the appurtenances of riches.

An outstanding figure of the boom was George Hudson, the Railway King, as he came to be known. Starting from a fairly humble origin in Yorkshire, he was bequeathed a sum of £30,000 in 1827 by a distant relative. The whole of this legacy he invested in North Midland Railway shares, and from that time his connection with the railway world became increasingly close. There were few large companies of which he was not a director, and in many others he was a shareholder. So great did his fortune become that he was able to

53

The Royal Railway Carriage (1849)

buy one of the vast new houses adjoining Albert Gate in Knightsbridge; thus extinguishing the name given to the two expensive buildings flanking the gateway: "the Rocks of Gibraltar", since no one could take them. Here he entertained on a lavish scale, the Queen and Prince Albert even honouring him on one occasion with their presence at dinner. He was an early example of a self-made man penetrating into the closely guarded circles of early Victorian society. There was special reason for this, however; not only were his parties desirable, but he also was in a position to make money for his friends. Thus the most exclusive doors were immediately thrown open to this bountiful Croesus.

Unlike the instantaneous bursting of the South Sea Bubble in the previous century, the collapse of the railway boom began slowly, but soon gathered speed. Late in 1845 there were falls, followed by partial recoveries, in the values of shares; in 1846 the falls heavily predominated; late in 1847 it was calculated that the depreciation in the shares of the ten principal companies amounted to seventy-eight million pounds. Many small companies were wiped out, and financial ruin entered houses of all grades including the sumptuous building at Albert Gate.

The railway boom, with easy money for many people, represented one side of the medal of the period; on the other was the distress and privation amongst the working classes, which gave this decade the name of "the Hungry 'Forties". The Corn Laws, which were intended to maintain a stable level in the price of wheat, had caused recurring trouble ever since their inception as long ago as the fourteenth century. The general intention was to tax imported wheat when the supply was plentiful in England and the price low, and to allow it in almost free when English wheat was scarce and the price high. It was hoped by means of this sliding scale to maintain the prosperity of agriculture and to ensure that no land went out of cultivation. The laws thus favoured the producer at the expense of the consumer, who could often barely afford the price of bread.

In 1845, for example, the average wage of a farm labourer was nine shillings a week, while a quartern loaf cost one shilling and twopence. A man with several children to feed could not possibly afford meat, and, with a few other vegetables from the garden, potatoes were the staple family diet; while burnt crusts would be put into the teapot to form a beverage which resembled tea only in colour. Workers in industry were slightly better paid; but they were unable to grow any foodstuffs for themselves, since there were seldom gardens or allotments amongst the crowded tenements which were being run up to house the workers in the many new industries developed with the utilization of steam-power. Thus the greater part of the working classes were living on the border-line of starvation. Agitation for the repeal of the burdensome Corn Laws had been increasing over a number of years, but decisive action had constantly been rejected by Parliament. At last Sir Robert Peel, the Tory Prime Minister, became convinced of the necessity, and the act was passed. Two years later the price of the loaf had been reduced to four pence.

The position of domestic servants was in some ways better than that of manual labourers in that they were at least unaffected by the rise or fall in the price of wheat. But their wages were exceedingly low. An under-housemaid, "tweeny", or general would have considered herself fortunate if she received a wage of eight or nine pounds a year, in return for about sixteen hours' work a day. When Prince Albert tackled the reorganization of the households at Buckingham Palace and Windsor Castle, which had hitherto been conducted on lines of extreme extravagance and confusion, he fixed the wages of housemaids at from twelve to eighteen pounds a year. This was considerably in advance of the usual rate.

The food in the servants' halls of larger houses was generally adequate, though very plain. When Augustus Hare went to stay with his grandparents in the early 'forties he noticed that the men and maidservants sitting at long tables had only large bowls of bread and milk to eat for breakfast: in the housekeeper's room there was bread and butter and tea. Sleeping accommodation was very austere. In small London houses, as at Mrs. Carlyle's in Cheyne Row, the maid slept in the basement kitchen; in larger houses, they were relegated to chilly attics. In big houses there were sometimes long dormitories for menservants and maidservants located high up in the pitch of the roof. This was a traditional arrangement of past centuries, but it is rather surprising to find it perpetuated in a house such as Mamhead, in Devon, which was built by Anthony Salvin in the 'thirties. Here there were two dormitories, one for men, the other for maids, divided by a securely fastened door, and they have remained unaltered to the present day. In each there is a long line of narrow beds facing the small dormer windows, each bed has its white, dimity curtains at the head; each its own little chest of drawers. To young servants, used to the squalor of cottage life, this must have seemed like comfort: the only amenity lacking was privacy.

In country districts servants were easily come by, but in and near industrial towns, where there was a continual demand for workers in factories, they were becoming scarce. London lay midway between these two extremes: millinery, sewing, and laundry work absorbed a large number of girls, but the necessary maids could usually still be found. An enquiry made in the middle years of the century revealed that there were 175,000 men and women employed in domestic service in London, and in the 'forties the numbers must have been approximately the same. The staffs in the big country houses were conceived on the most lavish scale. At Stratfield Saye, for example, the Duke of Wellington had an indoor staff of about thirty-five, and in houses such as Wentworth Woodhouse or Blenheim there must have been a considerably greater number. The domestic arrangements would be on the following lines: the male staff would consist of a house-steward, a groom of the chambers, a butler with an assistant, two or three valets, six footmen, an usher, a hall boy and several lamp-men; the female contingent would be a housekeeper, a cook with about six assistants, though both cook and some of the assistants might be male, several ladies' maids, fifteen or more housemaids, and in addition laundry-maids, and nurses and nurserymaids as required.

In a country house where there was a family of growing children it was not at all unusual for five sets of meals to be served daily. There would be the principal meals in the dining-room, for the older children and the governess in the schoolroom, for the infants and nurses in the nursery; and as soon as these were completed the upper and lower servants would have their repast in the housekeeper's room and servants' hall respectively. This was the order of the day throughout the nineteenth century, not only in the great houses, but also in those of no particular pretensions, and a large staff was essential to carry out the complicated programme.

The number of houses organized on a magnificent scale were naturally few, but the establishments with a dozen or so in service were many, while the average house in Bayswater or Belgravia would employ at least six. With wages so low, even the most impoverished could afford a "slavey" of a humble sort. Benjamin Haydon, whose latter miserable years were spent in extorting little loans of a few pounds from his friends, employed a maid to help his "dear Mary". The Carlyles, also, who lived in Cheyne Row without a shilling to spare, always had a maid to cook and clean, with an occasional daily assistant. In Mrs. Carlyle's letters there are constant references to maids. Helen, for example, a young Scots girl, seemed a treasure, until one evening extraordinary sounds were heard from the basement, and little Helen was discovered fighting drunk in the kitchen. She was severely reprimanded but forgiven; a second time the same catastrophe occurred with the same result; there was a third relapse and she was definitely given her *congé*. But her appearance was so woebegone as she came to receive her last pittance on departure, that Mrs. Carlyle was moved to give her one final chance. Her kindness was rewarded, and Helen remained with her for eight unblemished years.

It was already becoming rather difficult to find the sort of maid Mrs. Carlyle's small establishment required. On Helen's departure to act as housekeeper for an affluent brother, Mrs. Carlyle engaged a temporary servant, who drove Carlyle "to despair". An advertisement was then put into *The Times*, but only one applicant materialized, and she was unsuitable. There was an uncomfortable hiatus before "a little creature called Anne" was found to fill the gap. Clearly the supply of domestic servants in London was already becoming shorter. In the country, where it was still considered not only a good training but also an honour for the labourer's daughter to be employed at "the big house", the position was easy, and those who moved from the country to their London houses for a few months in the year would bring their households with them. Servants were beginning to realize the strength of their position, and jokes which were becoming popular in pages of *Punch* of pert slaveys and outraged mistresses were indicative of current conditions. A slightly subversive feeling was becoming apparent in the lower orders. It was generally agreed that it must be crushed at all costs, or where would it lead to? We, three generations later, see the attainment of the ultimate objective.

It was thus against a very unequal background, a background of intense chiaroscuro, that the smooth, upholstered, early-Victorian homes were created. On the one hand was the increasing opulence, and the rising commercial families; on the other were the low wages and extreme poverty of the working classes. The Victorians were not uncharitable: there were many who shared the humanitarian views of Cobden and Lord Shaftesbury, but who felt themselves baffled by the vastness of the social problem. At the same time there seems now to have been a certain obtuseness in the approach towards the poor. They were not expected to have very sensitive feelings, and brought up as they often were, in circumstances of hardship and squalor, finer feelings had in fact little opportunity for developing. It was the generally accepted opinion that the poor should feel contented with their lot, even if that lot could be more accurately described as little. The Sunday school, which would be one of the interests of the lady bountiful and her daughters, afforded an admirable opportunity for inculcating a spirit of Christian resignation into the children of the village.

> *The rich man in his castle,*
> *The poor man at his gate,*
> *God made them high or lowly,*
> *And ordered their estate.*

Let the children learn this admirable Victorian hymn and take the well-expressed sentiments thoroughly to heart.

Taste during this decade was gradually veering towards the elaborate and the opulent; this was the taste of those who considered themselves in the van of fashion; many others still cast back their eyes to the simpler, more austere, style of William IV's reign. Very shortly, however, taste would be crystallized in the heterogeneous collection of objects displayed beneath the glass vaults in Hyde Park.

Cast-iron door porter
(c. 1850)

"Berlin Black Inkstand" (*c.* 1845)

CHAPTER III

GOTHIC TRIUMPHANT

1850—1860

IN the industrial cities of the Midlands the wheels were turning at high speed. Steam-power was now fully harnessed, and had been brought into use for the manufacture of a wide range of products, varying from the most complex and massive machinery to small articles designed for domestic use, in quantities and at a rate never previously thought possible. The machine age was in full swing, and methods of production were being entirely revolutionized. Never before had the domestic market been so copiously supplied with objects designed either to embellish or to add to the convenience of homes of all classes.

No new model can be produced without first being designed, and drawing-boards of the period must have been engaged to the uttermost in carrying out drawings of ever-increasing elaboration. Where an object was made in cast metal, it made little difference to cost or difficulty of production whether it was elaborate or simple in form, while the former, so it was generally accepted, gave a much increased air of opulence. Whether it was the manufacturers or the public who were responsible for this retrograde trend it is not now easy to distinguish, but no doubt the usual course was pursued of the purchaser demanding and the manufacturer producing. In any case products of both large and small cost were equally affected. Humble domestic necessities such as boot scrapers and coal-scuttles were loaded with flowery and unsuitable decoration in modest imitation of the massive ornaments and centre-pieces which were produced in precious metals.

59

Nº 9672.5
Japanned   13/ ...
French Bronzed 16/ .
Fancy Bronzed   16. .
Berlin Black   16/ .

Cast-iron Umbrella Stand (c. 1845)

These mid-nineteenth-century years were a great age for presentation plate, an embarrassment from which public figures of this austere age are happily preserved. Retirement from any important position was almost inevitably signalized by the presentation of a piece of silver or silver gilt as large as a monument. The design of the ornament would naturally bear some indication of the services which were being so handsomely rewarded: for a successful general a group of palm trees with some dying negroes beneath their fronds would be considered tasteful; for a master of foxhounds a hunt in full cry at the base of a rocky silver hill would be suitable. Here there was no mass production, and much good craftsmanship was often expended on these useless objects, but it was seldom that the general design was satisfactory. The greater number, embodying much work and good intention, have now returned to the melting-pot.

An example, which perhaps still survives, was the "gilt centre-piece" designed by Prince Albert and made by command of the Queen. It was a little less florid than most contemporary work. It consisted of what was called "a salver in antique taste" supported on an elaborate pedestal of vaguely Italian Renaissance style. On the steps at the base were grouped representations of four of the Queen's favourite dogs, on one side a greyhound and a rough-haired terrier with a dead hare at their feet, on the other a "turnspit" dog and another terrier gazing with interest at a rat in a cage. The animals were modelled by Mr. Cotterell and the remainder of the work was executed by Messrs. Garrard. These Victorian monuments were the descendants of the great *surtouts de table* such as those presented to the Duke of Wellington by a number of grateful monarchs, some of which are now on view at Apsley House. It was fortunate that the Duke's military achievements took place before the decay of taste had set in.

It became essential for manufacturers to devise some means of

"For Sale" (1852). From the painting by James Collinson

displaying their new and exciting wares to the public, some more striking and compelling method of salesmanship than commonplace advertisements in the newspapers. For they had much to show, and a stimulus was needed to attract the purchasing public. Midland manufacturers, therefore, decided to hold a grand exhibition in

Birmingham, the town which was the centre for the production of the politer forms of metal work, and to give objects intended for domestic use a prominent place in the display. The exhibition was happily timed to coincide with a meeting of the British Association and a musical festival which were taking place in the city. It was named the Exposition of Arts and Manufactures, and was opened to the public at the beginning of September, 1849.

The hall, in the grounds of Bingley House, Broad Street, had been specially built for the occasion at a cost of two thousand pounds; and the exhibits in this spacious hall were not confined either to metal work or to English products. There was to be seen china and woodwork, materials and wall-papers, as well as the "productions of France in metallurgy, and Bohemia in glass". This exhibition, however, was soon to fade into obscurity before the dazzle and glamour of the great undertaking in London eighteen months later; but it had its importance as forming to some degree a dress rehearsal to the latter, while the change in the taste of the exhibits, though the interval was so short, is striking. The majority of designs at Birmingham were imbued with a strong classical spirit, and, although a superfluity of decoration was often introduced, there was usually a simplicity of line more reminiscent of the work of the early years of the century than of a date verging on the middle. Some of Messrs. Messenger & Sons' metal castings might be quite welcome today: the reproduction of the "Petrarch inkstand brought from Italy by the late Miss Edgeworth" was distinctly pleasing, and the tall metal lampstands had undoubted elegance.

But perhaps the greatest interest in the exhibition lay in Messrs. Hardman's stand of objects of church decoration, for which Pugin was the principal designer. Here naturally the Gothic note was stressed, and perhaps for this reason the stand received greater praise than any other part of the exhibition. The *Illustrated London News* was particularly enthusiastic. "Collectively", wrote their contributor, "we have never before seen so complete an exposition of ecclesiastical ornament, and in such thorough good taste, brought together". There were candlesticks, reliquaries, censers, flagons, processional crosses, and a great number of other church ornaments carried out in gold, silver and enamel; while Messrs. Crace & Son had contributed many examples of church furniture. Here indeed Pugin gained useful experience for the arrangement of the Mediaeval Court in 1851.

Some time before the Birmingham exhibition took place, the Prince Consort had conceived the plan of holding a vast exhibition in London organized on the widest lines and designed to attract exhibitors from all over the world. The Prince felt, with justifiable confidence, that English productions could with advantage be placed in competition with those of other countries, and would thus be readily acceptable in the markets of the world. This represented the material aspect of the project: it was also designed to carry a profound spiritual message, to exemplify the high and humanitarian ideals which underlay the progress and prosperity which were so apparent in England. It is probable that the subtleties of this message were lost on the world, but in all other respects the Prince's plan was a triumphant success. The material achievements of manufacturers, the machinery and inventions, the rich and varied productions of the applied arts, were patent for all to see and for all, with rare exceptions, to admire.

"The results of the Exhibition are pregnant with incalculable benefits to all classes of the community", was written rather pompously in the preface to the catalogue; and it was not an excessive overstatement. Nevertheless, there was much painful and acrimonious skirmishing before the Prince's project was generally accepted as being desirable. However, Albert's energy carried all before it, and an influential body of Commissioners was selected for the organization of this huge scheme, and a site south of the Serpentine in Hyde Park was agreed upon. But the design of the exhibition hall excited intense controversy, and it was not until June, 1850, that one, out of the two hundred and thirty-three designs submitted in the competition, was eventually selected. The dominant feature of "this monster edifice", as it was called—the adjective referring rather to its size than to its appearance—was a huge central dome which was to be forty-five feet larger in diameter than the dome of St. Paul's; while the length of the whole building, which was to be constructed in brick, would be four times that of the cathedral. The publication of the design was greeted with conspicuous lack of enthusiasm, while to Mr. Paxton, who studied the drawings in a copy of *The Builder*, it caused positive dismay. He at once enquired from the Building Committee whether it was too late for him to submit proposals, and was told it was not. Within eight days Paxton's finished plans and drawings were in the hands of the Committee, and after considerable deliberation were eventually accepted.

There were obvious advantages in Paxton's design over all others submitted, both aesthetically and practically. A great building of glass and iron gleaming in the tepid London sunshine would have that appearance of festivity and gaiety which was essential for the setting of the greatest exhibition that had ever taken place; in addition the structure in itself, as much as the remarkable display which was to be housed within it, represented a triumph of art and engineering. From the practical aspect the points in its favour were manifest. It was to be made up of a great number of prefabricated

Visiting the Great Exhibition. From a contemporary painting

units, so that the skeleton of the structure could be turned out by the foundries, brought to the site, and immediately erected like the steel bones of a present-day reinforced concrete building. The glass, the majority of the sheets of which were of similar size, could then be speedily fitted into the metal frames. Here indeed were speed and economy in building to a degree which had never previously been envisaged. There was a further advantage: whereas a brick building could be dismantled only with a great loss of material, Paxton's building could be taken to pieces without the necessary loss of a single sheet of glass. Perhaps Paxton eventually regretted this last feature of his design, for he later advocated very strongly the retention of the structure on the Hyde Park site and its conversion to a winter garden for the enjoyment of the public: it would have been a unique feature of any metropolis.

The qualities and defects of the objects displayed, which were intended for the embellishment of the Victorian home, have been constantly discussed and reviewed, and it is seldom that they have received anything but unfavourable criticism. Regarded as a whole, it emerges clearly that taste in all the great countries of the world was on a similar plane. English taste was no lower than the others, and was perhaps even a little less preposterous than that of France. Craftsmen of all countries were united in their love of decoration and elaboration: everywhere was evidence of the exact contrary of Inigo Jones's wise axiom: "In all designing of ornament one must first design the ground plain as it is for use, and then adorn and compose it with decorum according to its use".

This admirable advice was not, it seems, entirely forgotten, but it had somehow gone adrift. A prize of one hundred guineas had been offered for an essay on "The Exhibition as a Lesson in Taste". It was won by R. N. Wornum, and his prosy article is printed at the end of the catalogue. "Ornament is not a luxury . . . but an absolute necessity", he wrote; and again, "ornament is essentially the accessory

Sociable (1851). Exhibited by J. & W. Hilton of Montreal

"A Wanstead Sofa" (1851). Exhibited by Gillow & Co.

to, and not the substitute of, the useful". The grammar may have
been a little faulty but the second sentiment, if not the first, would
have been accepted by Inigo Jones. It cannot, however, be maintained
that many of the designers kept these sound principles in mind.

The principal means now available to us for studying the great
mass of the exhibits, is the line drawings in the catalogue and in
contemporary illustrated papers. The representations are accurate
but not flattering, as can be deduced from those exhibits which are
still to be seen in the round. It is possible that if they had been
illustrated by photography our judgment might be less harsh. In any
case it would have required photography of the most expert kind to
conceal the overwhelming massivity and elaboration of the furniture,
some of which has appeared in recent exhibitions in London. It must
not be supposed that all the monumental pieces of furniture were
accepted as being beautiful specimens of art, even at the time of the
Exhibition, when the senses must have been bludgeoned into semi-
consciousness by the quantity and forcefulness of the exhibits. The
official catalogue naturally introduces no word of adverse criticism,
but the illustrated papers could adopt a more captious approach.
The firm of Gillow, for example, who with their fine tradition might
have been expected to produce furniture of sound design, were
awarded some very hostile remarks in the *Illustrated London News*:

> "The Library Table, Sofa, and Easy chair . . . are specimens
> of the more substantial class of furniture, in which it has been
> attempted to combine extreme solidity with elaborate adornment.
> We confess we are by no means well pleased with the result".

The paragraph continues with detailed and very just criticism
complaining particularly of the amount of space which the furniture
takes up in comparison to the useful accommodation provided. The
sofa, for example, with large winged griffins at the front corners is as
large and ostentatious as a Jacobean tomb, but provides sitting

space for only two. But all three pieces of furniture were so highly decorated, so encrusted with projecting ornament, that anyone spending much time in their proximity would inevitably be severely bruised.

A large area of precious floor space was given up to the Mediaeval Court which was under Pugin's special charge. Here a different note was sounded. The furniture and objects, both ecclesiastical and lay, shared the general ponderous quality, but at least they were not vulgar. The furniture produced by such craftsmen and firms as Myers, Crace, Hardman and others was reticent in design rather than ostentatious: outlines were four-square and directly in contrast to the bounding curves, the luxuriant polypi, the mixed metaphors, which shouted so noisily from other stalls and stands. Here alone, perhaps, was to be detected something of the message with which the Prince Consort had hoped to imbue the whole mammoth Exhibition. Here was to be seen a love of craftsmanship, a singleness of purpose, and in the collection of church ornaments a perceptible degree of spiritual feeling. But from the practical aspect, the lay furniture was

A Group of Ecclesiastical Objects
Designed by A. W. Pugin and shown at the Great Exhibition

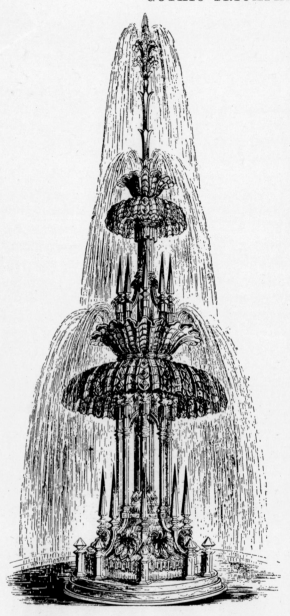

The Glass Fountain at the Great Exhibition

ill conceived, and it is difficult to guess for what settings it was designed. It would have looked singularly inappropriate in the polite drawing-rooms of South Kensington or in the rather noisy villas which were going up in suburban areas. Perhaps a suitable *milieu* could have been found in some of the large country houses which were being built, such as Worsley Hall which Blore had lately erected for Lord Ellesmere in the Elizabethan style; but on the whole, mediaeval furniture demanded a mediaeval setting and this was not always easy to find.

The furniture made by Myers was in general less severely mediaeval than that of his colleagues, though this tendency was not allowed to creep into his exhibits in the Mediaeval Court. He was primarily a builder, the assistant of Pugin, and his designs had an architectural quality which the others lacked. He was inclined to turn to the Renaissance for inspiration, and the varnished oak cabinets which he made were inlaid with panels of marble and decorated with twisted columns of ebony. On other occasions he would adopt a more Gothic spirit and inlay his tables with chastening mottoes such as "Waste ye not nor spoil the products of the fruits of toil". Here was a true disciple of Pugin.

There was one object in the Exhibition which excited universal praise and would probably do so still. This was the great glass fountain made by Messrs. Osler, which stood in the midst of the main transept. It was twenty-seven feet high and was so contrived that the whole of the metal structure which supported the glass was invisible. Water gushed from three tiers of fluted basins of decreasing size, and descended in a transparent curtain of water into the pool from which the fountain rose.

It had at first been proposed to reward successful exhibitors with financial prizes: it was, however, eventually decided that the presentation of a medal would be a more fitting, and certainly a more economical, reward. Here again was an occasion for competition, which was won by M. Bonnardel of France. The design consisted of a figure of Britannia, who was backed by a panoply of flags and held wreaths over the heads of two figures standing on a lower step before her. On the right was a majestic woman representing industry with part of a railway engine projecting from behind her, on the left was Mercury partially concealing the prow of a trireme. The female figure is thickly draped in voluminous garments, Mercury is naked except for his winged hat. The scene is reminiscent of those nightmares in which the dreamer finds himself inexplicably naked in a polite and fully dressed gathering.

Outside the shining walls of the Crystal Palace, as it had come to be called, stood an exhibit as interesting and important as anything displayed within it. This was the "Model Dwelling House" designed by Prince Albert. It consisted of a block containing four flats, two on a floor, with a central staircase between them. It was so planned that the building could be carried up another two floors if required. The exterior was vaguely Jacobean in design and amateurish in effect, but of the sound and extremely advanced planning of the flats there can be no doubt. The accommodation consisted of a living-room, scullery and three bedrooms, while such conveniences were introduced as heated linen cupboards, dust shafts, and well-ventilated larders. The main walls were constructed of hollow bricks which it was

A Cabinet of Oak (1851), *by "Mr. Myers of Lambeth"*

69

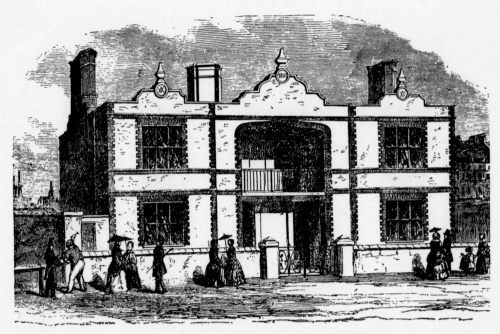

Prince Albert's Model Dwellings (1851)

said resisted both damp and cold. The Society for Improving the Dwellings of the Working Classes, under whose auspices the block was erected, maintained that it could be built and let at a price advantageous both to owner and to tenant. Unfortunately it does not appear that any capitalist was prepared to undertake the venture, and the living conditions of workers remained deplorably bad.

A rather similar enterprise, though one based on a harder financial foundation, arose with the construction of Victoria Street, which was opened for traffic in August, 1851. In the making of this new street a large number of poor dwellings had been demolished, and it was proposed that, to compensate for this destruction of living accommodation, lodging-houses should be erected each of which would house "no less than ninety poor families at a rent of four shillings a week each". It was computed that these buildings could be put up at a cost of £2,000 and give a return to anyone inclined to invest his money in this way of 10 per cent. per annum. The accommodation here provided must have been far inferior to that in the Prince's model homes. The Commissioners in charge of the works proposed also to put up small blocks of flats for the more well-to-do: these with four bedrooms and two sitting-rooms would be let at £50 or £60 per annum including rates, water and gas.

It was quite clear that the welfare of the working classes, which had until recently been so neglected, had become a matter of prime importance. Only a few years earlier, when New Oxford Street had been driven through a densely populated slum quarter, no provision whatever had been made for the many families rendered homeless. The result had been deplorable: instead of moving to other and more salubrious fields, the miserable families had merely crowded into the pullulating tenements of St. Giles's. Thus the brave new street, though a great convenience for traffic to the City, reduced the living conditions of many poor families to an even lower standard.

The Prince Consort was chairman of the Society for Improving the Dwellings of the Working Classes, which has already been mentioned, and his influence and enlightened views had done much to stir the social conscience of the upper classes and to bring forward the urgency of the housing problem in the great cities, a problem which has not yet been fully solved. It was not only housing which was being tackled during these exceedingly active years: there was also the construction of a wide variety of buildings designed for humanitarian objects. The number was positively bewildering: there were new hospitals, alms-houses, penitentiaries, grammar schools, asylums for idiots, public baths and laundries, work-houses, as well as a great number of new churches. Many of these benevolent institutions were erected and run by private charity, and the motives

The Prince Consort in "his" Study, with Lord Palmerston, about 1855
The interior is based on the Drawing-room at Hughenden Manor, Buckinghamshire

71

which brought them into being were doubtless of the highest. And yet, one questions whether the huge social problem was, even at this date, being tackled from the right angle. The attitude seems to have been that the poor could be lightly deprived of their liberty. The indigent, the mentally unstable, the sick, should at once be kindly but firmly shepherded into institutions, there to carry on their dreary lives until terminated by death. With the existing social structure there was little alternative, but the real trouble lay, as must have been clear to many, in the very low wages of all classes of workers, and the bad conditions in the factories. If these had been remedied there would have been fewer candidates for the institutions.

It was largely with the intention of bringing before the public the misery of the lives of a large section of the community that Charles Dickens started in March, 1850, the journal which he named *Household Words*. Mrs. Gaskell was a prominent contributor, and it was here, in serial form, that *Cranford* first appeared. For nine years the journal was produced, with the conditions of the poor as a background theme; but in May, 1859, the last number was published, and Dickens transferred his interest to the paper known as *All the Year Round*.

The age of contrasts was not yet past. While the popular taste for the lavish and over-decorated was reaching its zenith, the average lower middle-class home was run on very austere lines. Few of the high-priced products of the Great Exhibition entered the house of the average citizen: nevertheless the style exemplified in Hyde Park was the one to which all who could aspired. Crowded rooms represented security but they did not indicate comfort, and this was considered all to the good: for comfort came very close to self-indulgence and this was a sin. Austerity in the way of life, on the other hand, gave a sense of spiritual uplift. Thus while taste became riotous, in fact positively abandoned, the middle-class outlook became increasingly severe.

The middle years of the nineteenth century were a period of great religious revival. The Deity, who had suffered profound neglect during earlier decades and in the previous century, was now brought forward as a very real and formidable character. Fervent proselytizers, however, often found it difficult work to bring elderly people who had lived in a free-thinking atmosphere to a proper state of piety. An example was Dr. Protheroe Smith's interview with the dying Lord Palmerston at Brocket in 1865. The subject of faith was not an easy one to introduce, for Palmerston had seldom shown any signs of religious belief. However, the good doctor thought it his duty to attempt a last-minute conversion to a proper attitude of mind. A tactful approach was essential. "We might think of the Lord Jesus

Family Prayers (1864). From the painting by Samuel Butler

Christ", he remarked hopefully, "who, as it were, rose from the dead on a Sunday". "Oh, certainly", replied Palmerston politely. "May I hope that you believe in the Lord Jesus Christ?" continued the doctor. "Oh, surely" was the answer; but these rather enigmatic assents were the only evidence the doctor could obtain that the dying statesman was in a proper state to meet his Maker.

The *bourgeois* paterfamilias of the new era was inclined to model himself on his conception of God. His attitude towards the Almighty showed a proper humility, but to his family and his fellow-men he presented a front of just severity, and he would be highly critical of those who did not achieve his own high moral standards. Needless to say, a large section of the community provided exceptions to this generalization, but the righteous householder was the character typical of the period. Children would be brought up to fear God and their father in about equal proportions, though probably the latter, whose punishments were more direct and painful, inspired the greater respect and alarm. It was accepted that the proper education of children must inevitably include intense religious teaching, with much austerity and discomfort.

Augustus Hare's autobiography shows the extraordinary harshness with which a delicate boy could be treated in prosperous clerical circles, such as those in which his family moved. Poor food, no toys,

73

an ice-cold bedroom, severe whippings for small offences, together with a number of ingeniously devised schemes for destroying his happiness and wounding his self-esteem represented the principal features of the curriculum. It makes incredible reading, and one feels inclined to believe that the horrors of his childhood may have been a little exaggerated. In 1843, for example, when aged nine, he was sent to the small school kept by the Rev. Robert Kilvert and his wife at Hardenhuish Rectory in Wiltshire. The description of this little academy is a painful story, and Hare writes of Mr. Kilvert: "So intense, so abject was our terror of him, that we used to look forward as to an oasis to the one afternoon when he went to his parish duties". Robert Kilvert was the father of Robert Francis Kilvert whose diary, written over a number of years about a quarter of a century later, is one of the most charming in the English language. That a sensitive and gentle young man like Robert Francis should have been the son of a sadistic monster is possible, but that he should also have been a devoted son, as he undoubtedly was, to a man of that character seems highly improbable.

Whether Augustus Hare overdrew his early hardships or not, there is no doubt that the general spirit of the picture he presented was a true and a common one. The extreme severities were generally reserved for boys, but both boys and girls were satiated with an intense religious training: daily family prayers, constant church-going, and the reading of interminable and improving sermons on Sundays, were well designed to turn children into paths far other than were intended, once they escaped from the restrictive discipline. This draconian attitude to child education seems to have developed rather suddenly in the middle decades of the century. At a slightly earlier date children, at least of the aristocratic class, were allowed great freedom and pleasure. Biographies and letters, such as those of Lady Munster, Lady Cardigan and Lady Elizabeth Spencer-Stanhope, contain constant references to the brilliant parties arranged for children, their pretty frocks, their general happiness. Children, indeed, during the 'thirties were much brought forward, and memoirs contain many references to benign royal hands patting curly childish heads. By the 'fifties children as a social asset had severely slumped. A large family was still considered extremely praiseworthy, but no longer were the little brats tolerated as the life and soul of an adult party. They were kept carefully out of sight, except for an hour in the early evening when, self-consciously dressed in their best clothes, they would be introduced into the drawing-room. This remote control as far as the parents were concerned was maintained until the end of the century, and in many families considerably longer. Now the cycle

"Children at Play", in an interior of about 1855

From the painting by W. M. Egley

has turned and, largely owing to economic causes, they show signs of stealing the picture once again.

A side-issue of the religious revival which permeated the middle and, to some degree, the upper classes was an improvement in the social position of the country parson. During the early years of the century his status had been exceedingly humble, unless, as was often the case, he was a man of good family or of some wealth, in fact what Mrs. Edward Twistleton, writing to her family in the United States during the 'fifties, called "one of those aristocratic, clerical, younger sons, who are so numerous here". Good country livings were generally reserved for those already well endowed by birth or inheritance. Did not the Bible itself sanction the advancement of "him that hath"? Livings in the gift of landowners and squires provided a useful profession for younger sons, though it was seldom that any thought was given as to whether they had any qualification, let alone a vocation, for this service. When prosperously placed, the parson would be second only to the squire in the social structure of the village, and his life would be led on very similar lines. A curate, or several curates if the parson had been astute enough to gather a number of livings under his aegis, would attend to the spiritual needs of the community, and only the compilation of an occasional sermon need interfere with the pleasant occupations of a social and sporting life.

The position of the poor parson was different indeed. Penury was regarded as a shortcoming, and an impoverished vicar had little better social position in the eyes of the well-to-do members of his flock than a farm labourer. The clouds were now beginning to rise a little on this social depression, but advancement for a man of humble birth was still unlikely. It was the clergy themselves, rather than laymen, who maintained these social distinctions amongst members of the cloth, and it was early made clear to a young man taking orders exactly where his position lay. When Augustus Hare went as a boy to stay with his grandparents at Stoke Rectory the curates would be invited to a very ceremonious luncheon on Sundays, at which they were allowed to eat moderately but not to speak. They were expected to enter the house by the back door, with the single exception of Mr. Egerton who being "a gentleman born" was allowed to enter by the front, though it does not appear that even he was ever permitted to voice an opinion.

A long-overdue interest in the condition of the fabrics of parish churches was arising. For many decades the buildings had been neglected, and all over the country parish churches were in a condition of decay. In many cases the chancel of a church had been left to fall into ruin, and the bleak undevotional services were held in the nave without the presence of an altar. Here was a material outlet for revived religious feeling, and it gave comfort and pleasure to many to contribute towards the reconstruction of some decaying edifice. Little reverence was felt for the antiquity of a structure: few felt like Ruskin that old buildings "are not ours. They belong partly to those who build them, and partly to the generations of mankind who are to follow us". However, had enthusiasts wished to bring Ruskin to their support they could have advanced his slightly contradictory opinion that a restoration was a fake, and that if a fabric was decayed beyond a certain point it was more honest to pull it down and start again. The latter was in any case more closely in accordance with prevailing sentiment.

If a parish church was to be rebuilt, or a new church to be erected in an expanding suburb, there would be little discussion about the style in which it was to be carried out. Pugin's *Contrasts* had appeared as early as 1836, and exercised a growing influence on popular taste. Certainly the book was written and illustrated by a Roman Catholic, and one of singularly violent and bigoted views, views which were absolutely abhorrent to the average middle-class member of the Church of England. Nevertheless Pugin's partiality for the Gothic style found increasing popular support, and though his own buildings in the manner he so fervently advocated seldom quite achieved the success that might have been expected from the drawings, there was always the architect Gilbert Scott whose buildings were all that could be desired.

Further editions of *Contrasts* followed the original publication, and while the tone became more tempered the drawings became more subtly persuasive. The contrast between the town of 1440, with its city walls, battlemented gateways and soaring spires and steeples, and the same town in 1840 with its warehouses, gas-works, factory chimneys, and eighteenth-century church towers, provides forceful propaganda for a return to the style of the Middle Ages. But it is probable that if the City of London had been rebuilt according to Wren's plan after the Great Fire and had remained unaltered until 1840, Pugin, with his apparently artless drawings, would have contrived to produce a contrast almost equally favourable to the Gothic style.

The Queen led the way in what seems to us now a disastrous passion for church rebuilding. The new house at Osborne, which had lately been completed, lay in the parish of Whippingham. The little church of the parish, dedicated to St. Mildred, was a structure of many dates, but it had been given its final and singularly engaging appearance by Nash in 1804. The interior was plain, with side galleries supported on slender shafts and a pulpit set very high and centrally under the chancel arch, from which the preacher had an uninterrupted view into the curtained royal pew which lay on the south side of the aisle. It was not a very dignified or convenient arrangement, and no doubt contributed to the decision to demolish the structure entirely and start afresh. The Queen laid the foundation-stone of the new church, which was largely designed by the Prince Consort, in 1860. The hard, Gothic building which arose was not completed until after the Prince's death.

This was an exceedingly prosperous period for architects who specialized in ecclesiastical Gothic. There was not only the rebuilding or drastic renovation of existing churches, but there were also a very great number of churches being constructed in the new areas of building round London and the industrial towns. Almost every week the illustrated papers showed a drawing of a large church lately completed, sometimes on an old site, sometimes in a new area. The technique of church building seems, with constant practice, to have been brought to a fine art. The space of time between the laying of the foundation-stone by some local magnate until the consecration by the bishop of the diocese was often little more than a year. The large church of St. Edward, Romford, for example, was well and truly founded by Mr. Bramston, M.P., in July, 1849, and was consecrated by the Bishop of Rochester in September of the following year. No doubt, however, considerable work had been carried out on the site before Mr. Bramston, with his silver trowel, was called in to officiate. This was a spacious building with a nave over eighty feet long, and was lavishly finished. There was an oak screen, a richly carved reredos of Caen stone, filled in with illuminated texts, a pulpit and font of the same material and also highly decorated, the floor was paved with Minton's encaustic tiles, and the pews in the aisle were of deal stained and varnished to resemble oak. The structure with its tasteful contents was the work of Mr. John Johnson and was carried out for the moderate sum of £8,000.

The enthusiasm for ecclesiastical Gothic was having a marked effect on domestic building. The pretty fantasies of the Strawberry Hill manner were now entirely out of fashion and a more serious note, one more in consonance with the rigid moral outlook of the day, had swept in. Antipathy to the style of the early Revival increased with the years and led to the destruction of many attractive buildings after a short span of existence. The pinnacles and crockets of Porden's Eaton Hall, for example, were to make way for a bombastic monster which we will contemplate in a later chapter; and in the late 'fifties Louisa, Lady Waterford, removed the gay fripperies from the stout walls of Ford Castle in Northumberland and restored it to the rather uncertain likeness of a rugged mediaeval fortress.

Pugin, the pioneer of this change of taste, died in 1852 at the early age of forty, worn out by the fierce flame of his own spirit. The organization of the Mediaeval Court had been almost his last work: early in 1852 he became insane and some months later died in Bedlam. The leadership of the Gothic army passed to Gilbert Scott, a contemporary of Pugin, but a man of very different character. His addiction to the style had developed slowly, and had not been encouraged by his early training. However, a meeting with Pugin and a close study of his writings and drawings so strengthened his knowledge of the Gothic style that in 1840 he was successful in making the winning design for the Martyrs' Memorial at Oxford. From that time forward his feet were firmly set in the mediaeval path, a path from which he was only once, and that by the most violent duress, to make a major deviation.

Gilbert Scott's influence was strong on the architecture of his age, but his actual contribution to the field of country houses was small: he built only three or four, none of which particularly enhanced his reputation. Lesser architects, however, were showing a rather alarming versatility in designing houses in styles showing many aspects of Gothic: there was English Gothic, Italianized Gothic, French Gothic, Tudor Gothic. Such books as Blackburne's *Suburban and Rural Architecture* offered suggestions for elegant villas in all these styles, with the addition of a number in various Continental vernaculars. Yet, though the names given to the designs were so different, the effects seem curiously similar. They share a like uncertainty of inspiration with the tedious historical pictures which were so popular with artists— and also presumably with clients—of the period, in which it is almost impossible to guess at what point in history the scene has been fixed. Are the costumes Plantagenet, Tudor or mid-eighteenth century? The only style to which they indubitably subscribe in most details is mid-Victorian. Blackburne differentiates between "English-Gothic" and "Tudor-Gothic". His villa in the first style is constructed

"Design for a Villa—English Domestic Gothic". E. L. Blackburne, Architect

Orchardleigh Park, Somerset (1855). T. H. Wyatt, Architect

of Kentish ragstone for the ground floor with brickwork above, cunningly masked by a timbered effect produced by cement beams coloured to represent oak with rough-cast in the interstices. The roof is tiled and the gables are decorated with carved barge-boards. Tudor Gothic he saw as a more austere style: plain red brick walls, stone mullioned windows and a steep pitched roof covered with slates, and with a cresting and pinnacles at the extremities; the chimneys should be tall and suitably embellished with mouldings. The French—or Composed—Gothic villa seems indistinguishable from the last, except that it is adorned with a tower, the roof of which "is of the spire-like character prevalent in French architecture". Here is a parody which might make the school of Fontainebleau die of shame, and perhaps provides a balance to the melancholy little areas of fir-trees and rough grass which habitually pass by the name of *jardins anglais*.

Much architecture of this sort was perpetrated during the busy 'fifties, but even by the standards of the time it was not good work. In general these vulgar villas were built for rising families who had little criterion or experience on which to found their taste. Had these houses been conceived half a century earlier they would certainly have possessed charm and prettiness; but now lightness and grace had vanished, and an elephantine whimsey had taken the place of imagination.

The architecture of the larger country houses can be said on the whole to show slightly better taste. Charles Eastlake, in his *History of the Gothic Revival* published in 1872, gives examples of several large

80

country houses erected during the 'fifties which he considered had merit. There is Orchardleigh erected from the designs of T. H. Wyatt in 1855. The style was late Tudor, and Eastlake kindly says of it: "Mr. Wyatt has shown of what artistic treatment the style is capable". It might be said, however, that it was the architect rather than the style which possessed the capabilities, for a number of unwarrantable liberties were taken with the style. The building nevertheless has certain virtues, it is not vulgar: it is well grouped and has dignity of a rather heavy order. But even the passage of a century has not endowed it with charm.

It is much to be preferred to the two examples of J. L. Pearson's country-house style of which Eastlake gives drawings: these are Quar Wood of 1857 and Eatington Park dated one year later. The François I style seems to have inspired the first, though it has not very much in common with the famous *châteaux* of the Loire valley. Probably Eastlake is correct in supposing that "the saddle-back roof and open loggia of the tower suggest the influence of Continental study", but the architect was obviously determined to give his own

Quar Wood, Gloucestershire (1857). J. L. Pearson, Architect

interpretation to a well-known style. It seems unlikely that anyone will again share Eastlake's partiality for Quar Wood; while of Eatington, poor Eatington, one can say with certainty that it can never be looked on as anything but one of the greatest monsters of the age. There was already a house on the site when Mr. Pearson was called in, and to the existing structure he gave a skin, a thick, highly coloured, exceedingly elaborate skin of Venetian Gothic. Eastlake's comment on the result was this: "Perhaps it is not too much to say that it is a wall-veil which Mr. Ruskin would have approved".

There seems to be no record as to whether Ruskin approved or not, but in any case his was the heavy responsibility for the popularity of Venetian Gothic. It was he, in *Stones of Venice,* who had induced the English to admire the buildings of Venice and persuaded them that the style, so different from the sombre English manner, was beautiful and not merely pretty. How diverse were the effects of Ruskin's writing. On the one hand it led to such travesties of architecture as Eatington, on the other it was an important factor in the formation of Proust's literary style, with its extreme sensitivity and meticulous observation of detail. "*L'univers reprit tout d'un coup à mes yeux un prix infini*", wrote Proust, after studying Ruskin's works.

Pearson and his client were no doubt inspired by the Oxford Museum, which was in course of erection when plans were being prepared for Eatington. The project of a museum for the study of natural science had long been considered, but it was not until 1854 that it was finally decided upon, and a competition opened for designs for the structure. Of the two favoured schemes one was Palladian, the other Venetian Gothic, and it was the latter, the work of Messrs. Dean and Woodward, which gained the day. Though the design was not Ruskin's, he became closely connected with the work, and his advice was sought on all points. Much of the stone carving on the Museum is beautiful in design and fine in workmanship, and under the master's eye the façade achieved considerable distinction; but both planning and construction were soon found to be faulty. But in general the style is not one which can be very happily translated into buildings of moderate cost. It was usually thought sufficient merely to reproduce the principal ingredients: the striped wall surfaces in red and yellow brick, granite columns to form central window mullions, while if the Gothic arches, which would have been indicated above the columns, presented difficulties, then a flat stone transom with chamfered edge could take their place. The sky-line generally abandoned Venice entirely for England and put up a fine show of decorated gables such as had never been seen near the Grand Canal.

This was the style, in a rather chastened form, which was considered suitable for the large number of rectories and vicarages which were being built at the time. With many buildings in this cultured manner being erected at the Universities, it seemed a safe choice for the many new parsonages required both in country districts and to serve the new churches in suburban areas. A little later, fashion transferred to English Gothic, and it was this perhaps which particularly merited the name Vicarage Gothic. There was nothing reminiscent of Italian sunshine or gaiety about the solid but economical homes provided for the clergy in the former style: rather, as the strident tone of their brickwork darkened in the damp English air, did they suggest the righteous but austere lives led within their walls. Whether the exteriors were Italianate or mediaeval, the interiors were uncompromisingly English nineteenth century: pitch-pine doors and wainscots, heavy cornices, chimney-pieces in coarsely moulded dark marbles in the principal rooms, or in plain white marble in rooms of lesser importance; and wherever possible would be found the chamfered corners which Victorians seemed to find so irresistibly attractive. A sheltering belt of Corsican pine-trees would then be planted round the structure, and all was prepared for the new occupant.

The interior aspect of the average rectory was seldom typical of mid-Victorian taste, since money was generally in short supply, and the furniture would largely consist of unfashionable objects dating from a few decades earlier. As usual one must look to the villas of the well-to-do to find decoration and furnishings which could be said to exemplify contemporary taste, to those homes where contents and appearance were not unduly hampered by financial considerations. No longer are we entirely dependent on written descriptions or on rare water-colours painstakingly carried out by the young ladies of the house, for photography was beginning to become a less specialized accomplishment. The photography of interiors, it is true, still presented difficulties owing to lack of light, and it was rather a family group at the entrance porch or a little party on a croquet lawn which were fixed for the benefit of posterity. Time-exposures of rooms, now so fascinating after the lapse of a century, seemed very naturally much less worthy of perpetuation than the figures gathered in the sunshine. The drawing-room was there for all to see, while the photograph of a group preserved the ephemeral gathering of an afternoon. Thus interior photographs of the 'fifties remain rare, and one must draw all possible information from the few that exist.

There were two features which affected rooms of the period: these were the taste inculcated at the Great Exhibition, and the new aniline dyes which broadened, and rather unfortunately brightened, the range of colours used in materials for furnishing, though the latter are not betrayed by photography. Everywhere there would be

From a "Comic" Photograph of about 1855

pattern: in the wall-paper, in the carpet, in the curtains, in the covers of sofas and chairs. Tables would be covered with chenille cloths, hearths were often dangerously draped with curtains hanging from a pelmet board supported on the shelf of the chimney-piece. When there was no fire, the grate, which for some reason it was thought necessary to conceal, would disappear behind festoons of rep. Over the chimney-piece a large looking-glass in a heavy gilt frame was almost a universal feature in the upper middle-class house. The great area of undivided mirror was still something of a novelty and gave a sense of space and added light to a room—both of which were acceptable where there was much crowding of furniture, and daylight was often obscured by draperies round the windows and Nottingham lace curtains over the openings themselves. It was through one of these mirrors that some years later Alice was to clamber into the romantic world of animated chessmen, passing carefully between the clock and a vase of artificial flowers which, sheltered by glass domes, decorated the chimney-piece.

Materials treated with aniline dyes came on the market about 1856. Until that time colours were usually the product of vegetable dyes, dyes produced from all parts of plants, from the root, the bark, the wood, the leaves, the flowers, the seeds. These colours were usually soft in tone. The aniline dyes, however, struck a more strident note; they were chemically produced from the distillation of coal-tar and provided some striking effects for the mid-Victorian drawing-room. Prussian blue, malachite green, a rather savage chrome yellow and several other uncompromising tints were available to brighten dingy rooms, while wools for needlework were produced in the same sharp colours. Though large expanses of these new dyes were apt to be overpowering, the effect on gros-point was much less unfortunate. Time has now mellowed the bouquets and the ribbons, the cabbage roses, the peonies, and the lilacs; and whether stitched as carpets, as the tops of ottomans, as fire screens, or as swirling wreaths on the backs and seats of sofas, they seem to us now the happiest and most attractive domestic production of the mid-Victorian years. In following years needlework pictures were inclined to rival the flower pieces: a Spanish girl at her devotions in a cathedral, indeterminate Tudor scenes representing great ladies with pages and falcons, and suchlike sentimental scenes, found more favour than the charming, if outrageous, horticultural effects of the 'fifties.

The brightness of the colours used in a room depended naturally on the taste of the owner.

"Through the Looking Glass" (1872)

From the illustration by Sir John Tenniel

Princess Beatrice's Sitting-room at Osborne

But that they were sometimes very brilliant, even before the introduction of aniline dyes, can be deduced from the Queen's rooms at Osborne, which still remain much as they were before the Prince Consort's death. The Prince, with the assistance of Mr. Cubitt, had begun the rebuilding in 1845 and, though the house was enlarged at different times, the main block which contains the royal apartments was completed before the end of the decade. In these rooms, which are neither very numerous nor very large, all is brilliance and colour, in paint, decoration, draperies and furnishings, with a strong emphasis on crimson, gold and white. Though the detail is far from refined, the general effect is one of robust and cheerful gaiety, which is extremely attractive.

The elaborate exhibits in Hyde Park represented an ideal to which many rich householders endeavoured to attain; but the average house in one of the genteel new quarters of London, or a Venetian Gothic villa in the countryside, was generally furnished on a less elaborate note, particularly in the rooms of lesser importance. The drawing-room would be as crowded and showy as possible, but the bedrooms, where the furniture was more utilitarian, must often have been very pleasant. Simple objects like chests of drawers and wardrobes were plainly designed and admirably made, though generally rather ponderous in scale. Four-poster beds with stout uprights were still made, but the half-tester in wood or iron was gaining popularity and, when not too massive, could look charming if hung with the flowered chintz or cretonne which vied with needlework in being the prettiest products of the age. A favourite design was the Victoria and Albert, in which the profiles of the Queen and her consort could be discovered, outlined by tendrils, amongst garlands of flowers. Patchwork quilts, and dressing-tables flounced with white muslin over a pink or blue foundation would contrast agreeably with the solid forms of mahogany pieces.

The Exhibition furniture naturally displayed the advanced designs of the period: there would have been little to gain by occupying valuable space with simple everyday productions of the manufacturers, such as the mahogany tables and chairs, the rosewood work-tables, the buttoned sociables, and other objects of a similar commonplace sort. By the turn of taste it is these humdrum chattels and not their high-flying brothers which now seem to us attractive. They are massive rather than elegant, and mouldings and detail are coarse, but they possess a solid integrity and suitability to the purpose for which they were designed, which will always ensure them a place where room can be found for them. Their scale seems often to have been a little over life-size, even when intended for rooms of moderate proportions. Those monumental dining-tables, for example, with legs stout enough to support the most massive display of

Osborne: The Drawing-room

87

silverware, the paraphernalia of gargantuan feasts, on their broad, thick surfaces, can now find a useful place in very few houses.

It is curious that at a time when furniture was made from such good quality wood it was considered essential to cover all tables in sitting-rooms with heavy cloths which hung in luxuriant folds to the carpet. A leg, it seems, was something to be concealed, whether constructed of wood, or of flesh and bone. Certainly the latter became even more demurely concealed than during previous years. By the middle of the decade steel hoops for displaying the skirts were generally worn in place of the starched linen petticoats which had previously been thought adequate. Crinolines increased in size, and the metal frame beneath the flounces made compression difficult. A crowded party became like a popular beach, with bathers bobbing in a sea of foaming tulle. A rigid deportment was required in order to obtain the maximum of effect from this exacting fashion: a tomboy style accorded very ill with these dignified garments, while careless lolling on a sofa might easily lead to a social disaster.

It was an appropriate period for Mrs. Bloomer to introduce her clothing of more rational design. The baggy trousers she proposed were fastened round the ankle with a ribbon and frill, while over them was worn a full short skirt, a little crinoline, of rather greater length than a kilt. There was nothing very masculine or revealing of the figure about this costume, but papers such as *Punch*, in mock horror, professed to believe that the donning of trousers by women was destined to alter the social structure of the country. The pages of 1851 contain drawings of dashing young women in ball-rooms, their slippered feet twinkling below the frills of their bloomers, inviting modest male wallflowers to partner them in a polka; or a determined girl on her knees offering her hand and fortune to a young man who gazes pensively at a carnation. The year ended with "Bloomeriana: A Dream" in which women had invaded many professions hitherto the preserve of the male sex: there were women soldiers, women jockeys, women undergraduates and dons, women cab-drivers and train conductors. The whole idea, indeed, of women abandoning their domestic vocations for these broader fields was made most laughable and absurd.

Although in the race between the styles Gothic was leading so handsomely in the country in general, the classical style won all along the line in the restricted but important area of clubland. Only one amongst the many new buildings which were erected during the middle decades of the century in St. James's was ventured in the former manner. This was the New University Club, which was built from the designs of Alfred Waterhouse between 1866 and 1868. The tall façade, based on the architecture of the thirteenth century,

Grand saloon of the Steamship Atlantic (1850)

was not without merit, but the long severe lines of the Portland
stone elevation must always have contrasted unfavourably with the
chubby, genial, classical, club-houses which adjoined it. More
suggestive of clerical asceticism than of lay conviviality, as was
perhaps intended, it lost its appeal in the mundane atmosphere of
this century, and after less than seventy years of existence it was
demolished.

In the 'fifties clubs had already a century of tradition behind them,
and the design of Victorian buildings generally kept closely to well-
known requirements. A different situation arose in the steamboats
which were now being built to make the Atlantic crossing, for in this
case there was no very exact precedent to indicate on what lines the
first-class saloon should be devised. Something very different to the
accommodation provided on the old sailing vessels was clearly indicated. The largest steamship afloat in 1850 was the *Atlantic*, which
with her sister ships bearing the chilling names of *Arctic, Antarctic* and
Baltic, formed the principal part of the Cunard Line's fleet. The saloon
of the *Atlantic* was extremely spacious, being sixty-seven feet long
and twenty feet wide and, since the liner style had not yet been born,
it was furnished in much the same way as a villa drawing-room.
Sofas and armchairs of florid design and rococo in inspiration lined
the walls, their generous curves taking up the maximum of room
while providing the minimum of seating accommodation. Mirrors in
arch-topped recesses lined the walls, which must have been a grave

trial to queasy passengers, and a vast writing-table, vaguely Louis XVI in form, with some fringed and tasselled footstools, occupied a prominent position in the middle of the brightly patterned carpet. On a rough passage this heavy, and apparently untethered, furniture must have reduced this genteel saloon to a scene of sad chaos. Only one feature seems to have survived from the long tradition of sailing vessels—the artificial lighting. From a central beam crossing the low ceiling swung a conventional oil-lamp with globe, glass chimney and metal smoke shield: only a large tassel suspended below the lamp gave a touch of ostentation to a traditional and refreshingly utilitarian object.

Chandelier for a Summer-house (1851)

Exhibited by Messenger and Sons

A house in the "Cottage Style" (1864)

CHAPTER IV

MATERIAL PROGRESS

1860—1870

URING the decade following the Great Exhibition the prestige of Prince Albert had steadily increased. He was not a man ever to gain great popularity with the upper classes as a whole: he was too studious, too pedagogic, too serious minded, too lacking in easy conviviality to engage in comfortable social relations with average members of the mid-nineteenth-century aristocracy. Like Mr. Waterhouse's Gothic club-house, mentioned in the previous chapter, he was not quite at home in those upper-class circles where a degree of robust eighteenth-century rakishness still persisted. But by the nation as a whole his remarkable capabilities were recognized, and the triumphant success of the Exhibition in all material directions greatly enhanced his reputation. If the public failed to perceive the moral lesson, this was a disappointment to few besides the Prince. None could any longer question his penetrating business acumen, and it was also becoming generally acknowledged that his views on various aspects of art were not to be despised.

Few at that time shared his enlightened interest in German and

91

Balmoral: the Queen's Dressing-room, about 1875

Italian primitives, but his excursions into the architectural field not only accorded with the better elements of public taste, but were also slightly in advance of it, so that in this direction he was an accepted leader, although his practical acquaintance with this highly specialized art was rudimentary. His design for the "People's House" was a marked step forward in planning for the working classes, while the new royal residence at Osborne had considerably more charm both inside and out than the majority of contemporary houses. The Prince's next architectural venture was the rebuilding of the modest house at Balmoral which the Queen had bought in 1852. The royal pair had first leased the old stone and rough-cast house in 1848, and the small size of the place, and the fact that they could live there in almost the simple way of any Scottish laird, particularly appealed to the Queen's romantic spirit. But Albert decided that the unpretentious house must be turned into a royal castle, and so it was.

With the aid of an architect, Mr. Smith, a formidable pile arose in the Scottish baronial style. Towers, turrets and battlements were used to give the great building an air of haphazard asymmetry, though the lay-out, in its general lines, was as rigid and rectangular as that of classical Osborne. Whether the Prince Consort's much admired common sense was strongly in evidence in the planning seems doubtful. The kitchen, for example, was placed at the furthest possible distance from the dining-room, and the food had to make a long journey, not only the full length of two corridors, but also for a space under a covered way open to the air. The intention to keep the plebeian smell of cooking out of the main part of the house was doubtless successful, but at the cost of cold food and a great deal of labour. The Prince's sensible taste was shown to better advantage in the decoration of the sitting-rooms than in the design of the exterior. The scarlet of the Stuart tartan was well to the fore in carpets, covers and curtains; but the furniture and fittings, such as bookcases, were restrained in design and had little of the florid exuberance which had pervaded the Great Exhibition. By 1855 the Castle was ready for occupation.

It can be said, then, that the Court under Albert's leadership was influencing public taste. It cannot be maintained that the court of Victoria was any parallel in this direction to the court of the Tudor monarchs, whose leadership in the promotion of the arts was out-standing; but circumstances in the nineteenth century were entirely different, and the progress of the arts depended more on practitioners than on royal patrons. The Prince was a practitioner in a modest way as well as a patron, and, with the Queen's hand in his, was the most important figure in the country. Whether his knowledge and taste would have had any decisive effect on the paths along which the arts were to move must remain undetermined, for on the 14th

Balmoral: the Prince Consort's Sitting-room (1875)

93

Balmoral: the Queen's Bedroom about 1875

December, 1861, he died at Windsor Castle. From that day the Queen, who in any case had little artistic appreciation, retired into many years of seclusion, and the Court ceased to have any influence on the development of the arts.

The Prince's death caused sorrow and dismay in all classes, and his qualities and unremitting industry were never so fully recognized as on his death. The sentiments which Lady de Rothschild expressed in a letter to a friend were the feelings of many: "What a loss . . . so active, so good, so gracious—we could think of nothing else; it gave us terrible headaches".

Meanwhile, unaffected by royal bereavements, architecture and the many attendant arts which are enlisted in the embellishment of the home advanced smoothly on the lines formed during the previous decade. The Pugin tradition remained very strong for a number of years after his death, and it was well maintained by Gilbert Scott who at the age of fifty was at the zenith of his powers. The altercation over the design of the new government offices had been no more than a temporary reverse, while the ultimate result increased his prestige. Building commissions in embarrassing quantities continued to flow into his office: by far the greater number were ecclesiastical projects, and were evidence of the urge which existed in all parts of the country to build new churches or to repair old, and the

94

former proposals, which were much more congenial to the architect, largely predominated.

During the mid-'forties Scott admitted into his architectural office as a young assistant George Edmund Street, who remained with him for five years. Street, who was born in 1824, was thirteen years younger than his master and assimilated to the full the older man's passion for the Gothic style. Street's practice was largely ecclesiastical, though his best-known work is the Law Courts in the Strand. A competition for designs for the new buildings was opened in 1866 and, as seems to have been inevitable with contests of this character, two years of strife and unpleasantness ensued, in which the architect was unavoidably involved, before the commission was finally given to Street. It was unfortunate that time should have been wasted, for Street died in 1881 before the building was completed. As usually happens where construction is carried on over many years, the style was already a little out of date before the work was finished, while from the first the disposition of the interior was said to be inconvenient, so that Street received little praise for a design which has many merits. At last, however, it would seem that sentiment is veering in its favour, for the posters of London Transport display the Law Courts as one of the attractions of the metropolis.

Except for some of his parsonage houses, which had less of the grim austerity so strongly stressed by other contemporary architects, Street's excursions into the domestic field were not on the whole very fortunate. His most important work was Dunecht House in Aberdeenshire, a gloomy, towered pile with a Gothic mortuary chapel attached to it. The macabre story of the theft of the embalmed body of the first occupant of the vault below the chapel was a sensation of 1881.

These references to Street's architectural work would not suggest that his influence on the Victorian home was very marked, but a special interest attaches to him owing to the fact that two young men, who were to become prominent members of the Pre-Raphaelite Brotherhood, received an architectural training in his office in Beaumont Street at Oxford: these were Philip Webb and William Morris. Under the leadership of these men of highly original genius, architecture, furniture and the applied arts developed in a manner very different to anything envisaged by Street. But though the work of the master showed now signs of being influenced by that of his former brilliant pupils, personal friendship endured until Street's death.

Morris joined Webb in the Beaumont Street office in 1856, but his talents were too varied and diffused to be concentrated happily on architecture alone. He soon found that painting, poetry, writing and the designing of furniture and fabrics were more satisfactory outlets for his versatile genius than long concentration on the complicated detail required for an architectural career. With his passionate nature he possessed few of the qualities of tact and patience essential for the successful architect; and in any case he could please himself, as he was in the fortunate position of being in no necessity to earn a living. A year's training in Street's office, however, gave a useful architectural basis to his talent for design, which showed clearly in much of his furniture—too clearly on some occasions when simple objects would be conceived with a massive solidity suggestive of a well-founded structure, rather than of a piece of utilitarian furniture. Possibly Morris himself was aware that his excursions into joinery lacked grace, for he seldom embarked in this field of design after his early years. Philip Webb, however, continued to design furniture for the firm in much the same simple, massive style, though his work is less cumbersome than Morris's early pieces.

On leaving Street's office, Morris joined his Oxford friend Edward Burne-Jones in a studio in Red Lion Square, but on his marriage to Jane Burden two years later, he decided to build a small country house for himself and his bride. Philip Webb, who had lately set up as an architect on his own account, was very naturally invited to provide the design. The Red House at Upton, near Bexleyheath, was the outcome of this harmonious partnership, and was also Webb's first commission.

The style of the building was to be a break-away from contemporary conventional standards; it was also to form a fitting background for Morris's furniture and decoration. The house was to be neither a stone Gothic structure, such as Scott or Street might have designed, nor a stuccoed, slate-roofed essay in what was supposed to be the Italian style. It was an L-shaped building and, as its name indicated, was built in red brick with a steep tiled roof and a staircase tower surmounted by a louvre at the junction of the two short wings. A well with a tall conical roof supported on robust timbers was an important feature of the court formed in the shelter of the wings. The style, if it has any particular derivation, might be said to descend from some Normandy *manoir* of the seventeenth century. This was the simple little building which, with its contents, was to have such a profound effect on the course of English taste.

The mental approach of Morris and his friends to the problems of architecture and the applied arts was essentially different to that of the average contemporary practitioner. Ardent supporters of the Gothic style were convinced that they were returning in their work to architectural fundamentals; but in the opinion of Morris and his colleagues the whole subject of architecture and the applied arts was clogged and vitiated by all sorts of spurious principles and traditions.

Morris's Oak Settle

Even Pugin, who was meticulous in his choice of mouldings and other detail, was quite insouciant in the use of materials. If cast iron could successfully simulate carved stonework, it was welcome to do so. Morris was determined to throw aside all these artificial accretions and get back to the real essentials, back to the earth which was to be the foundation of all his varied works. The aim of the Pre-Raphaelites was, in a sense, narrow, but it was deeply founded, and as it has turned out it was the tap-root from which the modern arts have developed; while the Gothic stem, after a rich flowering during the middle decades of the century, expired unregretted.

In the Red House every single article was to be specially designed; no piece of furniture, no hangings, no wall-papers, no glass or china, was to conform to the current taste; no offspring of mass production was to be allowed within the chaste new walls. But how to obtain these furnishings: that was indeed a problem. It was a problem which led to the founding of the firm of Morris, Marshall, Faulkner and Co. in April, 1861. It was not until 1940 that the firm, the name of which had been shortened to Morris & Co., went finally into liquidation.

The Red House was gradually furnished and decorated on the desired lines. Some of the furniture was brought from the studio in Red Lion Square. There was the famous oak settle, which combined a seat with bookshelves and cupboards behind it with a canopy above.

Owing to an error in the measurements it had crowded the studio rather embarrassingly, but the large drawing-room on the first floor of the Red House was able to accommodate it more happily. This was the room which Morris announced he was going to make the most beautiful room in England, an ambitious statement with such formidable competitors in existence as the Double Cube Room at Wilton and the Ante-Room at Syon. Much trouble, however, was taken with its embellishment, and constant improvements were made to it over several years. Burne-Jones, Madox Brown and Rossetti lent their talents to give colour and interest to it, and Morris's own wall-paper and fabrics provided a rich background to the furniture and ornaments which were slowly assembled.

Meanwhile the firm was enjoying a modest prosperity. A number of its products had been shown at the International Exhibition of 1862, and sales to the amount of £131 had been effected. It was clear that there was at least a small section of the public which preferred the honest craftsmanship of Morris & Company's workshop to the florid productions of the average manufacturer. In 1866 the firm received its first important commission for the complete decoration of a room. This came from the Department of Science and Art, and resulted in "The Green Dining-room", which provided an opportunity for all visitors to the museum—then known as the South Kensington, now the Victoria and Albert—to see work which was so different to that of the conventional decorators. The dining-room represented a harmonious union of the talents of the principal artists of the firm. Morris devised the general scheme, Philip Webb designed the plasterwork of the ceiling and the walls, and Burne-Jones the stained-glass windows. These last were unfortunately destroyed by blast in 1940, but the remainder of the room is still intact. It has a sombre, mellow beauty with its high oak dado, and intricate leaf pattern in many shades of dim blues, greens, and Indian red all over the upper walls. Its charm must always have melancholy, and for the taste of today the decoration is too all pervading and oppressive. There is no note of festivity: to eat a hearty meal in such a room would be to disturb coarsely the aesthetic atmosphere. It seems more suited to blessed damozels able to exist on purely spiritual food.

Morris's antipathy to the work of the popular Gothic architects was increasing. He was particularly incensed by Gilbert Scott's and other ardent ecclesiologists' drastic restorations of famous churches, restorations which were constantly inclined to degenerate into complete rebuilding. It was Scott's proposals for the restoration of Tewkesbury Abbey which led Morris to write his powerful letter to *The Athenaeum* advocating the formation, before all was lost, of a society for the preservation of ancient buildings. Within a fortnight of the appearance of the letter a society, with Morris as secretary, had been formed, particularly designed to combat the destruction envisaged by well-intentioned mediaevalists. The influence and achievements of the "Anti-Scrape" society, as Morris called it, during the past three-quarters of a century have been constantly increasing. Morris's interests were limited entirely to the work of the Middle Ages, and he had no sympathy for post-Renaissance work in this country: the buildings of Wren, for example, seemed to him to have no merit at all. It was distinctly a reverse when Thomas Carlyle joined the new society, stating very clearly that his reason for doing so was the grave neglect into which Wren's City churches had been allowed to fall.

Possibly Morris's dislike of classical building grew a little less with the years, for in 1878 he bought an early eighteenth-century house on the Upper Mall at Hammersmith which he renamed Kelmscott House. This remained his London home until the end of his life. It was a pleasure to Morris to feel that he could make the journey from Kelmscott Manor, his country house near Lechlade, to his house in London by water, both houses being on the banks of the Thames. The Hammersmith house contained simple but spacious Georgian rooms, but Morris made no compromise with the eighteenth century in his decorations and furnishings. Much of the solid oak furniture which had been at the Red House was installed, and the drawing-room, with five long windows overlooking the river, was hung with tapestry woven in his workshops at Merton. In other rooms were his trellis and pomegranate papers, some of the happiest designs which he ever produced. In whatever shell Morris's life was contained, the style remained true to his early ideals. His accomplishment in design improved with practice, but his taste remained remarkably constant throughout his life, and at no time did he deviate in his decorative output from the intransigent ideals of his youth.

Not all the members of the Pre-Raphaelite Brotherhood shared Morris's singleness of outlook in the decoration of their rooms. Rossetti, for instance, a close friend and colleague in early years, though they were estranged, later had a more catholic taste. In 1862 he came to live at Queen's House, a fine, late seventeenth-century building in Cheyne Row, but there was none of the chaste austerity of Morris's rooms. The house was filled, according to his brother, with objects from many countries and of many dates: English mirrors and chandeliers of the seventeenth and eighteenth centuries, Chinese tables and chairs, Dutch tiles, draperies from Africa and the Orient (but none it seems from Merton), while all about were knick-knacks and ornaments of every conceivable sort. Queen's House could not be advanced as an advertisement for the wares of Morris & Company,

Cloverley Hall, Shropshire (1862). Eden Nesfield, Architect

but it was even more remote from the average mid-Victorian home, those overladen houses furnished with pieces directly descended from the objects displayed at the Great Exhibition. Only in their crowded condition did Rossetti's rooms conform to popular taste.

Meanwhile, the more conventional exponents of the applied arts were carrying on a brisk trade. There were many architects at work during this decade, but the majority faded swiftly into obscurity. Their works are now little admired, and public interest in the personality of an architect is seldom long maintained unless his output reaches the extremes of beauty or ugliness. In any case the names of architects have always in this country been allowed to fall easily into oblivion. How slowly and painfully, for example, are the identities of the highly capable but minor architects of the post-Restoration period being carefully dug out of the dark recesses of history. Were it the general practice for an architect to leave his name on a building, in the same way that painters sign a picture or sculptors a statue, how much trouble and uncertainty would be saved. To ascribe a building to an architect purely on the basis of style is more dangerous than a similar method would be with any of the other arts. Victorian architects, however, are better recorded than their Stuart colleagues; and, with interest in the works of this period increasing, names are being brought out of the mists which have been cast over them by the passing of a century.

Amongst those who were enjoying prosperous careers during the 'sixties was Alfred Waterhouse, whose name has never been forgotten.

He was born in 1830 and achieved his first major success by winning in 1859 the competition for the new Assize Court in Manchester. It was a great achievement for so young a man. But the elaborate and formidable Gothic building which arose did not meet with universal approbation. Even Charles Eastlake wrote a little defensively in its praise: "It will be time enough to criticise when any better modern structure of its size and style has been raised in this country". In any case it was sufficiently admired to form the model for several harsh and flamboyant public buildings in the county towns of England, such as the Guildhall at Winchester. Some of his important domestic works will be described in the next chapter.

William Eden Nesfield was a highly-regarded architect of the 'sixties and secured a number of architectural plums. In 1860 he was commissioned by Lord Craven to make alterations and additions to Combe Abbey, work which was to cost about £60,000. The tall Gothic wing, dominating the remainder of the house, was the result, and shows the architect's weakness as a collector, as it were, of Gothic bric-à-brac. Nesfield had extensively studied and sketched the mediaeval Gothic buildings of the Continent, and the formidable structure at Combe incorporated detail culled from many sources without subscribing to any very definite style. The same criticism could be made of Cloverley Hall, which he designed two years later, though there was greater simplification. This high house, of four stories on the garden side topped by tall finialled dormers in the François I manner and with high fluted chimney-stacks, has some merit as a design; but its heavily mullioned windows must have made it dark and melancholy to live in. The decorative features of the interior, such as the oak-panelled entrance hall modelled on the hall

Knightshayes Court, Devonshire (1869). William Burges, Architect

William Burges's own house in Kensington (c. 1870)

at fifteenth-century Ockwells, with the upper part of the panelling decorated with a pattern in the oriental style, and the stained glass in the windows, must have been singularly lugubrious. It is doubtful whether the garden hall which was lined with amber-coloured tiles, with a frieze above them representing birds painted on a white ground, was any more attractive. How refreshing the homespun effects of the school of Morris seem compared to all this.

An architect who favoured a rather different style either to the conventional Gothic, or to the fundamental manner of Morris and Webb, was William Burges. The style, if such it can be called, for which he showed preference was a romantic castellated which derived from the mock castles of which a number were built during the early years of the century. Even such a sober building as Knightshayes Court in Devon, which Burges designed in 1869, has a muted note of fantasy in the battlemented bow-windows and high dormers, though Eastlake's description indicates that fantasy was in this case kept well under control. "Massive walls, bold gables, stout mullions nearly half the width of the lights which they divide, large and solid looking chimney shafts, corbelled from the walls or riding on the high pitched roof, are the principal incidents which give this building dignity and effect". A certain dignity indeed the house has, but the "effect" is not a happy one.

A congenial commission was the building of a huge tower at Cardiff Castle which was twenty-five feet square and one hundred and thirty feet high. Here Burges was allowed free rein to his devotion to the castellated style, not only on the exterior, to which he gave a fabulous, fairy-tale aspect, but also in the rooms contained within the redoubtable walls. In these strange apartments chimney-breasts groan with machicolations and groups of mediaeval figures, while from miniature crenellations and loopholes little figures of archers and serfs peep out, waving flags, blowing fanfares on long trumpets, and in every way giving a hearty welcome to any startled entrant to the room. There was much in the same strain to be found in his own home, Tower House in Melbury Road, while the furniture which he designed for his own use had a character unlike any other contemporary work. His earlier furniture had, perhaps, a little in common with the designs of Morris and Company. A bookcase, for example, made in 1862 had flat surfaces which were painted with romantic scenes by eleven different artists, including Burne-Jones, Poynter and Simeon Solomon; but the bed and washstand designed in 1879 and 1880 respectively owed nothing either to precedent or example. The vast wooden bed was gilded and inset with small pieces of mirror, miniature paintings, and fragments of vellum and textiles under glass. The whole conception was graceless and confused. The washstand with its marbles, mirrors, bronze taps and fittings, maintained the same lavish theme with the same lack of elegance. Indeed vulgarity rather than splendour seems the dominant note of these strange pieces of furniture.

There were many other architects sufficiently well known during the 'sixties to receive important commissions for the building of huge country houses, but whose names are now little remembered by any except the expert. Ferrey, for example, spent nine years from 1861 to 1870 supervising the construction of an enormous house in the Tudor style for the Duke of Somerset at Bulstrode, while simultaneously Teulon was erecting a formidable building in the fourteenth-century style, but in the medium of typically nineteenth-century brick, for the Duke of St. Albans at Bestwood in Nottinghamshire, as well as a house containing about a hundred rooms for Lord Ducie at Tortworth in Gloucestershire; Clutton was also engaged on Melchet Court, a large brick house in the Elizabethan manner for Lord Ashburton. All over the country the rich were active in building huge structures, at a cost of hundreds of thousands of pounds, which less than a century later proved to be worth little more than the demolition value of the materials with which they were built.

During the seventeenth and eighteenth centuries a number of books had been published offering all manner of information and

suggestions for the building of country houses and villas, while during the early years of the nineteenth century the stream of publications became a flood. Many architects, both successful and unsuccessful, produced illustrated books as an advertisement of their wares, and a means of bringing their capabilities to the notice of the public. Some of these contained much technical matter useful to a working builder, but none was quite so comprehensive in the breadth and depth of advice given to laymen and professionals alike as Robert Kerr's *The Gentleman's House*, which was first published in 1864. Here there are no hints on actual construction, but every other aspect was fully dealt with: siting, planning, drainage, domestic working, outbuildings, gardens, with an introductory chapter on architectural styles. Kerr's interest, like our own, lay more in large houses than in small, and it is in his advice on the planning of great houses, houses designed to be staffed by thirty or more servants, that he is so particularly interesting about the *train de maison* of the very rich.

The complex world of the vast nineteenth-century house seems now far more remote and improbable than that of the great Palladian mansions of the eighteenth century, perhaps because it is so near in time, and yet so very far in spirit from life of the present day. One sympathizes with the sentiments of Thomas Carlyle expressed in a letter to his wife written from a Yorkshire country house in which he was staying:

> "I have never lived before in such an element of 'much ado about almost Nothing'; life occupied altogether in getting itself lived; troops of flunkeys and bustling and becking at all times, the meat-jack creaking and playing all day . . . and such champagning, clareting and witty conversationing. *Ach Gott!* I would sooner be a ditcher than spend my life so".

Carlyle was then a beginner at country-house life: later when he paid constant visits to Lady Ashburton at The Grange this critical attitude evaporated, and he recognized the pleasure of being a social lion.

Economy, that sobering word which takes first place in every present-day description of a building enterprise, was not apparently considered by Kerr: indeed it might have been looked on as indifferent taste to refer to such a plebeian necessity. The size of a projected house might be regulated by the length of the owner's purse, but once that point was decided the financial aspect was forgotten. The small house came in for some rather patronizing remarks. On the subject of drawing-rooms the author wrote: "In suburban villas and other small houses where the accommodation is radically insufficient for the numbers occasionally received, it may be required that the Dining-room shall be connected with the drawing-room . . . a grievous informality". How formal indeed was social life in the 'sixties.

Hints on decoration and furnishing are of a general nature. A dining-room, for example, should have furniture which is massive and simple, and so be in keeping with English fare, but an unbroken line of chairs along a wall should be avoided or the room will look like a tavern. Kerr gives a long list of objects designed to bring elegance to a drawing-room: chairs and couches, occasional tables, sofa tables, chiffoniers, fancy cabinets, pier tables, what-nots and so forth. A collection of this sort would make a small drawing-room look elegant and welcoming, but if the room were a large one, the number of pieces of furniture must be doubled; while the "cabinet pianoforte" would be replaced by a "grand". The useful hints cover a wide range of reception rooms, and assist owners to avoid social solecisms, such as introducing statuary or busts into a morning-room when they are only properly suited to a library. The cooking apparatus in the kitchen of a moderate-sized house is interesting: there should be a roasting range with a boiler, a roasting screen, stewing stoves heated by charcoal, hot-plate, broiling stove, hot closet, and a hot table.

These suggestions may now appear rather ridiculous, but at the time when the book was written they were useful and sensible. Whether architects acknowledged much debt to Kerr is doubtful, for with their professional training they would claim to know what was required in a huge establishment without his assistance. But to the newly rich, contemplating building a house commensurate with their increased fortunes, the book must have been invaluable. Without previous acquaintance of the workings of a large country house they could, after perusing Kerr's closely printed pages, indicate to an architect exactly what was required.

Kerr was obviously catering with enthusiasm principally for the rich; but simultaneously during the 'sixties the lot of the poor was slowly improving. Disraeli's saying that England was divided into two nations, the rich and the poor, was still true in some degree, but the gap between the two was narrowing slightly; or perhaps it would be more accurate to say that the edges of the two groups were becoming blurred by the rise of a prosperous lower-middle class which linked the two groups, though the extremes of high and low remained as far apart as ever. The industrial prosperity of the country was at last beginning to percolate down to the workers, and the various acts, which had been with difficulty squeezed through Parliament during the late 'forties and 'fifties, were at last ameliorating the conditions of their lives.

In the country-side the situation was also improving. The gloomy prognostications which had accompanied the repeal of the Corn Laws had turned out to be entirely misplaced. Farming, so far from being brought to a state of ruin, was enjoying a solid prosperity it had never previously known, and the lot of the labourer was showing signs of brightening. But it was a very slow progress, and meanwhile there was a considerable exodus to the Colonies of rural workers, who saw little prospect of materially improving their status in England. In the majority of cases their decision was the correct one, and they brought benefits both to themselves and to the countries to which they migrated; but it was the beginning of the drift away from the farm-lands of England, which has continued ever since. It was a happy period for landowners, for during this decade farm rents rose to heights they had never previously, and it may be added have never since, reached. Even allowing for the diminution of the value of the pound, farm rents today remain in general slightly lower than they were during the peak period in the latter part of the 'sixties. A small proportion of this prosperity was passed on to the farm labourers, and the level of their wages rose by about twenty per cent. between 1848 and 1865; but since the average wage at the former date was no more than seven shillings a week, an increase of one-fifth did not amount to a very great deal.

This halcyon period for landowners was not of long duration: in the middle of the following decade there was a sudden and sensational collapse in agriculture, and from 1875 onwards the possession of a large landed estate indicated poverty rather than wealth.

During the 'sixties, however, there seemed no presage of coming disaster, and landowners, with an unaccustomed quantity of money in their pockets, turned their attention to improving the housing conditions of the rural workers on their estates. It was a congenial task, for English landowners have been, in a general way and according to their lights, good landlords. Architects were not slow to perceive this philanthropic trend, and a number of helpful books were published containing drawings and plans for all manner of estate buildings. These compilations show a very different spirit to such books as Robinson's *Rural Architecture* of thirty-five years earlier, in which the only aim was to provide designs for housing a dutiful peasantry in picturesque buildings which would form a pleasing feature in the landscape. The convenience of the cottages was at that time only a secondary consideration.

G. A. Dean's *Selected Designs* of 1867, for example, sounded the new note: "No chapter in the history of national manners", he wrote, "would illustrate so well . . . the progress of social life as that dedicated to Domestic Architecture". And this progress is here exemplified by his intention to "awaken a better sense of the importance of

"Residence erected at Moorland near York" (c. 1860). G. A. Dean, Architect

providing improved Residences for labourers". "The farm labourer", he continued, "has degenerated both morally and physically: at last there is a general desire to improve his condition". Beneath the rather sententious phrases and the high moral tone, which was typical of the age, there was sound sense; and the accommodation in the labourers' cottages he proposed was much in advance of the normal run. But how unfortunate that while the principles of Mr. Dean and others were so excellent their designs should have been so ugly. Robinson's *cottages ornés* fully achieved their aim of fitting happily into a landscape, but Dean's essays in the "old English style" were devoid of all charm. Groups of cottages, which were supposed to have the haphazard, unselfconscious air of a Tudor manor, were fussy assertive buildings which, with their tall meagre chimneys and spiky gables, were clearly straining desperately to be picturesque.

Hand in hand with material progress came a more humane attitude towards the employment of children. Since 1842 it had been forbidden for women, and children under ten to work in mines; but not until twenty-two years later, when the public conscience had been deeply stirred by Kingsley's *Water Babies*, was an act passed designed to prevent the use of small boys as chimney-sweeps. This well-intentioned act, however, was largely disregarded until reinforced by another in 1875, by which the scandal was effectively crushed without apparently causing a notable increase in fires due to soot-laden flues.

The position of women during these mid-Victorian years was becoming more important in the social structure. During the previous two decades the most desirable attribute of a girl wishing to secure a good place in the marriage market was a submissive temperament. Whether she remained gentle and yielding once her objective had been achieved was a different matter, but it was considered attractive and becoming that she should appear so, at least to the public eye. Human nature in fact changes very little, but an air of devoted and clinging domesticity was the fashion amongst the great masses of the middle classes, and *Kinder, Küche und Kirche* were considered very adequate interests for the average married woman.

That young women were not always satisfied with their ineffectual lives is clear from the extracts which Cecil Woodham-Smith quotes from Florence Nightingale's unpublished novel *Cassandra*, which was written in 1852. The dreary, stifling daily round in the average upper-class home is described in detail. The morning is spent "sitting round a table in the drawing-room, looking at prints, doing worsted work, and reading little books". The afternoon is passed "taking a little drive", while the evening no doubt followed the same plan as the morning. All but the most lymphatic must have suffered from the pernicious effects of these aimless days, and some suffered, Miss Nightingale declared, "even physically". ". . . The accumulation of nervous energy, which has had nothing to do during the day, makes them feel every night, when they go to bed, as if they were going mad; they are obliged to lie long in bed in the morning to let it evaporate and keep it down. . . . Some are only deterred from suicide because it is in the most distinct manner to say to God 'I will not do as Thou would'st have me'."

The Crimean War, which was proclaimed against Russia in 1854, had a marked effect on this social question. Florence Nightingale's remarkable achievements in nursing and organization led to a general realization that there was a place for women beyond the domestic hearth. And this was reinforced by the remarkable career of Elizabeth Blackwell, the first woman doctor of medicine. Though English by birth, she carried out her medical training in the United States; but in 1859, at the age of thirty-eight, her name was placed on the English medical register, and from that time forward until her death in her ninetieth year she divided her energies between America and this country, in lecturing, writing and the organization of such undertakings as the National Health Society and the School of Medicine for Women.

Nursing was naturally, and very properly, the first choice for those seeking a career, but others soon followed; and perhaps, as *Punch* had feared, Mrs. Bloomer's innovations, with the assistance of Miss Nightingale's and Dr. Blackwell's examples in a different field, had started a new era in the life of women.

Their contributions to literature began to turn in new directions. As novelists they had, of course, been long established, and it was perhaps the sole field in which their contribution was seriously considered. The *British Women's Review* now provided an opportunity for articles on highly serious subjects, on education, health and other social problems of public interest. The review, which formed stiff but uplifting reading, contained articles such as the following: "Education by means of Workhouses", by Louisa Twining; "Local Schools for the Poor", by Barbara Collett; "Principles of Education in Lower Class Schools", by Mary Carpenter; "The Conditions of Women Workers in England and France", by Bessie Parkes; "Slavery in America and its Influence on Great Britain", by Sarah Redmond. The subjects discussed show that women were in some cases looking far beyond the restricted limits of their homes; but the majority of the writers were unmarried, and so were free from the dependence and subjection which were the accepted conditions of the marital state.

Up to this period a married woman had possessed no property of her own. On marriage her possessions, apart from property held in trust, passed to her husband, and many wives had the unhappy experience of finding their portions dissipated by an extravagant husband, without having any legal means of safeguarding their assets. It was this anachronic condition which led John Stuart Mill to publish his *Subjection of Women* in 1869: it was a condition which greatly startled the Frenchman Henri Taine. Describing English life in the early 'sixties he wrote of married women: "*Elles sont sujettes ici, de par la loi, la religion, les moeurs*", and he went on to explain how the average wife, having nothing to command except a small allowance of "pin money", was usually kept in absolute ignorance of her husband's financial affairs. So complete was it indeed that they were sometimes faced with ruin without having had the least premonition of approaching disaster. Mill's determined advocacy, though received with hostility in many, perhaps interested, quarters, led directly to the passing of the Married Women's Property Act which effectively released women from financial bondage to their husbands, and allowed them a degree of independence, if they were fortunate enough to possess any assets.

A substantial dowry was a rarity even in this age of prosperity. A self-made industrialist might obtain good marriages for his daughters by endowing them well, but the daughters of an average upper-class, land-owning family were seldom able to advertise anything but the smallest portions. Families were often large. The eldest son would have the upkeep of a big house and estate, the second might be able to lead a life of moderate ease in the family living, another might earn his livelihood in one of the services or perhaps in the law; but in any case these younger sons would be largely dependent on what they were able to earn, while the daughters had seldom much beyond such sweetness and gentleness of temperament as they could muster to attract the eligible male. It was not an easy rôle to play—to attract by passive virtues—but at no other period perhaps had the feminine art of encouraging the male, while appearing to withdraw, been more highly developed.

Mr. Punch had envisaged women joining the fighting services, but this situation, which then appeared so risible, was to be delayed for rather more than half a century. Early in the 'sixties, however, the Volunteer Movement which provided a masculine army of amateur soldiers was given great impetus. The intentions of Napoleon III, just across the water, were highly suspect, and the purpose of the volunteer army was to create an impression of an England bristling with martial ardour and fully able—indeed anxious—to deal with aggression. This was not the first occasion during Queen Victoria's reign on which there had been a similar scare: in 1852, soon after Louis Napoleon's *coup d'état*, there had been a parallel anxiety. James Pope-Hennessy in his book *The Flight of Youth* describes how that exceedingly unmilitary figure Monckton Milnes hurried off to Yorkshire in the autumn of the latter year to instil a little discipline and enthusiasm into the Pontefract volunteers, and was rewarded with a letter from Lord Palmerston praising his patriotism: "You were quite right", he wrote, "to buckle on your armour. The sight of gentlemen joining the Militia is a great encouragement to the lower classes to do the like".

That either the Emperor or his advisers at any time had any thought of invasion now seems highly improbable, since they were fully occupied with other difficulties; but at least the apprehension stimulated a useful movement in this country which was destined to become a permanent part of the defensive structure. The croquet-party atmosphere, with crinolines as much to the fore as the ill-fitting tunics and rifles of the volunteers, which pervaded the early stages of the movement, was gradually dissipated, fortunately without having to be extinguished by the cold test of actual combat; but undoubtedly the social, gregarious style of its inception led to the wide popularity of what might otherwise have appeared a tedious burden.

Although the threat from across the Channel was not very imminent, the dislike of Napoleon III by the people of England had become very real indeed. The days when he and the Empress had paid a state visit to England and charmed the Queen, who had found him "so gentle, so full of tact, dignity and modesty", were long past, and the papers of the early 'sixties contained ribald cartoons showing him in all manner of deceitful and scheming guises. In the pages of *Punch* he shared an equally violent opprobrium with the Pope, Pius IX; and it is difficult to gauge which of the two Mr. Punch, with his militant Anglican outlook, considered the greater menace to the peace of Europe.

The Roman Catholic faith was fast gaining ground in England. In

A Family Group of the late 'sixties

1850 a Roman Catholic hierarchy had been established in this country, and fifteen years later Manning was consecrated Archbishop of Westminster. The success of his activities was viewed with alarm by staunch supporters of the Church of England. Miss Emily Eden voiced the fears of many when she wrote to a friend in 1851: "The Pope has us beat and taken us . . . England will be a Roman Catholic country". Religion remained, as it had been for the past two decades, a highly important factor in family life, and in the average home an iron discipline of daily prayers and Sunday observances continued unabated. Whether it was still considered desirable to turn pictures to the wall, as it had been in Ruskin's home when he was a boy, is doubtful, but the ban on games and toys for children was still rigorously enforced.

The strict maintenance of the austere English Sunday was regarded by staunch Anglicans as evidence of their religious strength, but already their ranks had been seriously divided and weakened by the increasing vigour of Anglo-Catholicism. Manning, when Archdeacon of Chichester, had been a leader of the movement, which made great headway within the Church of England; his defection to Rome and ordination as a priest in April, 1851, provoked intense hostility, as well as dismay, amongst his former friends and associates. What was looked on as an act of treachery was never forgiven, and for the rest of his life he was considered by Anglicans as a danger to the stability of their Church and country. Augustus Hare writes of meeting Mr. Gladstone at breakfast in 1874, when "the great topic was Manning. About him and Catholicism in general", he adds, "Gladstone seems

111

to have lost all temperance". The religious controversies which were maintained during the middle decades of the century, though no doubt eventually destructive of spiritual feeling, were at the time evidence that religion was more than a superficial attribute of Victorian respectability, and sprang from deeper and stronger sentiments which were far removed from the rationalist attitude of the Georgian era.

During the 'sixties the photograph album, that enduring feature of domestic life, began to take its place on the drawing-room table. There were in general two varieties: there was the chubby leather-bound volume fastened with a brass clasp, which was designed with windows in its thick leaves for *carte-de-visite* portraits by professional photographers; but there was also the larger, folio-sized book for the groups and views taken by amateurs.

In the previous decade the pleasures of photography had been limited to a few, but now it was becoming an absorbing hobby for those with money to buy the expensive apparatus which was required, and the time to deal with the complicated process of developing the plates. The results achieved with large calotype plates were remarkably good, though they lacked the crisp light and shade of modern photography. Societies were formed, and members exchanged copies of their successful work. Thus a sense of rivalry was engendered amongst enthusiasts, and much trouble and thought were given to the production of suitable scenes. There was then no question of snapshots taken at random: on the contrary, parties were carefully grouped and arranged so as to form interesting compositions —some standing, some sitting on the ground with crinolines gracefully billowing round the wearers. Those, both men and women, who fancied their profiles, would resolutely turn this aspect to the camera; and at least one young man, in a deerstalker and with a heavy moustache, would lie in front of the party in an attitude of studied abandon seldom found in twentieth-century groups. The principal aim was that the group should look natural and unposed, and though this was seldom achieved these photographs have great charm.

Landscapes, highly artistic still-lifes, and "studies" of young women thinly disguised as peasants or oriental sultanas, formed almost equally popular objectives for the camera; but these have now little beyond technical interest compared to the straightforward groups which, with their mannerisms and fashions, give penetrating insight into contemporary ways of life. But even more fascinating are the photographs of interiors, which in this decade came within the scope of the average amateur, so that from this period one can see rooms exactly as they were. Paintings and drawings of this subject are highly illuminating, but with these one often has the impression that

"Engaging the new Page" (*c.* 1869)

A Conversation Piece of the 'sixties

a certain sense of selection was exercised, and some of the furnishings excluded. In these early photographs, however, the rooms appear in their normal crowded state. And how strange a confusion they present: the most striking feature of a drawing-room of the 'sixties is to our eyes the complete lack of organized arrangement. Whether the room portrayed was large or small the effect was generally the same, with chairs, tables and little what-nots dotted about as if the removers had dumped the furniture into the room, and it had been left where they had placed it. The style of the setting made little difference: an equal chaos would be found in a contemporary Gothic drawing-room as in a formal eighteenth-century saloon, though probably in the latter symmetrically disposed pier-glasses and consoles would form a disapproving background.

This effect is so persistent that there can be no doubt that it was deliberately arrived at. The apparently haphazard air of the rooms was as carefully contrived as that of the portrait groups. A room filled with furniture and knick-knacks produced, it was felt, a sense of comfort and opulence, and gave a generous, welcoming air to hospitality. How crinolines, which reached their largest proportions in the early 'sixties, were negotiated amidst these dense archipelagos without constant disaster is a mystery.

114

The quantity of furniture in the average drawing-room was no less astonishing than the poorness of its quality. In many rooms, obviously in large houses and belonging to wealthy owners, there would be nothing to be seen which would now be worth more than a few pounds, if subjected to the cold test of the auctioneer's hammer; but even where some fine furniture from a happier period survived it would be mixed, in complete insouciance, with worthless bric-à-brac. Amongst the commonplace throng a few first-class pieces might stand out, aloof and dignified, but apparently as little prized, in spite of superb workmanship and design, as the varnished oak tables and basket chairs which surrounded them.

Naturally all rooms were not like this. Those, for example, showing the influence of Morris would be far different; and even some conventional rooms were more methodically arranged, though all sense of quality would be lacking. Elaboration and ostentation, which had begun to submerge craftsmanship at the Great Exhibition, were continuing on a victorious career. In needlework almost alone did a sense of design still prevail, and it is this above all products of the period that is still valued today. How astonished a mid-Victorian needlewoman might be to learn that a small carpet made up of flowered squares at which she had stitched for a few years would be worth a thousand pounds or so a century later.

Small easy chairs were a prominent feature of sitting-rooms of the 'sixties. In the Great Exhibition there had been chairs designed for

"*Paris Fashions for March*" (1869)

moderate ease, but on upright lines with turned mahogany or walnut legs. Chairs of the following decade were of different character: though still upright they were low, with well-sprung seats and padded backs, and were clearly a development of the prie-dieu, without which no well-arranged bedroom was complete. They were admirably adapted to women's fashions of the day: nothing could be more graceful, more suggestive of elegant relaxation, than the appearance of the wearer of a well-controlled crinoline seated on one of these comfortable little chairs. The back would be supported on the resilient upholstery, while the billowing skirt swept in long and concealing folds from waist to floor. How well the young George du Maurier, whose drawings were beginning to raise the rather plebeian tone of the pages of *Punch*, realized the beauty of gentle, well-poised repose.

The fashions of the middle decade of the nineteenth century may have had practical drawbacks, but they afforded extreme dignity and grace to those who were able to wear them with advantage. The drawbacks, too, may have been slighter than one is now inclined to suppose. Gwen Raverat, in her book of childhood reminiscences *Period Piece*, describes how she once asked her aunt what it had been like to wear a crinoline. "Oh, it was delightful", the old lady replied, "I've never been so comfortable since they went out. They kept your petticoats away from your legs, and made walking so light and easy". Those unmentionable limbs, legs, may have been successfully concealed by the crinoline, but at least they had a freedom of movement which was denied them by later, and less extravagant, fashions.

During the first years of the 'sixties the crinoline increased in size, and there were subtle changes in its form. At the end of the previous decade the swelling lines of the skirt had sprung directly from the waist, so that the figure from the waist downwards was entirely concealed. In compensation the shoulders and bust were exposed with a freedom which seems a little out of keeping with the Victorians' reputation for demureness. It could be extremely alluring. "*Le ton de la peau est éblouissant . . . le cou et les épaules semblent de la neige, ou plutôt de la nacre*", wrote Henri Taine, who considered an Englishwoman's skin was her principal beauty. It was regarded as unsuitable for a woman who was in mourning to expose her shoulders in evening dress, but age on the other hand imposed no restrictions. Two or three years after her husband's death, Lady Palmerston wrote to her daughter: "I think, Fanny, I must really begin low bodies again in the evening". She was then over eighty years of age, but her period of mourning was ending.

About 1863 skirts became sufficiently close-fitting round waist and hips to give a discreet indication of the figure, but opened to an immense span below. It was in these fashions that Princess Alexandra of Denmark arrived in England for her marriage to the Prince of Wales. "Dear Alix, looking like a rose, wore a grey dress, with a violet jacket trimmed with fur, and a white bonnet", wrote Queen Victoria enthusiastically on her arrival; but the frumpy English Court, which lagged far behind Continental modes, was inclined to be startled by the size of the Princess's crinolines. A few years later skirts had assumed more flowing lines, with folds gathered at the back so as to form a sweeping train. A contemporary and rival fashion to these impracticable garments was the short full skirt which was said to have been introduced by the Empress Eugénie. It daringly displayed not only feet but also ankles with an occasional glimpse of the frilled edge of long drawers. These two divergent fashions maintained a hot rivalry until the extinction of the crinoline about 1867.

A "Scent Fountain"
Shown at the 1851 Exhibition

"A State Party" (1864). From an engraving after Richard Doyle

CHAPTER V

COMMERCE ENTERS SOCIETY

1870—1880

SOCIAL changes are seldom conveniently adjusted to the decades, and the opening of the 'seventies seemed to promise no alteration in the comfortable tenor of English life. At home, both industry in the towns and agriculture in the country were in a condition of gratifying prosperity; many humane reforms designed to improve the state of the working classes were before Parliament; and all were agreed that a little, but no more than a little, of the great wealth which had come to many should be passed on to the workers, to whose efforts the success was largely due.

In a wider field, there seemed no serious clouds on the international horizon to divert the country's energies from the rewarding task of money-making—and money-spending—into the dull and expensive channels of defensive or offensive operations. The Services were organized on a scale adequate for existing conditions, while the volunteer movement remained an important feature in the life of all classes, particularly in the country. It had emerged from its fumbling and amateurish start, and no longer provided such easy jokes for the comic papers. As the menace from across the water which it had been inaugurated to combat faded, so the movement rather unexpectedly became more serious and efficient.

118

Altogether the country seemed safely set on the path of prosperity and security, and there seemed no reason to anticipate any deviation from this broad and easy road. At this propitious opening of the new decade it was impossible to foresee that a number of unexpected twists and turns would interfere considerably with the smooth progress of English life.

The first shock to complacency came with the outbreak of the Franco-Prussian war on the 15th July, 1870. It might have been supposed that it would be a pleasant new rôle for John Bull to be a spectator rather than a participant in a war, particularly when one of the parties had lately seemed to be menacing our own shores. Indeed there was a certain satisfaction in observing that the French aggressors were not gaining the initial advantage they had anticipated; but when their reverses turned to utter defeat and humiliation at the hands of a country which had not hitherto been very highly thought of by the average Englishman, a certain feeling of unease crept into the cosy, upholstered parlours of this island. It was a sensation which, with varying intensity, was to remain a constant and uncomfortable background to English life.

At the height of Victorian prosperity, the average Englishman felt sufficiently secure in his country's ability to deal with any conflict not to be fundamentally disturbed by potential threats from the Continent. A few years later, however, there came a more direct, a more domestic shock, though one which was limited in its effects to only part of the community. About 1875 the prosperity which agriculture had enjoyed, apparently so unassailably, for a number of years past, suddenly collapsed, and the industry, on which a large section of the population had depended in one way or another for its livelihood, ceased to provide employment and support. The cause of the disaster was the importation of large quantities of foreign wheat, chiefly from the new corn-growing areas of America where costs were low and space unlimited. The market was flooded with cheap corn, and by an unfortunate chance English farmers suffered a succession of three ruined harvests, so that home-grown corn was scarce. The effect on the farming community was immediate. Few farmers had any capital to fall back on and they thus were unable to carry on. The rents of farms fell heavily, but even at low levels they were unlettable, and owners were compelled to leave them derelict. Thus many farm labourers found themselves suddenly out of work and without means of subsistence: in fact the whole structure of country life, which a few years earlier had seemed so thriving, fell swiftly into ruin.

Strangely enough the Government took no effective steps to remedy the deplorable situation. Free Trade was the mainstay of their policy and had, until now, brought great national wealth. The Corn Laws, which had led to the prohibitive price of bread and the virtual starvation of a large section of the community during the "Hungry 'Forties", were still well within the memory of many. Cheap imported corn, and hence a cheap loaf, was of great benefit to all, except to those engaged in or dependent on agriculture; and in addition the urban population represented not only the larger section of the community, but also infinitely the most vocal. In any case farm labourers had no votes and did not obtain them until 1884, so that their hardships were unlikely to shake the stability of the Government.

The direct effects of the agricultural collapse were obvious and inevitable. The drift away from the land was much accelerated. Workers either emigrated, or moved into the towns where expanding industry was always ready to absorb them. Thus in 1881 it was computed that one hundred thousand fewer men were employed in agriculture than there had been when times were good. Small farmers, particularly those who had bought their farms at high prices during the good years, were faced with a ruin as complete as that of the labourer —and the fall was greater. Landowners who were dependent for their income on rents rather than on investments suddenly found themselves faced with the necessity of a drastic alteration in their way of life. The large houses which they had built during the happy days when their estates provided a clear income of one pound or thirty shillings for every acre, became an embarrassment as the means of maintenance suddenly dried up.

To the country squire and his family the necessity for a reduction in the scale and standard of living was a bitter blow, particularly at a time when some of their vulgar acquaintances were amassing fortunes in industry. In these austere, mid-twentieth-century days this process is recognized as a great inconvenience, but it carries no social stigma, indeed it is perhaps less suspect than expansion; but in the 'seventies, when the importance of individuals was gauged, even more definitely than now, by what they possessed rather than by what they were, a reduction of income became an overwhelming social reverse.

These, then, were some of the obvious results of agricultural collapse, and though the range was limited, in some directions the effect was permanent. There were also other consequences, slower to develop and more indirect, but which nevertheless radically modified the structure of Victorian Society, and so of the Victorian home which is the principal theme of this book. With the acute distress in the country-side the position of even the great land-owning families, unless they were fortunate enough to possess coal-mines, or ground-rents in London or some prosperous provincial city, was seriously affected. Their power in the country as a whole, which had once been paramount, had been lessening for some time: now the pace quickened, and as the social position of the landowner declined, so that of the industrialist and the man of commerce improved. All who possessed any social sense, and it was a sense very highly developed at this period, could see that money was beginning to count as much as lineage, indeed rather more. Whereas the latter was of little value without the former, the former had obvious merits on its own. A union of the two was clearly the most desirable, but it was a losing and extremely impolitic battle for those of high birth to try to exclude the new rich from society.

The numbers of the rich were constantly increasing. In spite of foreign competition and other difficulties industry was booming, but the money-making centre had moved for ever away from the countryside, where it had been fixed in earlier centuries, into the cities. A new class of men, those who controlled industry, were coming to the fore; and their wives and families, and often themselves, were gradually infiltrating into a society which had for so long considered itself highly exclusive. In the past the wisest course for a newly rich man, intent on climbing the steep path into society, would have been to buy an extensive country estate and to live there in grand style: this was far more respectable, more suggestive of a solid financial background, than merely owning a large house in London. After all there was the unfortunate example of the Railway King, George Hudson, whose huge house at Albert Gate and lavish entertainments had not, as it transpired, indicated a well-founded financial background. But with agriculture in the doldrums, astute industrialists were chary of investing in such a declining commodity as land. Thus they were more likely to favour comparatively small estates, though the houses might be extremely large; while shooting, which would attract distinguished guests, could be rented from some adjacent impoverished landowner. Thus the transference of money made in industry into the land was less than might have been expected; far less, for example, than has occurred during the middle years of this century; and the countryside remained starved of the blood which might have brought back to it some degree of prosperity.

The entry of self-made men into the rigid ranks of existing society was no new feature of English social life. Since the times of the Tudors new families which had made fortunes by various means—often at the expense of their fellow men—had perforce been accepted as the equals of those of ancient lineage; and the children of these families, if not the founder himself, had married freely into social strata which a generation earlier would have been far above their aspirations. The Stuarts were on the whole inclined to dispense their favours to those of good family rather than to rich parvenus, though Charles II's mistresses, who founded several ducal families, were a striking exception to this generalization. During the eighteenth century East India merchants, who were sometimes younger sons of old but impoverished families, but equally often men of no social background at all, would return to this country after twenty industrious years in India with large fortunes, but without wives. These men in young middle age were eagerly sought after for their daughters by mothers of the utmost distinction. There seemed to be something particularly respectable, even romantic, about fortunes made in the East Indies, or for that matter about those made, as many were, from plantations and properties in the West Indies; and wealth which came from banking or brewing, and they were often allied, seemed to impart an almost equal distinction.

The numbers of the new rich during the eighteenth century had been relatively few, but in the middle years of Queen Victoria's reign an increasing number of men were making fortunes from industries which had neither romance nor tradition to recommend them. Families would make their appearance in polite London drawing-rooms whose wealth was derived from the most inelegant origins; from the distilling of spirits, for example, an enterprise which possessed little of the wholesome atmosphere of brewing, or from a chain of stores, from the making of soap, or laxative pills. How different these sources of wealth were from fortunes amassed in the fabulous Orient; and the fact that they may have been more meritoriously gained was neither here nor there. But money counted none the less, even if its vulgar origin gave an opportunity for social titters.

Du Maurier's familiar character, Sir Gorgius Midas, who delighted the readers of *Punch* during the 'seventies, was essentially a real type. He was obviously overdrawn, or there would have been little that was funny about him, but he represented an important feature of social life of the period. The top level of London society admitted, almost without blenching, a number of paler replicas of the successful pork-butcher and his spouse; they were less ostentatious, less stridently common, but were often given, like Sir Gorgius, to an inordinate display of wealth, and to considerable boasting to compensate for a lack of social self-confidence.

It seems now a very remote distinction, the question of being in or outside "Society", but mid-Victorian society was still what Lord Frederick Hamilton described in his memoirs as 'a sort of enlarged family party'; and until at least the later years of the nineteenth century English society entrenched itself within a firmly defended barricade. Within the fortress there were a number of excluding circles—*coteries excessivement exclusives* they were called by a contemporary French author—into which only the privileged could penetrate; but it was a definite step, and the only one which many could hope for, to negotiate the exterior bastions. On the Continent, society maintained its exclusive structure much longer than in England, so that the foreigner's anxious question: "Mrs. . . ., is she received?" could be answered in many European capitals long after it had ceased to be possible to reply to it in this country. The circles have not yet disintegrated, but the outer fortifications have long since crumbled into ruins.

An outstanding precedent for the toleration of social newcomers was provided by the circle in which the Prince of Wales moved. Since his marriage in 1863 he had become emancipated from the rigid control of the Queen, and had embarked on a social life of which his royal mother gravely disapproved. She had no sympathy with racing and gambling, and the slightly raffish Continental life which particularly appealed to the Prince, and in which the new industrial millionaires played an extremely useful part. These rich friends possessed—and to spare—the wealth which was necessary to make the wheels revolve smoothly and swiftly, and they for their part counted it good value for their money to be admitted to the Prince's circle; while their excellent social contacts could be turned to great profit in the City.

It was not only with Aryan financiers that the heir to the Crown consorted: his broad cosmopolitan outlook made the cultivated mentality of Jews extremely sympathetic to him. In addition, the fortunes which some of them had amassed in the money-markets of Europe were greater than those of the majority of industrialists. To this section of the Prince's circle the Queen could raise less objection. They were intelligent and highly respectable—which could hardly be said for all his Aryan friends—while her own admiration and affection for Disraeli disarmed criticism in this direction.

At the general election of 1874 Mr. Gladstone and the Liberals had been decisively routed, and the Tory party found itself firmly in power for the first time for forty years. This triumph was clearly due to the brilliant leadership of Disraeli, who was soon as successful in overcoming the initial prejudice of the Queen as he had been in winning the support and trust of his own party. The Queen, to her surprise, found the subtle workings of her Prime Minister's oriental mind as beguiling in matters of state as the Prince found similar characteristics in his social circle.

The entry of Jews into English society had been an uphill task, but Disraeli and contemporary financiers and merchants were not the first to achieve this goal. In the previous century Sampson Gideon, the son of a Portuguese Jew who had amassed a huge fortune as a stockbroker, played an important part in the social life of his time. It was true that he had been baptized, and that he later dropped the plebeian-sounding name of Gideon for the essentially English appellation of Eardley, but the Jewish blood remained well known to all, in spite of an Irish peerage granted to him by Pitt in 1879. All London society flocked to the parties he gave at his beautiful house of Belvedere, overlooking the Thames as it turned southwards towards the village of Erith; and yet he remained an outsider: he never achieved the social position of the Rothschilds, for example, in the nineteenth century.

It was perhaps Lord Eardley's attempts to appear so thoroughly English which prevented him from being accepted on quite equal terms by the extremely snobbish society of his day. The Rothschilds, on the other hand, remained true to the Jewish faith and made no effort to conceal their Continental origin and connections, yet the family reached a position almost unique in the social life of England. The wealth they amassed was immense, and it was spent with extreme lavishness on their houses, on the collection of works of art, and on the splendid entertainments they gave in their sumptuous settings. There were few, if any, houses in England which could rival the hospitality of the Rothschilds, and it was not surprising that the heir to the throne, to whom a life of luxury made a particular appeal, should have been their constant guest.

Though the Queen had no personal objections to the Rothschilds, she firmly refused Mr. Gladstone's request in 1869 that Baron Lionel de Rothschild should be given a peerage. "To make a *Jew a Peer* is a step she *could not* consent to", the Queen wrote in her usual emphatic style. Later, however, her views changed, and in 1885 Sir Nathaniel de Rothschild became the first professing Jew to enter the Upper House.

A letter from Constance de Rothschild to her mother, when visiting her cousins, gives some indication of the elaboration of the house-parties. "In the house", she wrote, "we have the Duchess of Marlborough, and Lady Sarah, the Wagrams, the Owen Williams, the Sandys, Lord Wolseley, Lord Rodney, Seymour Finch, a Mr. Walsh, Member for Radnor a very nice young Welshman, a clever Mr. Spring Rice, and last but not least H.R.H. and a youthful equerry". "The Christie Minstrels and a Hungarian Band", she continued, "perform alternately and give great satisfaction, particularly the latter. But the house itself with all its wonders and pictures, *objets d'art*, magnificent couches and satin cushions, and palms, and photos of crowned heads with autograph signatures are a never ending source of pleasure".

What a picture this letter conjures up of a Victorian house-party conceived on the most abundant scale, and moreover by a family which a generation earlier was entirely obscure. But the Rothschilds possessed not only the power of making money but also the rare gift of spending it with supreme grace.

As the century advanced the week-end house-party became an increasingly important feature of social life. In earlier years long and probably monotonous late summer visits, or a week's stay for shooting in the autumn, had been the usual form of country-house entertainment; but in the 'seventies a journey by train into the Home Counties was no longer an arduous undertaking, and this convenient means of transport could comfortably carry guests from London into the depths of the country-side on Friday afternoon, and return them to the metropolis on Monday. Furthermore, a number of the larger houses were provided with their own stations, a condition on which astute landowners insisted in return for permission to carry the railway line across their properties. A word to the station master, and an express would be stopped at the wayside station, so that the distinguished guests forming the house-party could be decanted on arrival, or collected on departure. The privileges of the great landowners may have been waning, but they were as yet by no means extinguished.

In some ways the inauguration of the week-end visit was a retrograde step. Memoirs of the period contain many descriptions of these entertainments with the names of those important people who were gathered for two days beneath a single roof: there are accounts of "The Pet's" prowess with the pheasants, or of "Poodle's" amusing practical joke, but little seems to have emerged from these elaborate and perhaps scintillating gatherings. They provided pleasant memories for those who enjoyed them, but were on the whole sterile in lasting effect. The spirit seems from this distance to have been very different to that of the eighteenth century. Then the great country houses played an important part in the promotion of the arts. Practitioners of literature, architecture and painting found ample opportunities within spreading Palladian walls for developing their talents, while the leisure and security, essential for the flowering of genius, were willingly provided by rich patrons. A boisterous Victorian week-end party may have been stimulating to the spirits, but it can seldom have been conducive to the development of the arts.

Perhaps alone architects benefited from the week-end habit. With easy communications between London and the country many new houses were being built, or old ones were being altered, to bring them into keeping with contemporary standards and taste. Many simple Georgian houses, which had satisfied their owners for a century or more, were demolished to make room for a building in painstaking renderings of the Tudor style, which was then much favoured; or the attractive products of the early Gothic Revival would be shorn of

125

"An Imp of Mischief". From a painting by C. Hunt

their pinnacles and tracery, and adorned instead with massive detail of mullions and battlements, in much the same manner that Georgian buildings had in their turn been given a Gothic air by the addition of pointed arches to the windows and a few filigree crockets on the roof.

The domestic architects of the 'seventies, however, were far more serious in their intentions than their colleagues of the early Revival, who had made little attempt to give their buildings the true appearance of the style they were professedly imitating. Alfred Waterhouse, for instance, was a noteworthy example of this intransigent, and indeed honourable, spirit. He obtained the most important domestic building commission of the age when he was invited by the third Marquess (later first Duke) of Westminster to transform the Perpendicular style building of Eaton Hall, which William Porden had erected less than half a century earlier, into a structure more in consonance with contemporary taste. The stupendous monument to nineteenth-century prosperity which emerged is well known. Though the detail was based on the surest precedents, the whole great building, both inside and out, is devoid of all charm, and none can greatly regret its diversion from domestic to military use.

A more interesting work of Waterhouse's, and one more typical of its age since it is reasonable in scale, is Blackmoor in Hampshire. The house was designed for the first Lord Selborne in 1872, the year in which its owner became Lord Chancellor for the first time. It is large by present-day standards, but has none of the ostentation which is so salient a feature of Eaton; instead it is inclined to veer in the opposite direction, and is rather pinched and crowded in its haphazard grouping. The architect might have had Compton Wynyates in mind when drawing up his design, but in any case the general rendering of the Tudor style is a comparatively free one, though doubtless all the detail was copied with a scrupulous correctness. The quality of the workmanship, particularly of the woodwork of the interior, is excellent, and it is in this direction that Waterhouse, in company with other Victorian architects of the first rank, is impressive. As with many contemporary painters they had a thorough knowledge of the technique of their craft: in the one it was the efficient use of materials, stone, brick and wood, in the other it was good drawing and competent paintwork; but in both that essential germ—a sense of beauty, charm, good taste, call it what one will—seems to us to have been almost always lacking. Thus in the rooms at Blackmoor, the beamed and heraldic ceilings, the light oak chimney-pieces inset with coloured tiles representing the seasons, or scenes from Aesop's Fables, a frieze depicting the parables, the heavily traceried window containing heraldic glass which casts a sombre light on to the staircase, all this could only have been produced by a man of insensitive taste. And yet in scholarship and in technical knowledge Waterhouse was in advance

Eaton Hall: the Ante-drawing-room (c. 1867). Alfred Waterhouse, Architect

of most of his contemporaries. This at least can confidently be said of his work at Blackmoor: there is no vulgarity about it, and it possesses a solid dignity which made it a suitable background for a distinguished Victorian Lord Chancellor.

The eighteenth-century practice, by which a capable architect designed not only a house for his client but also the decoration and the furniture, so that the whole became a single composite scheme, was not in general carried on by the academic architects of the mid-nineteenth century. William Morris and his company of craftsmen and architects were so closely united and worked so much in sympathy with each other, that with them the tradition was largely maintained. But these idealists stood apart from the normal run of practitioners. At Blackmoor, however, Waterhouse designed the furniture for the principal rooms, and it is this which makes the house a particularly interesting product of its period. On the whole the furniture has similar characteristics to his architecture, except that in the former he was more inclined to indulge his own initiative and fancy, not always with the happiest results. The greater part, in light oak, is reminiscent of the furniture which nearly forty years earlier Salvin had designed for his Gothic houses, but for the drawing-room he perpetrated a majestic piece in which he allowed his imagination free play. It is a large affair intended for the display of china: there are cupboards in the lower part, and above them are vitrines surmounted by open shelves. But it is the great variety of materials employed which make it so remarkable: the framework is of mahogany, and this is inset with decorative panels of ebony, mirror, brass, and—a strange introduction—brown leather. It is perhaps one of the most curious domestic productions of the period.

In general lines Waterhouse's furniture showed affinity with the principles advocated by Charles Eastlake, whose *Hints on Household Taste* had considerable effect on furnishings and decoration of the 'seventies. Eastlake was determined to break away from "the meaningless curves" which had been an outstanding feature of the furniture of the Great Exhibition period. Of the average sideboard of the 'fifties he wrote with sarcasm: "It was bowed in front and 'shaped' at the back: the cupboard doors were bent inwards; the drawfronts were bent outwards, the angles were rounded off; tasteless mouldings were glued on; the whole surface glistened with varnish". It was a just condemnation, and no similar reflections could be cast on the rigid, upright pieces of furniture which the author himself designed. His productions had an uncompromising four-square appearance, in which the form was dictated by the solid framework, and a minimum of unnecessary mouldings or decoration were allowed to soften the angular lines, though perhaps a few flourishes would be permitted in the forged-iron work of the hinges. His furniture indeed was primarily functional, and as such had merit, but it is doubtful whether it now seems more sympathetic than the buxom contours of a generation earlier.

A direction in which it is difficult to find any sympathy for Eastlake's taste is his advocacy of encaustic tiles. He recommends this deplorable medium for covering floors and dadoes, which, in his view, "for beauty of effect, durability, and cheapness, has scarcely a parallel". One might have indulgently supposed that he had in mind some of the less distressing examples; but no, he boldly provides coloured illustrations of the styles he particularly favours. They are productions with which we remain all too familiar, and which can barely be looked on without nausea. The patterns are geometrical and

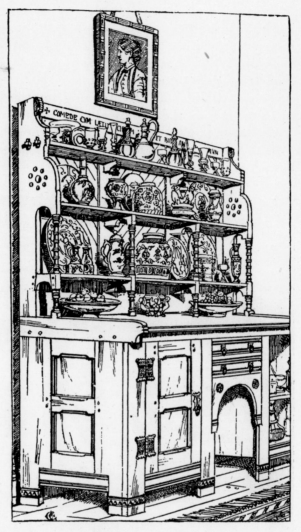

"Dining-room Sideboard" (1878)

Designed by C. L. Eastlake

are carried out in Indian red, gamboge, black and white—a singularly bilious combination of colours.

Eastlake's opinion was widely shared, and few houses of the period were built without a porch or entrance hall paved with these strident tiles, which the favourite addition of "Ave" in turquoise blue across the middle of the pattern did little to relieve. More serious was the disastrous damage done in the course of restoration to old churches. Uneven stone floors in chancels and naves were torn up, and encaustic tiles would be found to make the happiest foundation for the new brass altar rails and lectern, and for the pitch-pine pews in the nave.

Eastlake expresses his views with extreme force: he is as violent in his attacks on the taste of a generation earlier as he is in advancing his own principles. And there is little doubt that in most directions his principles were correct. He was against all shams, all unnecessary ornament, he was insistent on a return to fundamentals in the construction of furniture. Everything for the house should be designed with an eye on the practical, the hygienic, and the durable; good craftsmanship was essential. These views indeed were highly laudable; but here one is faced by the almost insoluble problem of taste. How was it that when intentions were so excellent productions were

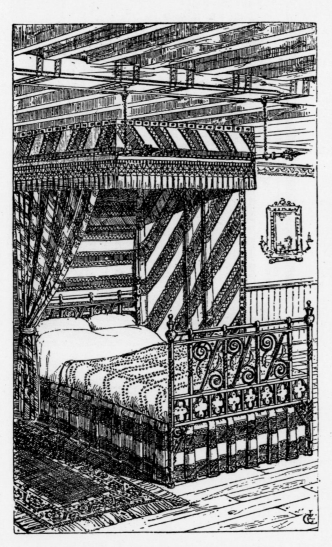

"Iron Bedstead with Canopy" (1878)

Designed by C. L. Eastlake

so unattractive? Almost every generation would believe they were actuated by views similar to Eastlake's: even the makers of the elaborate furniture shown at the Great Exhibition persuaded themselves that the luxuriant decoration in which they indulged fulfilled some useful purpose. We still subscribe to Eastlake's axioms, and produce the rather trashy objects which presumably represent the taste of today. However, no pretence is any longer made at good craftsmanship.

In one direction, however, we have perhaps advanced. We have lost that bold assurance which buoyed up the Victorians: we no longer have confidence—we have no confidence at

An Undergraduate's Room at Cambridge. About 1875

all—that our productions are the most beautiful, the most tasteful, the most useful that have ever been created. We accept with resignation the fact that economic conditions make it impossible to produce objects of good quality, and those who can afford it decorate their houses in the styles of the past. Never has the cult of the past been stronger, never have the productions of the present been less generally admired. It is an infertile attitude of mind, and one which must eventually give way to a new phase in the cycle of taste.

A change was slowly coming over the rooms of the 'seventies. The heavy materials of rep and velvet in dark colourings of turgid greens and deep crimson, varied with the shrill note of aniline dyes, which had been an outstanding feature of interiors of the 'fifties and 'sixties, and had formed a harsh ensemble with chocolate-brown paintwork and lincrusta dadoes, were being cast aside. A number of new stuffs appeared on the market, such as cotelan, algerine, and cretonne, of which only the last was destined to find a permanent place in the English home. The two former were light in colour, if not particularly attractive in design, and introduced a gayer and less ponderous note. Thus in up-to-date drawing-rooms shining white paint would cover, and greatly improve, the heavily moulded woodwork, and chintz or cretonne, which at first had been considered only suitable for bedrooms, would clothe the bulbous chairs and sofas. It was a slow

From a design by Lewis F. Day (1880)

132

process, the infiltration of these flowered materials into reception rooms, although many of the patterns were extremely pretty and showed Victorian designers at their most inventive and best. More usual in the average sitting-room of the mid-'seventies would be materials dyed the crude colours which represented another avenue of escape from the muddy tones of the previous decade. Prussian blue and canary yellow were daringly contrasted, and other striking combinations of opposed colours were introduced to give a gaudy air to previously dingy drawing-rooms.

As velvet lost favour, its near kinsman plush was found suitable for use in all manner of unexpected directions. That mantelboards and table tops should be covered with this material was inevitable, but it was a more daring notion to stick it on to picture and photograph frames, and to set china plates for wall decoration in cosy roundels of blue or crimson plush. Once the idea was accepted there seemed few limits to the decorative uses of this soft and rich material: it made a sumptuous background for many elaborate objects in metal or wood, it covered wooden stands for glass domes over clocks and other ornaments, it concealed the unfashionable marble tops of any tables which had survived from an earlier, a more coldly classical, period.

There was a further use to which plush was put, without which no properly conducted home could have been carried on: it was used for the knee-breeches worn by footmen. In the country footmen generally wore trousers with their liveries, except on special occasions; but in London, even in houses of no great aspirations, knee-breeches and white stockings were absolutely *de rigueur* during the 'seventies, while the livery coats were usually of the elaborate style which had been in fashion since the beginning of the century. A little later simpler liveries with plain coats and contrasting waistcoats and trousers took the place of these relics of eighteenth-century splendour; and even these have now—seventy-five years later—disappeared into limbo with so much else which provided colour in life.

During previous decades it had been a usual custom to close-carpet the principal sitting-rooms and bedrooms of a house. The patterned products of the Brussels factory, which were close woven, hard and durable, or the richer-piled Axminster carpets, would cover rooms from wall to wall and creep into all corners and recesses. But that rich mine of domestic information *Beeton's Housewife's Treasury*, which was published in the later 'seventies, advised strongly against this comfortable practice. "At the present day", the anxious housewife would learn, "in very many houses where tasteful effects are studied, carpets are tabooed to a considerable extent. . . . The old style is now giving place to the far more healthy and cleanly mode of

"The Dining-room"

As illustrated in *Beeton's Housewife's Treasury*

134

An Oxford Undergraduate's Sitting-room. About 1885

laying down a square of carpet in the centre of the room". Here was one more indication of the wish to escape from the oppressive, upholstered aspect of earlier rooms and to promote a cheerful air of lightness and hygiene.

Large expanses of uncarpeted boards would make necessary, particularly in bedrooms, a number of mats, and here the *Treasury* is once more to the fore with an unexpected suggestion included in the description of a bedroom: "In the room the skin of a favourite brown setter of Irish breed lay before the washstand in perfect harmony and keeping with the time-tempered browns of the bedside carpet". Here, indeed, was a method of perpetuating the memory of a faithful pet—by performing one's ablutions each day on his pelt. Is it an increase or a lessening of sentimentality about animals which makes this suggestion now seem uncongenial?

The practice of smoking was gaining ground, and was leading to various innovations in the planning of houses. It was not until 1845 that smoking was allowed at White's, but other clubs of St. James's followed this audacious lead so slowly and reluctantly that the foundation of the Marlborough Club in 1866, under the auspices of the Prince of Wales, was largely determined in order to provide a place where members could smoke without restrictions. Kerr, in his compendium of 1864, suggests that a smoking-room should be "a

135

chamber . . . detached from the main house", or a "prospect chamber in a tower". The latter proposal is repeated in the *Treasury*, with the further suggestion that it might be combined with an observatory in "the topmost room of a campanile".

All this made the habit of smoking seem a very complicated and expensive affair, but fortunately the *Treasury* on a later page abandons its ambitious notions, and recommends that the smoking-room should merely be "a little snuggery, cheerfully but not too delicately decorated". After a few hints on suitable furnishings in order to achieve this objective, it concludes with the prudent advice: "a couple of neat salivariums are necessary adjuncts".

Many subtle changes were almost imperceptibly creeping into the way of life in the Victorian home. For example, needlework, which in previous decades had filled the long leisured days of women of the upper classes, was losing a little of its appeal, and women began to direct their interest to other arts and crafts, to other means of embellishing their rooms. A useful hobby was the knotting or crocheting of thread into a coarse lace, which could find a useful place in sitting-rooms as antimacassars, or as little mats for tables; linen and muslin embroidered with flowers or names could be utilized for similar purposes; photograph albums, and blotting-books for the writing-tables, could be made with their purpose clearly indicated in coloured silks on the linen covers of their exteriors. Handiworks of this sort were endless. Women were also becoming rather bolder in their choice of crafts, particularly perhaps those who had little natural aptitude for needle and hook. The fretsaw, for example, opened a field of endless possibilities. The industrious worker could produce all manner of little knick-knacks—book-rests, shelves for china ornaments, little over-mantels—none of which called for any high degree of skill, and yet gave a more acute sense of creation and production than needlework.

Some women, though their number was not great, went in for serious wood carving, thus impinging on a masculine occupation. Panels of carving could be made up into boxes or cupboards, but better still, old furniture could be given an added interest by incising designs on any surface which the makers had decided to leave plain. Tudor and Elizabethan chests lent themselves particularly well to this treatment, a treatment by which busy chisels rendered these ancient pieces of oak more or less worthless. But old furniture was little valued at that period, either sentimentally or commercially, and the average rich man was prepared to pay much higher prices for ambitious contemporary furniture than he would for the finest English products of the eighteenth century.

There were many other hobbies to fill the idle hours. For those not very clever with their fingers there was poker-work, which had the advantage over carving that it required both less art and less equipment. Many hours could fairly harmlessly be devoted to this pastime. The pressing of flowers and leaves provoked a constant interest, and the seared and desiccated results could be used for a number of decorative purposes.

Music came into a slightly different category. All well-brought-up young women were expected to be able to entertain an evening party by playing a few pieces on the piano or singing some sentimental ballads, and it was not looked on askance that they should thus perform in public although their standard of accomplishment was low. It was accepted as an unavoidable feature of a small soirée, however tedious it might be. Another outlet of enduring popularity was water-colour painting, but here some talent was advisable. It is very seldom that these amateurish little land- or sea-scapes have any interest or merit, though they must have given pleasure to the painter; only on the rare occasions when a house or garden, or better still a drawing-room, provided the artist with a subject have they interest, even if, as has already been said, they are otherwise without merit.

In addition to the amateurs there were many professional artists who devoted their talents to the embellishment of the home. There were such as the sculptress, Mrs. Freeman, whose works are described in the *Magazine of Art*:

"Her studio is full of delightful models for rendering home surroundings elegant and poetical. Her model for a chimney-piece has on the entablature a frieze of babies representing the Happy Hours, and another frieze of Household Genii on the marble fender".

One feels inclined to hazard that Mrs. Freeman was childless. But there was much else in her studio to delight and surprise, particularly perhaps a drawing for a piano "in a Gothic form, to be executed in carved wood", while the house which she adorned "with designs emblematic of photography" must have been exceedingly remarkable.

This expenditure of energy, usually so ill but occasionally well directed, indicated the increasing restlessness of spirit amongst women of the richer classes, and their desire to pass creative and useful lives beyond the narrow limits of their homes. Those with real talent, those with indomitable personalities, were already, as has been said in the previous chapter, beginning to find a place in a world ordered by men; but the great mass of women with leisure had neither the upbringing nor the capability to make a career for themselves. And yet they resented their position of subjection to the dominant male. Why had women no votes, why had they not even this modest say in the government of their country? Why should they be considered inferior beings to the most crapulous man, who had a vote merely because he happened to be a householder?

Thus the long painful struggle to obtain votes for women began, but very many stormy years were to pass before the movement achieved its objective. At first it was treated with patronizing derision: it was amusing, even rather alluring, to see the little dears aping the ways of men—organizing campaigns, holding meetings, delivering discourses from platforms. But soon it became clear that these enterprising women were actuated by something more profound than a passing whim or fashion, and the many, both men and women, who disapproved fundamentally of the movement began to grow seriously annoyed. It might have been supposed that the Queen would have had some sympathy with this claim of women for what they called their "rights"; but on the contrary she viewed it with the gravest disfavour. She was Queen by divine right, and her position had no affinity whatever to that of other women, who should be satisfied with their home life and social amusements, and not attempt to interfere in matters far beyond their capabilities. She held the strongest possible views on the subject and did not hesitate to make them quite clear. To Mr. Theodore Martin she wrote in 1870:

> "The Queen is most anxious to enlist everyone who can speak or write in checking this mad, wicked folly of 'Women's Rights', with all its attendant horrors, on which her poor, feeble sex is bent forgetting every sense of womanly feeling and propriety. Lady —— ought to get a good whipping".

However, in spite of royal displeasure the movement continued, and grew slowly in strength.

Arts and crafts, or the public platform, were not the only pastimes for leisured women: during the summer months there was the fascinating new game of lawn tennis. About 1874 a game was devised— a gentle hybrid between real tennis and badminton—named sphairistiké. A net about five feet high, but sagging in a graceful curve to the centre, separated the two couples of players, who hit a rubber ball back and forth with long-handled rackets. The original name was soon abandoned, but the game caught on prodigiously. Croquet had been suitable to the crinolines of the previous decade, but now that skirts were narrower, though by no means any shorter and as tightly nipped as ever in the waist, young women could dash about the little area of lawn selected, left hand holding up flounces, right hand waving a racket, and derive not only amusement but also a healthy means of stirring the circulation. Moreover it provided a pleasant opportunity, and one less formal than the croquet lawn, for social contacts between the sexes.

Lawn-tennis Players of 1878. From an engraving after George Du Maurier

It was in any case a novel notion that girls and young women might benefit by gentle exercise. In high-class girls' schools games were not thought of, and the young pupils were educated to show a becoming feminine physical weakness: they should be as etiolated as possible, while a tendency to swoon was not at all out of place. If offers of marriage were not forthcoming at the appropriate time, it was sometimes found expedient to take to a sofa, and to gain attention as an interesting semi-invalid. Herbert Spencer in his treatise on education wrote rather sharply on the subject:

"We have a vague suspicion that to produce a robust physique is thought undesirable; that rude health and abundant vigour are considered somewhat plebeian; . . . that timidity which commonly accompanies feebleness is considered more ladylike".

Feebleness and timidity, however, began to lose their charms with the disappearance of the crinoline, and women became healthier and more natural.

Tennis was an exciting new addition to the summer pastimes of the 'seventies, but it by no means eclipsed the existing amusements such as croquet and archery. Tennis, in its novelty, may have seemed more fun, and to the young it provided a greater outlet for energy and high spirits; but undoubtedly croquet and archery were more becoming and less heating. Parson Kilvert's descriptions in his diary of

The Picnic. From the painting by Richard Doyle

croquet parties in the gardens of Clyro Court during the long summer days in the early 'seventies, followed by tea in the shade of the trees, depict the leisured atmosphere of country-house life at that time; while his account of an archery match brings the scene clearly before the eyes.

"The targets were pitched in the long green meadow which runs down to the river and the summer houses, one of the prettiest archery grounds I ever saw, the high woods above and the river below. It was a pretty sight to see the group of ladies with their fresh light dresses moving up and down the long green meadow and the arrows flitting and glancing white to and fro against the bank of dark green trees."

Another favourite way of spending a summer day was to go out for a picnic. The scale of the entertainment was often something more ambitious than the word now connotes. There would be a gathering of parties from several neighbouring houses, a footman or two to cope with the unpacking of hampers and the spreading of tablecloths and plates. Francis Kilvert was taken on an expedition of this sort to Snodhill Castle in the Golden Valley, and made full notes of the day's outing. It was a highly gregarious social affair, with four carriage-loads of neighbours and friends driving up a remote wooded glen to the ruins of the castle. The guests undertook the cooking of potatoes, which led to much chaos and laughter, but fortunately large quantities of other food had been provided as well. "There was plenty of meat and drink, the usual things, cold chicken, ham and tongue, pies of different sorts, salads, jam and gooseberry tarts, bread and cheese, splendid strawberries. . . . Cup of various kinds went round, claret and hock, champagne, cider and sherry, and people sprawled about in all attitudes and made a great noise".

The picture is complete—a Tissot scene—the women elegant in their long light dresses, the men in Norfolk jackets and narrow breeches or perhaps, if the day were exceptionally hot, in blazers and flannel trousers, with boaters on their heads, while up and down amongst the wooded hills, and round the grey stones of the ruined keep, echoed the cheerful voices and carefree laughter of the guests. One does not associate much laughter with the earlier decades of Queen Victoria's reign, the atmosphere was too sanctimonious, too restrained, but in the 'seventies there was a welcome loosening of the bonds. It would have been difficult, and perhaps unbecoming, to be hilarious in a crinoline; but the more normal fashions of the 'seventies imposed fewer restrictions on the wearers, and women were beginning to enjoy not only an added physical, but also a new social freedom.

There was cause for laughter and happiness in the easy *camaraderie* which was springing up between the sexes. The degree of liberty was indeed not very great, but it indicated an improvement in the hitherto dull lives of unmarried young women oppressed by stern parental control. Thus untroubled laughter rang freely amongst the hills and across the archery swards and over the croquet and tennis lawns; gardens were bright with geraniums and standard roses, and silver kettles gleamed and hissed on tea-tables set in the shade of trees. Taste may have been uncertain, but of how small significance this seems compared to the gaiety and happiness which were a feature of the age.

At its outset the game of sphairistiké may have seemed likely to be as passing a fashion as was diabolo at a later date, but it was destined to become an enduring feature of English home life and thus, though its *début* is worth noting, it has not the period interest of transient foibles and fashions. The middle years of the 'seventies were marked amongst the upper classes by two examples of the latter: the first—the foible —was the affected drawl used by both sexes, but particularly men, as a mark of the highest *ton*; while the second—the fashion—was the rather uncritical collecting of blue-and-white oriental china. There seems to have been no apparent link between these two crazes, except that both were considered artistic, and it was becoming modish to be thought to possess this attribute. The stylish drawl and the dropping of the "r" was no indication of effeminacy in a man, indeed this affected manner of speech would emerge from the bearded lips of the most virile characters.

The cult for blue-and-white china was a more serious affair, and comes essentially under the heading of a fashionable craze. It reached the country from across the Channel, where during the 'sixties it had assumed the proportions of a "rage". Many prominent members of intellectual circles were ardent collectors of both oriental china and pictures: Baudelaire, for example, and Zola, who was inclined to specialize in *Japanese* prints of a rather indelicate kind, while Edmond de Goucourt was an enthusiast for all phases of Japanese art, and records many sale-room triumphs and defeats in his Journal. Soon an interest in Japonnerie came across the Channel and found an enthusiastic exponent in Whistler, who was instrumental in introducing it to the Pre-Raphaelites and the supporters of the Aesthetic Movement. Its headway in these circles was not spectacular, though at least Rossetti added a number of Japanese objects to the extremely catholic collection which filled his house in Cheyne Row. It was Whistler who showed an unstinted admiration for the art of Japan in his painting during the last years of the 'sixties, and so widely influenced the English connoisseur public. His most famous picture of this period was his *Princesse du Pays de la Porcelaine* which was an occidental rendering of an oriental theme. A dark-haired girl in Japanese dress stands in the undulating attitude usual in Japanese woodcuts, and holds one of those fans which were soon to make their appearance in the drawing-room of every person who had aspirations to culture. The floor is covered by a rug of oriental design, and the background is formed by the folds of a painted screen.

Nothing could have harmonized more happily with a collection of "blue-and-white" than this picture, and in 1867 it was sold to a rich enthusiast for *Japonnerie*, Mr. Leyland, who was decorating his house, No. 49 Prince's Gate, in the style advocated by Morris and his school. *La Princesse* was intended to be the principal feature of the dining-room, but unfortunately the setting which had been provided by the architect, Jeckell, proved—at least in Whistler's eyes—to be entirely unsuitable. The walls had been covered at great expense with old Spanish leather, which was surrounded by dark and solid woodwork. Pre-Raphaelite paintings, with their crowded canvases and rich colouring, would have been here happily in place, but Whistler's painting, with its simple design and pale clear colours, was absolutely killed. In the absence of his indulgent patron, Whistler tackled the problem with vigour; and before the return of Mr. Leyland, who had

Prince's Gate, London: the Peacock Room (*c.* 1875). J. McNeill Whistler, Designer

been only casually informed of what was taking place, the mellow leather disappeared beneath a pride of peacocks and their feathers, painted in blues, greens and gold. When Mr. Leyland returned to London he found himself provided not only with a striking setting for *La Princesse*, but also with a background which completely destroyed the subtle tones of his fine examples of blue-and-white china.

The taste for the Japanese style was widely developing, though the full flood was not to come until the early years of the 'eighties; but already a few fans were found to mingle happily on the rich plush-covered mantelboard with the massive, and not very expensive, modern ware with which the enterprising orientals were flooding the market. There could be no doubt about the highly artistic quality of these productions since the illustrious Mr. Whistler, the prime exponent—in his own view—of good taste, had given them his aesthetic blessing. Mr. Liberty, who had lately opened a shop in Regent Street where oriental products of all sorts were obtainable, did a very brisk trade indeed. English manufacturers were not slow to note the drift of public taste, and soon the products of the Minton and Doulton potteries were taking on a subdued oriental guise. There was generally little merit in these objects designed purely for ornament: the forms were clumsy and the decoration elaborate and confused, and they

143

possessed little of the attractiveness of some of the china designed for use. In the latter, flowers were a very usual ornamentation; and decorators of the period in every field were at their best when reproducing the infinite variety of the forms and colours of nature, not only on china, but in wall-papers, in materials, in needlework, and the many other ways in which flowers could be turned to domestic use. Eastlake might cry out against the absurdity of covering the walls of a room with improbable bouquets, or painting sprays of flowers on coal-scuttles; but now it is these which seem to us charming and not the tight, hard geometrical patterns from which we utterly revolt.

It was no new event for the decorative arts to be inspired by the Orient. In the seventeenth century Chinese lacquer cabinets and a certain amount of porcelain, shipped home by the East India merchants, had formed highly valued ornaments in Caroline rooms. The great popularity of lacquer work led cabinet-makers of this country and in Holland to produce furniture so closely copied from the originals that the occidental and the oriental can barely be distinguished. In the following century the vogue for Chinoiserie was extremely strong, and the drawings of furniture, which William Chambers had made on his voyage to China, were used as a basis for furniture and decoration in this style. Much fine porcelain was imported, and much of the highest quality made in this country was decorated in the Chinese style. The nineteenth-century phase turned more towards the poorer art of Japan, and there was also this difference, that with improved transport the actual products of the Far East could be easily and cheaply imported, so that on the whole there was less advantage in producing furniture and ornamental objects in oriental style in this country. If there is any regularity in the cycles of taste, a twentieth-century fashion for Chinoiserie and Japonnerie would seem soon to be due.

There must presumably be some cause for these recurring bouts of oriental vogue, and it seems that they are inclined to arise at a time when the indigenous decorative arts are not developing in any very determined direction; but never has it been more than a phase, never has it had any very lasting effect on English design. By the 'seventies Gothic had run its long and varied course as a style of domestic architecture. In the ecclesiastical field, and to some degree in public buildings, the tradition was carried on for another two decades by Waterhouse, Butterfield and others; but before the first half of the 'seventies had passed it had come to be recognized that buildings based on the Decorated style made gloomy shells for family life. The styles advocated by William Morris and by Eastlake formed two distinct but parallel threads, and neither had the lightness and

144

sense of selectivity which were implicit in decoration based on the Japanese style. It was these characteristics, then, which came in with the fashion for Japonnerie and to some degree remained, though the vogue for the style itself died out; but it was only slowly that Victorian rooms, which had been crowded and crepuscular for a quarter of a century, were simplified and lightened. It was a tendency which developed with increasing speed during the following decade.

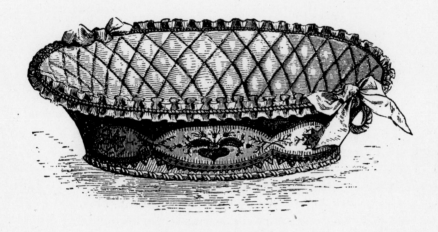

Basket for Reels of Silk
From *Beeton's Housewife's Treasury*

A Diaper of Daisies (c. 1880). By Lewis F. Day

CHAPTER VI

EMANCIPATION AND CULTURE
1880–1890

URING the first four decades of Queen Victoria's reign architects, craftsmen and decorators showed on the whole a robust
and unselfconscious gusto in the designs which they produced
for the wealthy. From the ruins of the Regency style, which survived
into the first years of the young Queen's reign, the arbiters of popular
taste plunged resolutely forward towards the amorphous and elaborate productions displayed at the Great Exhibition. New methods of
manufacture which had been introduced made the output of highly
decorated furniture and metal work a comparatively easy matter, and
these ingenious inventions received so much popular admiration that
the label "machine made" became a description of the highest
praise. Articles designed for domestic use or beauty, and produced by
up-to-date processes, seemed to the eyes of mid-Victorians, dazzled
by the advantages of industrial progress, to be far superior to objects
produced by the old-fashioned method of manual craftsmanship:
they were also a great deal cheaper.

Leaders of conventional taste looked firmly forward to a brave and
beautiful new world, created by machinery and inventions, which
would bring benefits to a much larger public than had ever previously
seemed possible. There was to be culture and beauty in every home;
rich and poor were to share in the widespread advantages of a great
mechanized age. There was no slackening of this laudable determination as the 'seventies passed into the 'eighties; and, with the

increased salaries which were being earned by an ever-expanding circle of workers, there seemed little reason why art in some form or another should not cast its beneficent rays over even quite modest homes. All who had the good of the nation at heart professed to agree on the importance of the place of art and culture in the social structure. No one who held a position of public importance, no one who wished to cut any sort of figure in polite society, would any longer dare to cast any reflection on the value of art in contemporary life. Private opinions may not always have been so whole hearted. But in that case a careful discretion was required, for art and beauty in the home were not only essential: they were also fashionable.

It had been the custom in previous decades to look back on past years, years perhaps half a century earlier, and feel comfortably certain that taste in those benighted times was exceedingly bad. It seemed unquestionable to mid-Victorians, for example, that the plain architecture of the late Regency was dull and ugly. How could anyone admire a severe stucco box bereft of all ornament, and containing unadorned rooms with none of the crowded, cosy atmosphere so much in vogue during the middle years of the nineteenth century? Taste had obviously been growing better and better since those unimaginative days, and seemed indeed to have reached an aesthetic climax at whatever date anyone considering the subject happened to be living.

With the 'eighties, however, an uncomfortable doubt began to blur the outlines of these accepted conventions. The importance of culture was so much in the public mind, and seemed to take so many different forms, that to the simple person, anxious to do the right thing and give voice to the right opinions, the situation was distinctly bewildering. Gradually the situation clarified a little: it was accepted that the taste which had been looked on as impeccable even a few years earlier was really very poor indeed, and that it was necessary to go back much further, perhaps as far as the eighteenth century, to find a solid basis of good taste.

The *Art Journal*, an informative publication which brought the latest views on culture to many a puzzled home, was highly contemptuous of a style of decoration that had been much admired only a short time before. A contributor in 1880 wrote firmly on this subject:

> "We are no longer afflicted by those monstrosities and absurdities which some years ago used to cover our walls, where humming birds and gigantic roses on a sea-greenish ground were quite the fashion".

While of furniture which was being produced by some of the well-known workshops we learn that "glaring defects have disappeared",

147

and that "ornament is now judiciously and not extravagantly applied". These optimistic phrases are accompanied by an engraving of a design for a sideboard which would seem to twentieth-century eyes, less attuned perhaps to the nuances of decoration, to be a riot of meaningless ornament.

The most favoured designs for large pieces of furniture, such as sideboards, had usually an architectural basis—the formidable structure being composed of a series of cupboards, shelves and recessions somewhat on the lines of a public building with a basement, *piano nobile* and reduced upper floors. The decoration of the woodwork would probably be vaguely in the Jacobean style but "purged from the coarseness which marked its ancestral features", as a contemporary writer gracefully phrased it.

The dining-room sideboard was often the most important object in a small house, and so set the note for much of the furnishings and decoration of the principal rooms. Its appearance was therefore a matter of great moment. The furniture in the drawing-room would be lighter in tone than that in the dining-room, but was generally conceived on rather the same lines. Display cupboards, designed to set off a collection of china or bric-à-brac to the best advantage, were given a prominent place, and they followed to some degree the lines of the sideboard. In many drawing-rooms much of the available space was devoted to the exhibition of ornaments, many of which were often far from deserving a place of honour, and an elaborate overmantel was found to make a very happy site for an array. The little shelves and niches of these complicated superstructures would be crowded with porcelain and faience ornaments, and were as complex in their arrangement as, though unfortunately far less successful in design than, the remarkable erections contrived by Daniel Marot two centuries earlier for the delight of William and Mary at Hampton Court Palace.

Robert Edis, whose *Decoration and Furniture of Town Houses* was published in 1881, was of the opinion that the chimney-piece and its inevitable overmantel should be the dominant feature of all living-rooms. He advocated cupboards and niches to give emphasis to the chimney-breast, or a "cluster of shelves" for the display of blue-and-white china. The fire-opening below this tasteful composition would be filled with a steel or cast-iron grate, and round it would be set a broad band of coloured tiles, which at this period were an almost inevitable feature in the construction of fireplaces.

Vivid colourings, peacock blues and greens such as William de Morgan had used in the splendid tiles he made a decade and more earlier, were now considered rather too dominant in rooms of the 'eighties, where colour schemes were generally soft and brilliant dyes

"An Escritoire, A Chair and a Side-board" (1880). Holland and Sons

were no longer the fashion. The harsh encaustic tiles produced by
Messrs. Doulton were too rigid in pattern, too serious in aspect, to suit
the average drawing-room, which was usually intended to strike a
note of gaiety; thus tiles decorated with arabesques, little landscapes
or figures produced in rather mawkish colourings became the usual
linings for hearths.

More highly prized than the machine-produced tiles were those
painted by hand—an art which was rapidly becoming an industry. As
a writer remarked rather patronizingly in 1884 in the *Magazine of
Art*, a rival compilation to the *Art Journal*, "This new art is not only
harmless and charming, but opens out a career for hundreds of
women". Tile painting, however, was not destined to develop on
quite such wide lines as the writer anticipated.

The painting of tiles represented only one small facet of the general
scheme of the decorative arts of the period; but in this, as in more
important directions, decoration and ornament remained excessive,
according to the standards of today, although contemporary writers
with one voice congratulated themselves that they had now reached
a stage when superfluous embellishments were discarded.

But if ornament was used almost as plentifully as ever, it was undoubtedly becoming less forceful in character. Those obtrusive carv-
ings which adorned almost every piece of furniture in the Great

Exhibition, those meaningless volutes, whorls and convolutions which were introduced into every form of ornamental object, were now rightly considered to be in execrable taste. The arbiters of fashion were beginning to look back to the delicate arts of the eighteenth century for inspiration, though their choice of what was suitable for admiration and emulation was highly selective.

For more than fifty years the work of the brothers Adam and their school had lain under a cloud. To the exponents of the robust styles of the middle decades of the century it seemed sugary and effeminate, and at the same time cold and comfortless: it was rated altogether far inferior to the architecture and furniture of the Tudor and Elizabethan periods, which were much more closely in conformity with popular taste. During those years journals devoted to the decorative arts would contain fully illustrated articles on such famous houses as Compton Wynyates, Knole or Hatfield, and in the reproductions of their interiors there would be found ample precedent for the contemporary reproductions which achieved such favour with the general public.

With the opening of the 'eighties a new note was introduced into these articles, and writers began boldly to describe and praise houses of the eighteenth century. They did not venture to interest their readers in houses designed by the Palladian architects: those, in their cold purity, were still considered as far beyond the pale. The buildings of the Adam brothers, on the other hand, in which both ornament and colour formed an integral part, were more to the taste of the age. Sensing the turn of the cycle, the *Magazine of Art* published long and moderately adulatory articles on the Adam rooms at Syon. That the work of Robert Adam should have been recommended for public admiration was satisfactory, but the writer's basis for this admiration was strange:

> "He succeeded in adapting with great elasticity and considerable originality the later Roman style to English uses, thus heading the reaction against the vulgarity of the French forms in fashion during the reigns of Queen Anne and George I."

How unexpected that the architecture and decoration of the first decades of the eighteenth century should have appeared vulgar to a writer in the 'eighties: it would seem the last epithet which could be applied with justice. At the same time, no doubt, the style prevalent round 1600 was thought to be essentially cultured and gentlemanlike. Robert Adam would have been startled by the innovations placed to his credit within less than a century of his death.

Owners of Palladian houses during the Victorian era were greatly to be pitied. No one looked on these large, chaste buildings as anything

150

but extremely ugly; and only towards the end of the century did it begin to dawn on popular taste that a large Palladian mansion could be anything but a "barrack". A writer of 1882, in the same publication which found tepid praise for Syon, described Prior Park at Bath as "terrible" in style, and Hawksmoor's brilliant façade of Queen's College at Oxford fronting on to the High as "unspeakable". It is not to be supposed that everyone felt such violent antipathy to the classical style as this author; but that a magazine devoted to the exposition of public taste should have printed an article of such strong abuse indicates that a large section of the public—of the public, that is to say, who took an interest in architecture—felt that the style was beneath contempt. It is in any case difficult for this tolerant age to reconcile a hatred of Palladian architecture with an admiration for the work of Robert Adam. To prefer one style to the other is natural, or to see no good in either might be logical, but to hold such drastically opposed views is puzzling.

The puzzle, however, is not insoluble, and the probable key lies in four words in the description of the style in the article—"total want of colour". Taste in the 'eighties was essentially bright and cheerful; rooms were expected to be light and harmonious, with clear colours and a plentiful supply of gilding in furniture and picture frames. There was an echo here, a distant muffled echo, of the subtle colour schemes advocated by Adam: there was not the faintest whisper of the severe, white decoration admired by the Palladians.

Rooms were beginning to be adorned in what was supposed to be the Adam manner, but there was no hesitation at all in treating it with that "great elasticity" which the originator was himself said to have used. Pseudo-Adam chimney-pieces were easily reproduced in composition, swagged friezes in lincrusta, while wall-papers were designed on complex architectural lines with pilasters and arches, which were a sharp break-away from the bouquets and cabbage roses of a few years earlier. These, with a few more details, would, it was hoped, complete a setting having a refined Adam atmosphere. But as usual the Victorians reckoned without the strength of their own personality. They might reproduce furniture and decoration with the utmost care, or build houses which were exact replicas of Elizabethan manors, they might disguise themselves in period fancy dress, but invariably the result was unmistakably nineteenth century.

In a *milieu* based on the eighteenth century, the light oak furniture, the robust display cabinets and sideboards which have just been described, would be entirely out of place. The "Adamesque" decoration, it is true, was usually kept for the drawing-room, and in such a setting only furniture which was thin and light in design was suitable. The style of Sheraton was especially favoured: it possessed those

"Octagon Boudoir: Adams Style" (1880). Messrs. Gillow, Decorators

qualities which were beginning to be admired. It had undoubted elegance of form, it was both decorative and decorated, the inlay with woods of many colours was particularly attractive, while the alternative ornamentation of painted plaques in the graceful style of Angelica Kauffmann seemed highly cultured. As Eustace Balfour, an expert on the decorative arts, wrote in 1883:

> "In recent years a fashion for Sheraton's furniture has sprung up, and has so widely spread that modern cabinet-makers have found it worth their while to reproduce many specimens, and even to attempt original work in the same style."

Victorian designers and craftsmen never lost the happy conviction that they could always improve on the work of former ages. It was obviously dull merely to make reproductions of existing pieces of furniture, particularly when these reproductions made no attempt to deceive a purchaser into supposing he was buying an original eighteenth-century object; so the temptation to improve, to elaborate, to beautify was understandable. The amount of imitation Sheraton furniture produced during the 'eighties and 'nineties was very great, and now it has even less interest than the robust light oak pieces simultaneously recommended by Mr. Edis. Less interest, but not less value: bogus Sheraton can still be introduced into the average sitting-room without causing undue disturbance, but Mr. Edis's oak, which had the merit of some originality, is far too assertive to be easily accommodated, and so has practically no market value whatever.

Emulating the amateur wood-carvers of previous decades, who had industriously mutilated straightforward early furniture by incising decoration, the professional cabinet-makers of later Victorian years often saw fit to embellish genuine furniture of the Sheraton period which happened to be relatively unadorned. It would be inlaid with patterns formed in coloured woods, which were intended to be chastely Adam, or painted with elaborately beribboned ovals depicting figures from Greek mythology, which had much more in common with the Royal Academy than with Olympus. So intent were the designers on improving the genuine article, that these late nineteenth-century pastiches can barely be included under the heading of fakes, and seldom indeed were they intended to deceive.

Although obvious reproductions of Sheraton furniture satisfied the majority of those who were decorating their houses in the latest mode, there were a certain number of connoisseurs who collected only genuine objects. There was Lady Charlotte Schreiber, for example, who, once she had unburdened herself from the cares of the Guest ironworks and of family troubles by encouraging into matrimony her large brood of children, gave up her life to the fascinating pursuit of

"A Dining-room Chimney-piece" (1880). R. W. Edis, Architect

old porcelain, and later of fans and ancient playing-cards as well. Her enthusiasm and her knowledge were exceptional, and the discomforts of long journeys all over Europe were undergone with perfect equanimity if there was a good prospect of a valuable "find" at the end. But even during the early 'seventies, when her travels began in earnest, she found to her annoyance that she was not always the first in the field. When scouring Holland, in 1873 for example, she mentions in her journal that a dealer named Duveen was preceding her everywhere and "making wonderful purchases". Each year competition seemed to increase, but Lady Charlotte's expert knowledge brought to light many treasures which others had failed to observe.

The first stirrings of transatlantic interest in the arts of Europe were becoming manifest. "Americans are now paying great attention to antiquities, and making collections everywhere", Lady Charlotte noted in 1879, and there are many other references in her journal to collectors from the United States. In particular there was a Mrs. Moore, whom the Schreibers were constantly meeting on the Continent and with whom they made friends. Mr. Moore, they learned, had bequeathed several thousand pounds to a museum to form a collection of antiques, and the widow had been given the task of spending this sum. Unfortunately, her purchases were disastrous, and Lady Charlotte was continually upbraiding dealers who had deceived her poor ignorant friend.

Lady Charlotte was by no means the earliest of Victorian collectors: there was Mr. John Jones, the affluent army clothier, who between 1850 and his death in 1882 amassed a superb collection of French *objets d'art* at his house in Piccadilly. He bequeathed his collection to the nation, and it can now be seen at the Victoria and Albert Museum. He must often have been a competitor with the fourth Marquess of Hertford who began his search for works of art, principally French of the seventeenth and eighteenth centuries, a decade earlier when prices were still comparatively low. Like a rapacious spider, in his apartment in Paris, Lord Hertford wove a web of agents and purchasers over England and the Continent, and thus secured the objects of unparalleled magnificence which now form the greater part of the Wallace Collection.

The market in antiques was largely a development of the nineteenth century. Sculptures, marbles and paintings had for many generations formed the loot with which travelling Englishmen had returned to this country from Continental tours, but the buying of English or Continental furniture made one hundred years or so earlier had not been a usual interest. About the middle of the century, however, an enquiry for the fine productions of French *ébénistes* began, and dealers quickly adjusted prices to the increasing demand. At the

Middle-class Cottage Residences (1878). R. Norman Shaw, Architect

Demidoff sale in Paris in 1870, for example, Lady Charlotte noted that prices reached new heights; she also particularly mentions a picture by Ary Scheffer, now in the Wallace Collection, which fetched £4,000—a sum much in excess of its present value.

The most famous sale during the period was that of the contents of Hamilton Palace in 1882. Many canvases, rather dubiously ascribed to the great masters, fetched several thousand pounds apiece owing largely to the distinction of their provenance, while the French furniture, which was unquestionably superb, was sold at a level rather above—pound for pound—that current today. A small Louis XIV Boulle cabinet brought £2,200, a secretaire by Riesener £4,620, and a writing-table by the same maker £6,000; a pair of Sèvres vases fetched over £1,500. The path of the collector was already a hard one.

As a fashion, the "China Mania" began to die out in the 'eighties. Those who had indiscriminately bought large quantities of ornaments in order to fill up their rooms as contemporary taste ordained were now inclined to view their purchases with a more critical eye, and to relegate their less handsome pieces to the lumber-room. Thus drawing-rooms were given a more elegant air, in which selection had played some part.

In so far as it is permissible to make a generalization on the taste of a decade, it may be said that the 'eighties showed a marked improvement. It was not only in decoration, but also in domestic architecture that there was a welcome lightening of style, though this was

156

not at first very pronounced. Alfred Waterhouse lived until 1905, but the style of domestic architecture which he represented, the style of Eaton Hall and of Blackmoor, had been out of date long before his death and had given way to the more genial buildings created by the brilliant young Scotsman, Norman Shaw. Though nurtured in the school of the later Gothic revivalists, Shaw had early broken away into realms of his own creating. His style passed through many phases: an idealized Tudor, with deep oriel windows, ingle-nooks, quaint corners, and tall chimney-stacks; a bland version of the Dutch manner, with elaborate brick gables and high, small-paned windows; a rather elaborate Queen Anne in which brick and stone were united; and lastly a solemn Palladian, which was generally reserved for public buildings. Few of Shaw's designs seem entirely satisfactory to us now, but equally there are very few which are without many solid merits. Philip Webb at the Red House was the first to cast adrift from the thraldom of domestic Gothic, and Shaw carried the work nobly forward, so that before the end of his long career of forty years the whole spirit of domestic building had altered. That it would have changed during that period in any case is certain, but it was fortunate that a man of Shaw's abilities was at hand to become the instrument of the transformation.

Early in his career he had been given the opportunity of developing a suburban lay-out on lines which constituted an innovation in this style of planning. In 1865 the famous botanist, John Lindley, had

In Bedford Park (1878). From a lithograph by H. M. Paget

died, and his property of Bedford Park, covering a hundred acres to the north of Chiswick, was bought by Mr. Jonathan Carr, who had conceived the notion of founding here an intellectual colony where the arts could flourish in an atmosphere of harmony and fraternity. The lay-out which Shaw devised represented the first example of what came to be known as a garden city, and embodied principles which form the basis of many present-day housing estates.

The roads were planned so as to preserve the majority of the trees which Lindley had planted, and the houses were grouped to give a flavour of the haphazard growth of a village, rather than to appear as regimented rows of suburban dwellings. Both architect and owner were prompted by ideals beyond the mere provision of agreeable homes: the spacious lay-out, the differing styles of architecture, the leafy background, were particularly designed to encourage the development of individuality and the blossoming of genius, as well as to provide houses for those who, if not themselves practitioners, were sympathetically interested in the arts. There was a social club where the men and women of the colony could foregather for intellectual and gregarious evenings, there was the old English setting of the Tabard Inn for those more convivially inclined, and shops were provided where the necessities of life could be obtained.

Perhaps the high aim of creating an artistic colony was not fully realized, but at least the praiseworthy project resulted in houses which have survived the test of changing taste in a way that few buildings constructed within the decades on either side of 1870 can be said to have done.

The interiors which Shaw created were more suited to decoration in the style of Morris and his followers than to the emasculated Adam manner—particularly his houses in the Dutch style, such as the towering structures in Cadogan Square, containing rooms which seem to demand oak furniture, Morris wall-papers above the high and elaborate dadoes, and stained glass in the style of Burne-Jones in the little windows dimly lighting the ingle-nooks. But always it was essential to leave space for a large number of pictures.

No drawing-room of the 'eighties would have been complete without a lavish display of paintings in heavy gilded frames. It was no longer good taste to cover the space from dado to cornice with closely serried oils or water-colours, though this was still the method of hanging pictures at the summer exhibition at the Royal Academy. Like ornaments, pictures were subjected to a selective process and were so spaced as to give proper value to each painting. But still in many rooms it was the frames, making so rich a glow on the walls, which were almost as important and were certainly more dominant than the canvases which they surrounded.

It was much in the mode to buy the works of contemporary painters, and it is doubtful whether academic artists ever enjoyed a more prosperous epoch than the last three decades of Queen Victoria's reign. The rewards of those who caught the public taste were not merely financial—though these were very great—but honours were also heaped upon them. There were knighthoods for a considerable number, several baronetcies—the first given to artists since Sir Godfrey Kneller had been thus favoured—and even a last-minute peerage for Frederick Leighton, conferred within a few hours of his death. Successful artists enjoyed a social position which had seldom been accorded to their predecessors, while their affluence would have amazed even the most successful practitioners of the previous century. One of the most highly-paid artists of the period was Millais, who admitted on one occasion to having earned forty thousand pounds in the previous year. Few other artists rivalled either his output or his sensational success with his pictures: *The Boyhood of Raleigh, Cherry Ripe, The North-West Passage,* and above all *Bubbles,* which brought an equal renown to the artist and to Pears's Soap, made for him very large sums, both by the sale of the original paintings and for the rights of reproduction. It is probable that Leighton's earnings were on an even greater scale. How different, one reflects, would Benjamin Haydon's life have been had he lived half a century later. He might well have adjusted his large canvases and stirring scenes to suit the public

Old Swan House, Chelsea: the Sitting-room (1877). R. Norman Shaw, Architect

159

Marcus Stone in his Studio

taste, and thus have secured wealth and peace of mind instead of being driven to suicide by the worries of bitter poverty.

Victorian artists had an inestimable advantage over those of the present day in that the great size of a picture was no impediment to its sale. Leighton's painting entitled *Daphnephoria*, which was exhibited in 1876, measured seventeen feet in length by nearly eight feet in height, and filled the whole of one wall of Gallery III at Burlington House. Nevertheless, in spite of its outsize proportions, it found a delighted purchaser with a country house large enough to accommodate it. Where can *Daphnephoria* be now, and what would be its value? A few pounds, perhaps, compared to the ten thousand or so which must have been its original price. Other artists were not backward in producing large paintings. Edwin Long's *An Egyptian Feast*, shown in 1877, measured more than twelve feet by six, and was rather larger than his *Babylonian Marriage Market* which had caused a sensation two years earlier. A year or two later Edward Armitage exhibited a picture measuring nearly thirteen by ten feet entitled *After the Arena*—a melancholy canvas showing the body of a young Christian being lowered into the catacombs.

Even more surprising than the size of the pictures hung at the Royal Academy was the intense sentimentality of the subjects. The dead and the dying, the distraught and the miserable, figure in canvas after canvas. It might be supposed that Edwin Long's *Feast* provided a gleam of gaiety amidst the prevailing gloom, but on the contrary it did nothing so insensitive and vulgar: it showed an old Egyptian custom usual on these festive occasions of "the semblance of a body being carried round upon a bier to remind the guests of their mortality". The "problem picture", too, became very popular at this period, but it was seldom that the picture set a problem in happiness: the viewer was rather called upon to fathom the reasons for despair.

The preoccupation of popular Victorian taste with a lachrymose sentimentality seems to us now an unsympathetic aspect of the period. Artists such as R. B. Martineau and Sidney Waller, particularly the latter, had achieved immense success with their soul-stirring pictures. The classical scenes of Leighton and Poynter were solemn rather than sentimental, but the jejune works of Marcus Stone, which enjoyed wide popularity and were constantly reproduced as coloured supplements to weekly illustrated papers, reeked with pathos, though there was often the hint of a happy ending to the drama.

There seems to have been some quality in oil paint which led artists to specialize in harrowing scenes, for the popular illustrators were much less gloomy. The horsy subjects of Randolph Caldecott, for example, carried on the robust spirit of John Leech, while the drawings of Kate Greenaway, which enjoyed a transcendent renown, were

"*The Drawing-room and Conservatory*" (1883)

After a drawing by Randolph Caldecott

not gloomy though they were extremely sentimental. Austin Dobson celebrated the works of Miss Greenaway in playful verse:

> Mine be a cot, for the hours of play,
> Of the kind that is built by Miss Greenaway,
> Where the walls are low, and the roofs are red,
> And the birds are gay in the blue o'erhead;
> And the dear little figures, in frocks and frills,
> Go roaming about at their own sweet wills.

The poem continued at some length in the same strain. Novelists, too, with their ears to the ground, ensured a wide circulation for their books by indulging richly in sentiment; but the greater excesses remained always in paint rather than in print. The novels of Ouida or Mrs. Humphrey Ward, for example, were highly charged with emotion and romance, but it had a healthy, straightforward quality different from the distressing scenes exhibited for public enjoyment at Burlington House. The explanation of this vogue for sorrow would seem to lie in the pleasurable contrast afforded by these scenes, in which the human emotions were plumbed to the utmost depths, and the security and comfort of the purchasers' lives. In these less serene times there is less wish to indulge in vicarious suffering.

The very large fortunes made by artists who caught the public taste were usually reflected in the houses in which they lived: indeed the possession of a magnificent home became as much a token of success as a film-star's house in Beverly Hills is today, or perhaps was yesterday. Holland Park and Hampstead were the two favourite localities for a fashionable artist to build his house. In the leafy purlieus of Kensington were to be found the houses of Marcus Stone, James Shannon, Watts, Val Prinsep, all of which were handsome and spacious; but none of them was so magnificent as that of the admitted sovereign of the area, Frederick Leighton, whose success both artistic and social, from the Queen down to the humblest visitor to the Academy, set him above all competition.

The Hampstead contingent was rather less august, though the house of Edwin Long, designed on ample lines by Norman Shaw, equalled in size any of the artists' dwellings of Holland Park except that of Leighton. Two of the most famous artists lived just outside these circles: there was Millais in Palace Gate, and Alma Tadema in Regent's Park. The home of the former was described as being "stately and prosperous", as befitted an artist who achieved a pre-eminent social position. The interior was decorated on conventional classical lines softened with sweeps of rich curtains, and enlivened

Edwin Long's House in Hampstead (1878). R. Norman Shaw, Architect

with much china on tables and walls. Here there was nothing bohemian, nothing which could have caused the most critical eyebrow to be raised.

Alma Tadema's remarkable house in North Gate, Regent's Park was arranged on much more exotic lines. As its owner's pictures would lead one to suppose, the principal rooms were decorated in the classical style, but the whole conception was fundamentally different to that of Millais's home. In Palace Gate a few thin pilasters, some rudimentary pediments over the doorways, some shallow classical chimney-pieces vaguely in the Adam style, gave the building a non-committal classical flavour. But North Gate was more full blooded: there were marble-lined walls, stout scagliola pillars with gilded capitals, paved floors, low sofas heaped with many coloured cushions, and an occasional intrusion from the Orient in the form of a Japanese lamp, a Burmese table and clusters of fans. Even the prosaic shape of the Broadwood piano was made to conform as far as possible to this Roman-Oriental interior by having its case inlaid with coloured woods, "combined with ivory, brass and alabaster, in a rich Byzantine design".

163

"Mr. Alma Tadema's Drawing-room" (1882)

The lavish expenditure on pictures, which led to this happy prosperity amongst artists, was evidence of the increasing amount of wealth circulating amongst all those who had any connection with industry. Towns were constantly expanding in extent, and though the new working-class houses showed an improvement on the old, in that they were usually provided with main water and drainage, as well as sometimes with gas, the general lay-out of the new areas showed little advance. There was no official control of town-planning, and few of the speculative builders who undertook these enterprises were willing to sterilize precious ground area by leaving open spaces amongst the network of narrow streets. This was particularly noticeable in the growth of London, where the new Victorian streets have in many cases turned into the slums of today; but the situation was little better in the great provincial cities, which were developing with equal rapidity.

To many, an increase in fortune meant an increase in social activity. There were many like the famous journalist Kennedy Jones who remarked to Ralph Nevill: "I think of going in for Society—don't be surprised if you hear of my moving from Finchley to Grosvenor Square". In Kennedy Jones's case these aspirations were soon abandoned, but with many others the assault on higher social circles was carried out with pertinacity and success. The last two decades of the nineteenth century and the first of the twentieth probably saw English society at its zenith. The anonymous French diplomat who published *La Société de Londres* in 1885 admitted that *"ce que Paris a perdu depuis la chute de l'Empire, Londres l'a gagné...— la capitale britannique est la métropole la plus brillante de l'Europe".*

All circumstances were favourable: there was wealth, leisure, improved transport, easy domestic arrangements, nothing was lacking to make the path of the hostess easy; there was no battling in the face of conditions. During the summer season, indeed for the great part of the year except for August and September, the politer areas of London hummed with social junketings. Whereas the houses in the squares and streets in the vicinity of Hyde Park became the social centres of the evening, the park itself was the focus earlier in the day.

Rotten Row was the great centre of attraction for those who wished to see, and also for those who wished to be seen; and it was rather the pleasure of forming part of one of London's pageants which brought the greater number of young women out on horseback than any particular interest in riding. As Guizot, the French ambassador, wrote some years earlier, "Hyde Park is a Longchamps every day". What pleasure the elegant gathering along the rails experienced in registering disapproval of anyone with a tarnished reputation who was bold enough to take part in the equestrian procession. In the late 'fifties, for instance, Miss Adeline de Horsey and Lord Cardigan would ride together daily in the Row, while all respectable women's eyes were averted from the horrid spectacle of an unmarried girl who dared to ride—and also to drive, which was worse—with a man who had a wife living. Although they later married, this early indiscretion was never forgiven.

During the winter months the Row was crowded in the mornings; but in the summer season the early evening, the hours from five to seven, was the time when rank and fashion gathered most thickly. Not only was the tan then crowded with riders, but the drives were also filled with carriages—those discreet but beautifully turned out equipages in which the English specialized, and which surpassed in distinction the more flamboyant and elaborate carriages to be seen in the shaded roads of the Bois de Boulogne.

In addition to the charms of the Row, there was Church Parade past the Achilles statue, as sure an opportunity for happy social encounters as any in London; while the meets of the Coaching Club in the broad alleys near the Serpentine had a glamour of the highest order. On some occasions the Prince and Princess of Wales graced the meets with their presence, and added a royal lustre to what was anyhow a highly aristocratic reunion. To racing, too, the interest of the

In a Park. From a painting by Val Prinsep

Prince of Wales gave a social impetus which had been lacking since the beginning of the century. Queen Victoria never fully approved of racing; but the Prince acquired a small stable of horses in spite of maternal discouragement, and from that time forward the more important race meetings, particularly Ascot and Goodwood, became highly social events.

Across this happy scene of gaiety and security broke a seemingly unbelievable tragedy. During the first days of February, 1885, it became known that General Gordon and the famished garrison of Khartoum had been massacred on the twenty-sixth of the previous month. For 317 days the General had held out against the Mahdi, and only two days after the massacre the relief, which had been so long in coming, arrived. The poignancy of the disaster created an effect far beyond its international significance, and a wave of gloom was cast over the country. With the power of England at its height, it seemed incredible that such a calamity could have occurred except through the supineness of the Government. Very soon after Gordon's death Mr. Gladstone's government was defeated, to the outspoken relief of the Queen, who had been incensed at the tragedy of Khartoum.

With the return of a Conservative government under Lord Salisbury in 1886 the popularity of the Queen, which had been at a low ebb for several decades, increased, and she was persuaded to relax her long habit of seclusion and show herself more freely in public. Everywhere she received a tumultuous welcome, so that the rejoicings which in the following year accompanied the celebrations of the fiftieth anniversary of her accession were absolutely genuine. She became more beloved than ever before during her reign; and the Queen for her part found that the long years of mourning had miraculously ended, and that she was regaining an equanimity of temperament which she had not known since the death of the Prince Consort.

This alteration in the disposition of the Queen, this benign Indian summer, had perhaps no direct impact on the social scene, for the Prince of Wales, since his marriage in 1863, had been the acknowledged leader of society; and even the note of public criticism, which at times followed his behaviour, had not hindered him from becoming the most prominent figure in the social life of England. It was a prominence which was due not only to his position, but also to his remarkable gifts: the Prince was not entertained as a duty, as had been done, for example, in the case of several of the sons of George III, but as a pleasure. Nevertheless, the grey cloud of criticism and disapproval which was inclined to emanate from Osborne or Windsor Castle, and hovered over various sections of society, had a slightly chilling effect. It was a relief to all to find that, if it had not entirely disappeared, it was less inclined to obscure the social sunshine in general, and that it gathered thickly only over the heads of those who broke various sharply defined conventions.

The growing emancipation of women, which had been a salient feature of the previous decade, was continuing fast, and it was now generally conceded that young women occasionally possessed minds suitable for advanced training in serious subjects. In 1873 Girton

College for women had been opened, within a couple of miles of the centre of Cambridge, where instruction was given to about a hundred students in the classics, higher mathematics, moral science, history and so forth; all of them subjects which a few decades earlier would have been considered quite beyond the abilities of the female brain. At the beginning of the 'eighties, women students were admitted to university examinations; and though the authorities declined to be so rash as to confer degrees on successful competitors, degree certificates were handed out as a testimony of proficiency. Newnham, though opened to students about the same time as Girton, was at first organized on much smaller lines; while at Oxford Lady Margaret Hall and Somerville were simultaneously built to house resident students.

It was naturally not contemplated that girls of the upper classes should attend these university courses: they were expected to concentrate their attention on the London season. The attitude of the average father to this novel idea is shown in Lady Pentland's life of her mother, Lady Aberdeen. The young Ishbel Marjoribanks, encouraged by her tutor, Professor Meiklejohn, begged her father to allow her to try for entrance to Girton, which was lately opened. Her father was incensed, and rejected the proposal out of hand as "perfectly preposterous".

Still earlier than the university colleges, schools of an advanced type had been founded at which girls could acquire an education far in advance of that at the ordinary girls' school, and even further removed from what they were likely to obtain in their own homes from governesses, whose usual qualifications for teaching were merely poverty and respectability. However, under the auspices of those two remarkable educationists Miss Buss and Miss Beal, there came into being the North London Collegiate School for Girls and Cheltenham College for Ladies—the name of the latter being singularly evocative of the 'sixties during which it was founded.

In the 'eighties, then, it was possible for a girl of intelligence, and with some means at her disposal, to obtain a first-class education; but it was by no means easy for the majority of these capable young women to find posts worthy of their attainments, or which showed an adequate return on the money spent in ten years of education. The profession of teaching provided an obvious opening, but vacancies were not numerous and salaries were low. The average assistant mistress with full qualifications could seldom expect to earn more than £150 a year: only a few could hope to reach the highest positions in the profession.

The situation of these highly-trained girls, armed with their certificates, was often a depressing one. It was almost worse to have a knowledge of classics or higher mathematics and to be unable to find any suitable and rewarding outlet, than to be in the same position when comparatively ignorant. Provokingly enough, too, it was the ignorant who seemed to have the greater success in the marriage market. Gradually, however, new professions opened for women, though few of them were very glamorous and few gave much scope for exceptional ability. In 1881, for instance, the Post Office Savings Bank admitted women to clerkships, and this was the first step to the entry of women into the Civil Service where ever-increasing numbers were to be employed, and where the possibility of making a career was to be much improved in the course of years.

The invention of the typewriter in 1878 opened, though slowly, a tremendous field for the employment of women who had reached an average standard of education, and was eventually to absorb as many girls, probably, as any other single profession. It was to be a number of years before the girl was finally distinguished from her machine and became known as a typist. In H. V. Routh's *England Under Victoria* published as late as 1930 one reads of a "student . . . in love with a typewriter", and only perusal of the following passage indicates that it was the executant rather than the machine which excited the young man's affections.

With the development of the female mind there came also a development of the female body: indeed the latter was a more general and popular employment. Tennis, croquet and archery remained the three favourite open-air diversions for the summer, and tennis, which, as has been described, was the latest introduction of the three, began to assume a more regular form. It was no longer considered adequate to set up a loosely hung net across some patch of grass, and to lob the ball back and forth without any particular rules. Now the proper size of the lawn was laid down—though it varied with the years—the height of the net was lowered, the balls used were more lively. It was in fact becoming an altogether more vigorous and more exact game.

Swimming was taken up as a useful and beneficial exercise for women. No longer were bathers confined to summer dips in the sea, clad in voluminous serge dresses, from under the hood of a bathing-machine; but swimming baths were now opened in many of the larger towns where women, still dressed with the utmost modesty, could practise serious swimming and compete in women's races. Golf, too, was no longer a purely male pursuit and, in spite of the incommoding bustles of the mid-'eighties, a number of women managed to achieve a tolerable efficiency. Women's cricket was never a very serious affair, but it was indicative of their increasingly emancipated state that it was not difficult to raise two opposing teams amongst the country houses of any locality. Quite a number of these frivolous fixtures used to take place during the summer afternoons of the 'eighties.

Thus the advance of women into many spheres from which their mothers had been excluded, though gradual, was determined and successful. Nevertheless, the average male attitude towards their achievements remained both patronizing and jocular. Towards the end of the century it began to dawn on even the blindest male that there was nothing very funny about the competent way in which women were taking an increasingly active part in the life of the nation; but it was a slow, hard job for women to get themselves taken seriously. In the 'eighties erudite, bespectacled students would still be called "sweet girl graduates"; the muscular young women winning races in swimming-baths were, in spite of all evidence to the contrary, "water nymphs"; determined women with bows and arrows were inevitably "fair toxophilites"; while Lady Folkestone's Ladies' Orchestra, in which there were forty-six players including "many ladies of the nobility", was described in an illustrated paper of 1884 as "a very pretty sight". Whether the gentle devotees of harmony were able to produce any pretty sounds was left uncertain.

The resolute supporters of women's emancipation needed no stimulus to further their cause, but it is probable that they found some satisfaction in acting as a counterblast to the Aesthetic Movement which, during the 'seventies and 'eighties, made tremendous headway in the drawing-rooms of London. The slogan "Art for Art's sake" had been carried to surprising lengths since Whistler first used it, and the distinction between "aesthetic" and "effete" was swiftly becoming so fine as almost to defy definition. There had been nothing effete about the beginnings of the movement. No one could properly have applied the term to violent and irascible Whistler, while the early band of Pre-Raphaelites, from whom the movement descended, managed to be intellectual and aesthetic but at the same time exceedingly robust. Rossetti was a sturdy if eccentric figure, at least in his early years, and William Morris, with his wild energy and fighting spirit, must have been startled at the fantastic structures which were built on the strong, pure and fraternal principles of the Pre-Raphaelite school.

The paintings of Burne-Jones, however, provided admirable models on which enthusiastic aesthetes could base their appearances; and their intellectual outlook would, it was hoped, be moulded into a suitable form with their clothes and figures.

Women's fashions were not extreme as the 'eighties opened: bustles were small, and skirts, at least by day, were worn off the ground and without long, dirt-collecting trains sweeping behind the wearer. Thus the general lines were fairly simple, but at the same time dresses were complex and fussy in detail with much mixture of materials and colours, while waists were as small as intense restriction could achieve. The true aesthetes would have none of all this, and dressed entirely on lines of their own. Dresses were long and draping, covering the figure naturally, with no whale-bone corsets to pinch in one place and expand in another, as conventional fashion demanded. There would be the minimum of elaboration, and the materials used were mellow in colouring. If the wearer's neck were long — and slightly goitred in the way Burne-Jones and Rossetti admired—so much the better; and if nature

Aesthetes of 1880

From an engraving after George Du Maurier

had provided a complexion of a costive parchment colour, the fortunate possessor would have to be careful not to brighten it by indulging in any philistine exercise, such as tennis. The hair style presented few difficulties: a heavy fringe close down on the eyebrows, and a rich coil of hair on the neck. There was in fact much to be said for the unconventional style: it was simple, it was graceful, it was comfortable.

For women aesthetes, then, the situation was tolerably easy, but for men intent on showing a passionate interest in "Art for Art's Sake" the rules seemed less clear. Since he was a youth in his twenties Oscar Wilde had proclaimed himself a champion of the movement, and with his remarkable gift for publicity he had achieved notoriety early in life. But unfortunately nature had not cast him in the mould of a Burne-Jones picture. His face was pale, and his hair was dark, but even from early years there was little that was aesthetic about his figure.

171

Beneath the affectations and frills of the supporters of the Aesthetic Movement there lay a serious purpose. By no means all those who showed the most obvious signs of belonging to this intellectual band had a notion that there was any purpose whatever, except to be different from their neighbour. But the purpose *was* there: a determined endeavour to discard from life and from all forms of art the encumbering paraphernalia which had grown up through the years. This had been the aim of Morris and his friends, and it remained the fundamental aim of the next generation. But the vogue for the art of Japan had intervened; and this, which seemed to fulfil their principles so admirably, had infused a rather different note into their rendering of the arts. Had the exponents been less flamboyant, less determined to flaunt all that was conventional, their achievements would have been greater; but their extravagances led to constant ridicule in the hidebound pages of *Punch*, while the production of *Patience* in 1881 made it difficult for the extremists to continue in their former ways without appearing absurd.

The froth on the movement may have been blown away, but the decorative styles which its supporters had introduced crept into many homes where the Aesthetic Movement was unknown, and where it would have been looked on askance if it had been recognized. Peacock feathers, sunflowers, and lilies became a favourite motif of decoration in many forms and materials, and even the Queen herself had curtains made for Windsor of brown velvet adorned with a broad band of golden sunflowers. This, however, was the only royal concession to the Aesthetic Movement.

Cast-iron Door Porter
(*c.* 1850)

College Tutor's House, Oxford. Designed by Sir Thomas Jackson

CHAPTER VII

THE END OF AN EPOCH

1890–1901

IN retrospect a gentle, golden light seems to hang over the last years of a century. The dying eighteenth century, for example, in its arts, its literature, in its attitude to life generally, seems to have possessed the ripeness of late autumn, a rather disillusioned maturity of thought and feeling. Similarly, the nineteenth century during its last decade seems from this distance to have been passing into a peaceful decline, into a rosy sunset which adumbrated a brilliant opening to the new century. There is double reason for feeling that there was a pronounced sense of *fin de siècle* about these latter years, in that not only was the century ending, but the reign of Queen Victoria was also drawing to its close. The Queen was seventy years of age when the decade opened, and she had been upon the throne for over half a century: the majority of the people of England had known no other monarch, and the prospect of the inevitable disappearance of this venerable institution was probably a more potent factor in giving the impression of the end of an epoch than any measure of time.

It is easy to exaggerate this sense of the closing of a book, or perhaps more properly the turning of a page. Looking back from a point more than half a century later, it seems to have existed; but probably the majority of those living at the time were little conscious that they were witnessing the close of one of the most important eras in English history. At least they could not have known how turbulent a century was opening, and that their harassed descendants would recall the years of Queen Victoria's reign, which may have seemed to them full of effort and troubles, as a period of almost unadulterated peace, comfort and prosperity.

173

There were obvious differences between the closing of the eighteenth and the nineteenth centuries. The former drifted on in spirit well into the following decades, as if reluctant to accept the fact that it was no more; while its arts and manners, as the first chapter has endeavoured to indicate, had barely faded when Victoria ascended the throne. The nineteenth century in contrast closed with a snap, and the people of England turned briskly and expectantly towards the new age which was being introduced under the auspices of Edward VII.

The Victorian Age, indeed, had died in spirit some years before the Queen, and the last years of the nineteenth century had a closer affinity with the era about to open than with the decades which went before. Both socially, in the widest sense of the word, and in the arts great changes were evident during the 'nineties. For years past feudal England had been rapidly disappearing. The great families and the big landowners were still rich and important as seen by the measure of society, but their influence in the country was vastly diminished, while the introduction of Death Duties by Sir William Harcourt in 1894 was, in the course of years, to thin their ranks and empty their purses still further. The power of the State and the power of the people, on the other hand, were constantly increasing.

A number of the well-intentioned acts directed towards improving the conditions of the working classes, which were passed during earlier decades, have been mentioned in previous chapters; some had been failures, others moderately successful, but at last the cumulative effect of these beneficent measures was beginning to be felt. The measure which perhaps above all others raised the standards of the working classes was Mr. Gladstone's Education Act of 1870. At the time when the act was passed, about one million and a quarter children were receiving free education: at the opening of the 'nineties the number had risen to four millions and a half. This was highly satisfactory; but at the same time it led to a number of not very clearly envisaged consequences, one of the most unfortunate of which was to increase the drift from the land. Where an illiterate yokel was content to remain in the country village where he was born, the youth with a smattering of education was inclined to suppose that he could gain a better living by going into industry. Having once left the land, it was very rare that a worker returned, even if such jobs as he was able to obtain in a town were monotonous and unhealthy.

There was no doubt that the average lot of workers in industry was still far from pleasant, though the pay was improving. There had been much legislation to ameliorate industrial conditions: there was the Factory Act of 1891 which was designed to abolish sweated labour, and the act of 1895 limiting the number of working hours a week for a child to thirty, and for adults to sixty; while the Employers'

Liability Act of a few years later gave workers a security they had never previously enjoyed. Thus it came gradually to be accepted that the State had the right to interfere in commercial undertakings, so far as conditions of employment were concerned; and the workers realized that in necessity they could look to the State for protection. This was a great improvement on conditions in previous decades, when the individual worker was helpless to combat unjust treatment on the part of an employer. Wages, according to latter-day standards, continued to lag behind, for over these the State had no jurisdiction. In 1895 the average wage for a male worker, taking a level over both agriculture and industry, amounted to no more than 24/7 a week, while 24 per cent. of wage earners, and amongst these were included many farm labourers, received less than one pound a week.

The incomes of the vast masses of the middle classes were continuing to increase rapidly. The number of those whose annual incomes rose from the hundreds into the thousands was great, and with the high purchasing power of the pound a definite increase of a few hundred pounds a year would make an improved way of life quite feasible. With an assured income of between two and three thousand pounds, a man could keep his family in considerable style. A tall, solid house in one of the new quarters of London, Bayswater or South Kensington, would be well within his means, and he could afford a staff of five or six servants to run it; he could own his own carriage with a couple of horses, and employ a coachman to drive them; he could entertain discreetly, if not lavishly. All this would require careful management, and a wife who was not given to undue extravagance. But on making a fine show—*una bella figura*—depended social prestige, and it was well worth a reasonable degree of economy behind the stucco façade of the home in order to present a handsome front to the fashionable world.

The public conscience as to the necessity of helping the poor was more alive than it had been a few decades earlier. It was generally realized that it was not charity dispensed by Ladies Bountiful which was required, but a better reward for work. As a governmental policy this was absolutely accepted, regardless of party; but the attitude towards the less fortunate remained slightly patronizing, rather that of a patient schoolmaster dealing with backward children. Reforms were introduced for the good of the workers, and little attention was given as to whether the reforms were such as the recipients would receive with pleasure. That was beside the point: naturally the Government knew what was best for them, and it was essential that control should be exercised over them from childhood to old age, with the prime purpose of making them useful cogs in the humbler parts of the social mechanism.

The precept of Hannah More was still borne in mind that working-class people should be trained "in habits of industry and piety". This was all very well a century earlier, when the poor were illiterate and amenable, but by the 'nineties the spread of education had allowed them to form opinions of their own. Thus social reforms did not always develop as smoothly as had been anticipated, though this was no reflection on the benevolent concern which both the Tories and the Radicals genuinely felt for the lower classes.

Whether the concern of the average affluent member of the middle classes was equally genuine it is impossible to say, but at least it was not looked on as attractive to show heartlessness; a warm humani-tarian attitude was generally considered more becoming. The reply of the Victorian mother to her daughter who asked who lived in the slums of London: "Nobody who matters", showed an attitude to social problems which was fast dying out; though it is a human failing, equally pronounced in the twentieth as in the nineteenth century, to banish from the mind the misery of others.

It was proving of great assistance to many lower middle-class families that their daughters could now become wage-earners without being employed in a degrading industry. Girls were now becoming an asset, rather than a liability, as they had been at an earlier date. For those prepared to go into industry, domestic service, and occupations of a similar grade, there had always been openings; but the next degree upwards had been largely limited to serving in shops. Now, as described in the last chapter, girls could obtain posts in offices of all sorts. At first opposition to this innovation had been strong. Parents were dubious about allowing their daughters to take up work where their companions would be principally men; while employers were equally anxious about the effect the introduction of a few girls would have on an impressionable male staff. There was much shaking of heads: there would be less discipline and industry, the sober routine would be ruffled, there would be a marked increase in the illegitimate birth-rate, there would be all sorts of undesirable consequences to this mixing of the sexes in business. But these lugubrious forebodings were on the whole confounded, and women, with no ill-consequences to themselves, became as important in the lower grades of business as men.

Social conventions usually move from the top downwards, and it is rare to find the reverse process; yet it seems to have been the suc-cess of girls in commercial occupations which affected the position of their sisters in the leisured classes, and which brought them a freedom that the two previous generations had never known. Anxious mothers had accepted as axiomatic that their daughters could not remain alone for any space of time with a young man without the risk of their

A Bedroom of 1892

reputations becoming slightly tarnished. It was taken for granted that the mild-mannered, bewhiskered young men became uncontrollably amorous if they were left in the company of an unchaperoned girl; and many a mid-Victorian suitor found that it was a task of almost insuperable difficulty to obtain a few moments alone with a girl, so that he might make the most honourable offer of his hand. Since it was supposed that men were so rakish, it followed that no carefully brought up girl could ever be allowed to walk alone in London, except perhaps in a few of the quiet streets and squares of Mayfair and Belgravia; also it was highly undesirable that she should ever drive alone in a cab—a hansom was unthinkable—or make a train journey without an escort.

This attitude towards the relationship between young unmarried people survived from the raffish days of the Regency, when supervision was probably very necessary; but now that young men were able to work in the same City offices as young women without unfortunate consequences being inevitable, it began to dawn on parents that the same circumstances might prevail in their own polite drawing-rooms. It came to be realized that a rigid insistence on chaperonage cast a slur on the manners and morals of young men—and perhaps on those of young women as well. Thus at last girls were able to walk in the streets of London, or go shopping, without the unwelcome company of a duenna. No longer, if the family carriage had driven out

Cyclists of 1896

and there was no maid available, were they condemned to passing long afternoons incarcerated indoors—an unmerited penance which Mary, Lady Lovelace, writing in 1932, clearly recalled from the days of her youth. Some streets still remained out of bounds for an unaccompanied girl, and of these the principal ones were St. James's Street and Pall Mall, where they might have to endure the gaze of ogling clubmen seated behind their plate-glass windows. A girl's reputation would indeed have been besmirched if she had ventured alone near these male strongholds.

It was a happy chance that the increased freedom for young women should have coincided with the fashionable craze for bicycling, for here was a splendid opportunity for the young and active to escape from the critical eyes of parents and chaperones. While disporting themselves on a croquet or tennis lawn, the parties of young men and women were constantly under supervision; but with the aid of bicycles, the chicks could make long sorties from the nest, and the only hope was for the young to chaperone the young, and to trust that there might be some safety in numbers.

Considering the simplicity of its construction, the bicycle as a machine had developed rather slowly. The old "boneshaker", made of wood and shod with iron, had been designed by a Frenchman in 1867, and soon afterwards the young Prince Imperial was to be seen skimming along the paths of the Tuileries gardens in Paris. A few machines were imported into this country, but so uncomfortable, so inelegant were they, that they aroused little popular enthusiasm; and there seemed to be no future for the bicycle. About 1885, however, a new pattern was devised in Coventry, made of steel and with solid rubber tyres, which was a great advance; while a little later the pneumatic tyre provided a comfort which had been entirely lacking in the earlier models.

At first, cycling was regarded purely as an amusement, and one which also provided healthy exercise for the rich: it was not until some years later that the vast possibilities of the machine as a cheap form of locomotion for working people was appreciated, and by that time it had ceased to be a society craze. When the vogue began, bicycles were treated much as if they had been horses. The machine was sent in the charge of a footman to Battersea Park or Regent's

Park, whither the owner would drive in her carriage. Arrived at her destination she would leave her victoria and with a good deal of ceremony mount her machine, and ride gracefully round and round on the broad smooth roads. The exercise over, the bicycle was handed back to the keeping of the footman, and the lady would return home as she had come. The simple pleasure of bicycling entailed at that time a good deal of work on the part of a devotee's staff.

These two parks to the north and south of the social centre of the metropolis were the play-grounds of the more serious riders, those who were prepared to bicycle considerable distances, and even to negotiate the long gentle slopes to be found in the Outer Circle of Regent's Park. But Hyde Park remained, as it always had been, the fashionable centre, and here for a few seasons it seemed possible that the bicycle was about to oust the horse from its long-established place. It was claimed that a woman could look as well on a bicycle as on a horse. "As a cyclist she can be dignified, graceful and effective", wrote a contemporary enthusiast. She could also, of course, merit these three adjectives on horseback; but on the other hand she could never be certain that the wretched creature beneath her would make any of them applicable. There was much to be said for the machine as opposed to the animal, and though unbecoming spills occasionally occurred they were fortunately a rarity.

The gatherings of cyclists in the drive by the side of the Row became as social an occasion as the gatherings of horse-riders had been in the previous decade, and to many the machine became merely the means of joining a delightful party to which no invitation was required. A short spin from the Achilles statue to the Serpentine and back, and the rest of the morning could be given up to agreeable conversation. This new sport, too, had the advantage of requiring a special costume. It is sometimes supposed that tweed knickerbockers, spats, a mannish jacket, a high stiff collar, and a deer-stalker hat perched on the high coiffure of the period represented the usual get-up, but in fact anything so advanced would have been as much out of place amongst the fashionable crowd in Hyde Park as it would have been in a Mayfair ball-room. Across the Channel it was a different matter. The costumes in the Bois de Boulogne could be as eye-catching as anyone pleased, while the speed of riding was far more reckless and erratic than it was in the London parks. These Continental modes were not for London.

For Hyde Park, a cycling-costume in the mid-'nineties would be designed on severe but dignified lines: a close-fitting coat with full, mutton-chop sleeves, a skirt so long and voluminous that the busy, pedalling feet in buttoned boots would only just peep out beneath its heavy folds; a high, boned collar would entirely cover the neck,

"A fashionable pastime: the morning ride in Hyde Park" (1896)

while above this austere, tailor-made outfit would be a wide flat hat
luxuriantly trimmed with flowers and feathers, and tethered securely,
as was necessary, by strong hat pins and a spotted black veil knotted
at the back of the head. A boater would pass muster in the country,
but it would not be suitable for the Park. These clothes were quite
conventional; and the wearers, unlike their equestrian friends, would
look as well on foot as on their machines, though naturally if there
were no bicycle in the background their costume would normally be
far more elaborate, with a softening of feather boas and other
decorations.

Men, on the other hand, adopted a completely sporting attire for a
spin in the Park, probably a check coat, breeches, stockings and boots,
worn of course with a starched collar and a tweed cap. This was in
strong contrast to the immaculate suits of the male members of the
fasionable crowd leaning on the rails, who would not think of appearing in anything but morning or frock-coats and top-hats. Here was
one further example of the unjust liberty allowed to men, who could
bicycle at ease in more or less country clothes, while women had to
conform to the current fashion of wasp waists and full skirts. No
wonder the weaker sex was beginning to show the stirrings of revolt.

The bicycling craze caused some complication in country-house
parties. Lady Londonderry remarked in her memoirs that invitations
for week-ends in the 'nineties usually ended: "Please bring your

bicycle". Croquet mallets in velvet cases were trouble enough; now came this cumbersome addition to the luggage. The rich guest, however, travelled in comfort and, whether man or woman, would be accompanied by a footman in charge of the precious machine, who would spend his time polishing and cleaning after the outings along the drives or on the winding gravel paths of the garden. When going for a few days' holiday to a seaside resort, visitors would not fail to take their bicycles, and at Brighton the most august company, the Duke and Duchess of Fife for example, could be seen bowling, in patrician style, up and down the front.

The craze lasted several years but, like all such over-intensive vogues, began to lose interest for the fashionable world as it passed down to the lower strata of society. There developed, too, a new interest: "the horseless carriage". Quite early in the century steam carriages had been designed which had carried passengers at a speed of thirty miles an hour along level roads. But that this invention might become a dangerous competitor to the railways was at once clear to the business men who had these companies under their control. They prudently lost no time in exterminating this unexpected rival, by forcing through Parliament in 1836 the Locomotive Act which successfully strangled this promising new invention. The act remained in force for exactly sixty years, thus covering almost the whole of the Victorian era. But on its repeal, in 1896, several motor-cars were at once imported from France, where they had been running since the beginning of the decade. Two exhibitions of these curious new vehicles were held in London during the summer of 1896: there was one at the Crystal Palace, where a few examples were shown, in conjunction with horse-drawn carriages and coaches; and there was another—more specialized—at the Imperial Institute in South Kensington. At the latter the motors could show their paces by moving in a parade round the garden. The Daimlers from France were the most advanced in design, but the Kane-Pennington Motor Carriage from America also attracted much favourable notice. There were also two "remarkable petroleum motor tricycles" made by De Dion, and a tandem "which ran with wonderful ease and speed", made by Bollée.

There were several other makes of motor, but in general design they were rather similar. The lines followed were those of a wagonette or victoria, but the placing of the engine under the driver's seat necessitated considerable height, which was increased by the size of the wheels, which were wooden, and as large as those of a carriage. The bodies were usually designed for four, two on the front seat and two behind, with the driver manipulating the controls and steering with a tiller or a little vertically-placed wheel. In some motors the

"The Evening Parade of Auto-cars" (1896)

passengers faced each other, as in a landau, which must have effectively obscured all sight of the road for the driver. The tricycles had the extra comfort of pneumatic rubber tyres, but here also the passenger sat in front of the driver, and would have had the benefit of taking the full impact of a collision. None of these vehicles had the least protection from the weather. It was not until the reign of King Edward that the motor-car took its place as a useful form of locomotion.

Few can have foreseen at this time the extraordinary changes which the development of the internal combustion engine would create in the lives of the English. It was not difficult to envisage that transport would be revolutionized, and that with it the whole way of life of the greater part of the nation would be altered. That was fairly obvious: but that the security which England had enjoyed ever since it had possessed a fleet to defend its shores would, within twenty years, be destroyed was still hidden in the future. No longer was England to be a castle, unassailable within its wide moat, when the air above it could be penetrated by hostile craft.

Naturally in this era of increasing wealth and mechanical invention, architecture and the decorative arts were not backward in developing. The urge to build remained, as it ever has been with the English, very strong; and those who had been successful in making fortunes rushed with zest into the exciting world of bricks and mortar. Not many of the newly-rich were inclined to buy existing houses, however fine

182

their architecture might be, and to restore them: they preferred to erect a new building which would exemplify in brick or stone their own personalities. There was, too, the embarrassment for those with sensitive feelings of following in a country house the long tenure of an old family. The traditions which would have grown up through the centuries, the old retainers, the family monuments in the parish church, the ghosts in the corridors: none of these would give a cosy, homely feeling to new owners. To buy a house merely for the sake of the matured surroundings and to rebuild was less exacting, and carried with it a less obtrusive sense of the past. Occasionally, however, a newly enriched man, who had no interest in building or the acquisition of furniture, would buy a country house as it stood with the whole of the contents, including the family portraits hanging on the walls, which he would soon come to believe represented ancestors of his own.

As in the past, there were architectural books being published which aimed at guiding the ideas of those who were contemplating building. C. J. Richardson's *The Englishman's House* which went into several editions during the 'nineties was a typical example. In the Introduction he wrote:

"The erection of country mansions, villas and other residences, has of late years been greatly stimulated in our country. The enormous annually accumulated savings of the commercial portion of the community have induced a large amount of capital to be invested in such objects".

The author was right. Although there had been no time since the Restoration of Charles II when the construction of houses had not been carried on with enthusiasm, there were, during these late Victorian years, a far greater number of people in the happy financial position of being able to indulge this national trait. And furthermore, with new machine-made materials available, the costs of building were considerably reduced. Richardson explained the position:

"Tons of heavy and unsightly materials are now replaced by hundred-weights of decorative, and yet substantial, masonry and iron work. A number of modern elegant erections . . . are now made at an expenditure of stone or brick less by one-third in quantity than was employed in many old houses".

Here was the spirit of the age: new materials, new machinery, new methods, were leading to the abandonment of the laborious building of past generations, and the tedious process of manual craftsmanship was giving way to cheap machine-made productions. The author accepted the fallacy, a common one during the 'nineties, that thinness was identical with elegance, and that if the first were achieved the

second followed automatically. This tendency is shown in the examples he gives of his own work. In his early years, he had designed the pleasant classical lodges, much in the Decimus Burton tradition, on the south-west side of Hyde Park, but later he favoured an elaborate and finicking Tudor convention, as exemplified in his design for a small country rectory. This he called "the old decorated style of wooden architecture", while others were in "the domestic style of Henry VII", or were modelled on such houses as Rushton Hall in Northamptonshire.

The Englishman's House is not a work of great importance, but it is interesting as showing that the architectural taste of the 'nineties was not wholly influenced by the greatly improved work which Norman Shaw and his followers were now doing all about England, and that some were still looking back, at least in style if not in methods of construction, to the fashions of the middle of the century. There were backward glances too in decoration. "Stained deals, varnished", Richardson wrote, "afford a good material for panelling. It has been largely adopted in churches for pews with the best possible results."

Stained deal wainscoting was generally considered out of fashion as the Victorian era neared its end, but stained wood furniture was beginning to become popular. Mrs. Panton in *A Gentlewoman's Home* of 1896 advocated the use of furniture stained dark green, since it could be "easily renovated and altered", while "the unmoving surface of mahogany, walnut or ash" remains the same year after year.

Mrs. Panton provides schemes for all the important rooms of a house, but her proposals for drawing-rooms and morning-rooms have considerably less charm than parallel rooms of the 'sixties. The taste of almost a century ago may not be greatly admired, but at least it has now assumed some of the patina of age; the rooms of the 'nineties have not yet that advantage and we are prone to judge them by the taste of today, while to earlier rooms we allow the licence of being "period pieces". The colourings of the rooms of the 'nineties were generally pleasanter and more subtle than those of three decades earlier, but the thin, fussy furnishings have little to recommend them, in either quality or design. The general effect, even if the colourings were harmonious, was essentially restless, and the curious conclusion is reached that though taste was becoming more critical and refined, the attraction of the rooms was lessening. The thin furniture, which was aiming at elegance, achieved only an air of cheapness, and one thinks almost with nostalgia of the robust mahogany and brilliant chenilles and woolwork of the 'fifties and 'sixties.

"An end view of a Morning-room" (1896). Designed by Mrs. J. E. Panton

"A Corner of a Drawing-room (1896). Designed by Mrs. Panton

There were a few basic rules for decorating a room in the popular taste. Round the room there should be a panelled dado, preferably painted white, which would rise to the uncomfortable height of four feet six inches to meet a brightly patterned paper in contrasting colours, or perhaps a gold Japanese paper, or one of Liberty's "terra cotta damasque papers". Below the cornice would be a deep frieze bounded by a picture rail, and thus there would be a succession of horizontal lines round the room, designed to reduce any appearance of height, for height was considered an undesirable quality. If possible there would be arranged along one wall a fitment of shelves or cupboards with a superstructure of a fretwork arcade; or a "cosy corner" might be contrived, which would be separated from the main part of the room by a fretwork arch, partly Jacobean, partly Moorish in inspiration.

A mirror surrounded by a composition of niches and shelves still, as in the last decade, remained in favour as an overmantel, while the furniture would consist of attenuated objects in which the influence of Sheraton could be dimly discerned. A few tall wrought-iron lampstands would be topped by shades flounced, ruched, and trimmed with an elaboration reminiscent of fashionable hats of the day, while in a corner would rise a carved bedpost which had been transformed into a stand for a spreading palm.

186

The age of evergreens in the house had arrived. For many years the aspidistra had been a perennial ornament of humble homes, but now in polite drawing-rooms the curving, pinnate fronds of various sorts of sub-tropical palms became an inevitable decoration. There would be flowers as well, but no large bold displays: instead, small vases were put about an occasional-table, or a plant with a silk handkerchief tied round the pot would occupy a prominent position.

Progress towards an improved taste in decoration was indeed slow, but the standard of comfort, on the other hand, was advancing swiftly. Though the furniture of the period was so attenuated, the soft furnishings were in contrast fairly massive, and also were designed on lines more receptive of the human form than they had been earlier. The same can be said of beds, in which direction an improvement was long overdue. The average mid-Victorian bed was made without springs, the mattresses being laid on a lattice work of iron or wooden slats; and on this foundation, with so little resilience, a billowing feather mattress became almost a necessity. But various methods of springing were being introduced: the slats could be supported on springs on the bed frame, chain mattresses were devised, which were highly recommended for their hygienic qualities, but nothing was so satisfactory as the "French Spring Mattresses" which were the precursors of the box-spring mattress of today.

The general design of beds was changing as well, though the half-tester, from which merely token curtains hung from either side, maintained its preeminence over the fourposter which had been in vogue during the first decades of the century. But whereas the conjugal bed of a mid-Victorian house was made of mahogany, probably with a high panelled foot, in the 'nineties beds of brass or iron were introduced, which were more in consonance with the prevailing

"The Corner of a Cosy Sitting-room"
Designed by Mrs Waldemar Leverton

Lily Langtry's Bedroom (*c.* 1900)

fashion for lightness, and also had the merit of being easily moved.

More important than any of these rather minor additions to comfort was the increased convenience in planning to be found in houses of the 'nineties. Though in large country houses it was still possible to obtain all the servants required, it was becoming less easy in small houses where the servants led a less gregarious and cheerful existence, and where there were no man-servants to brighten the lives of the maids. Young architects, then, had to tackle the question of planning against a background of different conditions from their predecessors, and the first and most obvious compromise was to risk a few smells of cooking, and to put the kitchen in close proximity to the dining-room, rather than at the furthest end of the house. In London houses and in houses where there were basements—for houses, particularly in the suburbs, were still sometimes designed with this depressing variety of domestic quarters—lifts were introduced. They were cumbersome contraptions worked by hand, but at least they enabled coal, luggage and food to be raised from the basement to upper floors without undue strain.

An even greater advance was the improvement in plumbing and sanitation. Bathrooms had crept slowly into English houses. In the middle of the century a single bathroom was considered sufficient supply for an average house. The bath, made of copper or painted iron, would be a majestic affair raised on a step and encased in a generous surround of mahogany. Brass taps would allow an exiguous supply of hot water to flow into the bath. By the beginning of the 'nineties rather more than this would be expected in a house where many people were entertained. A popular arrangement was to fit baths into as many dressing-rooms as possible, rather than to put them in rooms of their own. The bath-dressing-room was at first claimed to be the height of convenience and luxury, but it soon proved to be otherwise. The room was generally cold, steam spread moisture on furniture and clothes in a damp mist, and in any case the presence of a bath was inclined to lend a slightly squalid air to the room.

Baths, however, were available; and the same could be said of W.C.'s, which were introduced more plentifully than had been thought necessary in the past. There were a few people who were convinced that earth-closets were more hygienic than those drained by water, and for these cranks there was an installation known as Moule's Earth System. In this arrangement the earth, which had first to be thoroughly dried, was carried to the top of the house—a lift would be almost a necessity—and deposited in a receptacle like a large tank,

A Drawing-room of the 'nineties

189

whence it descended through flues to the various closets. This system was advocated in books dealing with the construction of houses published as late as the last years of the century, but there can at that time have been few who preferred earth to water, except where there was a grave shortage of the latter.

An invention which brought added comfort to many houses in the 'nineties was electric light. Gas had been available for domestic use in urban areas from the first decades of the century, but incandescent lighting had many obvious advantages of which the principal was that of safety. As has been described in an earlier chapter, various forms of arc lighting had been successfully developed during the 'sixties, but it was not until Mr. Edison and Mr. Swan, working quite independently, invented the incandescent burner in 1879 that electricity could be put to domestic use. Development was swift, and within a decade current was available to houses in many parts of London and in the principal cities. As early as 1884 a visitor to Lord Randolph Churchill's house remarked that this was one of the few houses in London lighted by electricity, and added that it cost the owner at least fifteen times as much as any other form of lighting.

Simultaneously, plants were devised which could supply a rather dim light to the principal rooms of country houses. In 1889 Lord Wimborne installed electric light at his vast house at Canford in Dorset, and a few other country houses had been lit even earlier. It

"An Idea for a Bedroom" (1898). Mrs. C. S. Peel, Designer

was not until 1891 that the British Museum was illuminated by this convenient method, and an evening reception was held to allow the guests to admire the miraculous effect of the brilliant light in the vast, sombre galleries.

When Mrs. Peel published her book *The New Home* in 1898, some advocacy was clearly still necessary to persuade the reader of the superior merits of electricity over gas. "In any place where the electric mains are in the same street, it is not an expensive matter to have the house wired and connected," she wrote. And again: "The economy of electric light is due chiefly to the extreme facility with which the switches can be turned on or off". A public which had been used to gas-light for half a century was obviously not inclined to take up a newfangled invention without some persuasion.

Throughout the Victorian era there was gradual but constant change in taste and in fashion in all that pertained to average houses: architecture, planning, decoration, comfort varied almost as much as the dresses of the women who inhabited them. But while this slow evolution was in progress, the immediate surroundings of a house altered very little. Gardens, in fact, showed no more than a slight change in general design during a period of half a century. It was not that Victorians were uninterested in gardening, for a well-kept garden formed an essential prelude to a well-kept house, and also was not difficult to achieve when labour was so cheap. Moreover, a little delicate gardening was looked on as a suitable employment for the ladies of the household.

Horticulturally it was by no means a sterile period, for many new plants were introduced and others were greatly developed. Many varieties of trees were brought for the first time into England, the majority from the Far West of America where the country was being opened up by seekers after gold. There was the Wellingtonia named after the Great Duke, and Prince Albert's yew, which was given the Latin name of *Saxegothaea Conspicua* and was imported in 1849; two years later came the Western Hemlock known, in compliment to the Prince, as Albertian. Lawson's Cypress was soon after brought from the same provenance. But more beautiful than any of these was the cedar from North Africa, the Atlantic Cedar with its brilliant silver-blue branches, which was first grown in this country in 1845.

At the same time the general interest taken in botany was shown by the extraordinary success of Mrs. Loudon's book, *Ladies' Companion to the Flower Garden*. It was first published in 1841, and sold more than twenty thousand copies before the ninth edition, which appeared in 1879, was exhausted. Mrs. Loudon wrote a number of other popular books, but all were devoted rather to the science of

191

plants than to the general structure of gardens. She was the wife of John Loudon whose work is mentioned in Chapter II.

It is remarkable that during these active years there was so little alteration in garden design, but it may be that the Victorians were still a little dazed by the dramatic changes which had been brought about in gardens and parks by previous generations. The elaborate topiary gardens, with their straight walks and hedged enclosures, which had been devised when the later Stuart monarchs were on the throne, had been ruthlessly swept away by the devotees of the landscape school under the aegis of Capability Brown. For a time gardens had been entirely taboo, and the swards of the park, varied with groves and plantations, swept up to the very walls of the house. Humphry Repton, who lived until 1818, modified this draconian taste, and while maintaining the landscape lay-out in parks allowed an area of garden in the immediate vicinity of the house. These permutations seem to have left succeeding generations uncertain where to turn, and William Cobbett voiced the sense of bewilderment in *The English Gardener* which was published in 1829:

> "The present taste is on the side of irregularity. Straight walks, straight pieces of water, straight rows of trees, seem all out of fashion; but it is also true that neatness, that really fine shrub-beries and flower-gardens, have gone out of fashion at the same time. People, however, must follow their own tastes in these re-spects, and it is useless to recommend this or that manner of laying out a piece of ground."

There it was, then: all could do as they liked. But since no parti-cular direction or leadership had been forthcoming since Loudon's death in 1843, the average owner was content to maintain whatever garden he happened to possess, and not to alter its character in any manner. One very definite contribution to garden design was made during the Victorian era, but it was one which affected only a few great gardens: this was the introduction of the Italian style of formal design by Sir Charles Barry, as has been mentioned in Chapter II. These vast architectural schemes were exceedingly splendid and, where they survive, are probably more effective now, when the colonnades and flights of steps are given a romantic Piranesian character by the rampant growths favoured today, than when they were ornamented with the bright, tight bedding which the architect envisaged. On a grand scale these gardens succeeded, but when translated to small proportions, as was sometimes attempted, they were sad failures.

The average late-Victorian garden, then, remained for the most part an uncertain affair, little different from what it had been in the 'forties, with amorphous lawns, decorated probably with small flower-beds laid out in a geometrical design, and with gravel paths disappearing here and there behind groups of sad evergreens. Masses of laurel bushes would be ubiquitous, for not only were their glossy leaves admired, but it was believed that they distributed an uncommon amount of beneficial oxygen into the atmosphere. Anyone wishing to extend his garden—and a large garden was something of a social asset like a large house—merely enclosed another acre or two of the park, and carried on with the same formula of mown grass, gravel paths and conifers. There was a certain charm about these artless pleasure grounds, with their contrast between splashes of rather over-bright bedding and sombre evergreens, but there was little real beauty or variety, and seldom any horticulturist interest. Many people were quite aware that their gardens showed lack of invention and enterprise; and Lady Violet Greville, who contributed a chatty column each week to *The Graphic*, voiced a fairly general feeling when she wrote in 1896:

"I don't think we cultivate enough variety in our gardens. How tired we grow before the end of the summer of the eternal geranium and calceolaria border, of the bed of mignonette, or even of the strip of annuals and lilies which is supposed to be a concession to our artistic taste."

Gardens were indeed dull, but it was difficult to know where to seek new ideas.

Into the stagnant pool of the art of gardening there plunged the vital figure of William Robinson, who may fairly be said to have achieved for gardens what Philip Webb and his colleagues at the Red House achieved for domestic architecture a quarter of a century earlier. He wrote three most important books: *The English Flower Garden, The Wild Garden*, and *The Vegetable Garden*. The last of these was principally utilitarian, but the other two radically altered popular taste and introduced new life into gardens, both horticulturally and in design.

Robinson shared Capability Brown's antipathy to formal gardens. He came to London, he wrote in the first of his three books, at the time when the new Royal Horticultural Society's garden in Kensington was being laid out in a series of elaborate patterns, and the mock Italian garden was being constructed round the Crystal Palace in its new home at Sydenham. This would have been about 1860. Both these two gardens the young Robinson found highly distasteful, and it was a distaste he retained until the end of his very long life.

He may be said to have taken old-fashioned cottage gardens as the basis of his style, gardens in which flowers grew largely where nature had seeded them, and where one plant drifted into the next without rigid control or regimentation. "The foreground of English scenery", he wrote, "should not be daubed with a flower garden like a coloured advertisement." This was a frontal attack on the lines of scarlet geraniums, yellow calceolarias, and blue lobelias which formed the favourite Victorian border; and carpet bedding fared no better. He was as bitterly opposed to "all devouring privet and laurel" as he was to what he called the "railway embankment" style of landscape-gardening. By the latter he meant the favourite Victorian custom of bringing regularity into a steeply sloping site by creating terraces, on which formal beds could be laid out, with steep grass banks between them.

As is usual with innovators, Robinson's precepts seem rather excessively uncompromising; but without these intransigent opinions he would never have had so profound an effect on English gardening, for it is he who was the originator of the style of garden we admire today. He had able followers, such as Miss Gertrude Jekyll, who developed and broadened the principles on which he worked, but it was Robinson who first stimulated a popular taste for herbaceous borders and flowering shrubs, the two mainstays of present-day gardens.

It is perhaps not fanciful to suppose that Robinson's innovatory ideas had an effect beyond his own sphere. His gardens, emulating, but far surpassing, unsophisticated cottage gardens were, it was soon generally agreed, exceedingly attractive; yet equally it had to be admitted that many of the rigid modern houses and villas, which formed the focal points of these artful but apparently casual lay-outs, did not assimilate very happily with their arcadian surroundings. Even Norman Shaw's Tudor-style houses, though so romantic in intention, were inclined to exercise too dominant an influence over a garden. What was required was a true countryman's house in a style hallowed by tradition. What then could be better than to buy an old farmhouse or cottage and make a liveable house out of it? It was an idea which percolated slowly, and it was not until after the turn of the century that the notion of living in an adapted workman's cottage, however spacious, seemed quite free from a slight social stigma. However, once begun, the vogue for restoring redundant farmhouses and derelict cottages was to continue until the supply, which at first had been abundant, began to dry up several decades later.

There was the alternative, which many preferred, of building a new house in a "cottage" style; and from the beginning of the 'nineties the young architect Edwin Lutyens erected for his patrons buildings in the style of timber-framed Surrey cottages or tile-hung Sussex

194

farmhouses. These rather arty dwellings fitted peacefully into a casual setting of shrubs, grass walks, flagged paths, and herbaceous borders. Though Lutyens soon abandoned strictly traditional styles and stamped his buildings with his own strong personality, such a house as Munstead Wood which he began in 1896 for Miss Jekyll, who was often his collaborator, formed a pleasant unobtrusive centre for the garden which she developed round it.

How remarkable an advance in taste these houses of Lutyens's represented can be assessed by comparing them to the dreary designs, described a few pages back, which C. J. Richardson was advocating only a year or two earlier. They seem to belong to different eras: the former one judges by the standards of today, the latter seem to belong to the sombre years of mid-Victorian building. Essays in the vernacular were generally unsuccessful when attempted by less skilled hands, but half-timbered houses had rather unfortunately caught the public taste and were to be built in great numbers during the following decades: they thus belong—an acquisition of doubtful value—to the twentieth century.

Mock-Tudor cottages represented only a minor phase of building during the last years of Queen Victoria's reign: there were also at work a great number of highly competent architects who had the extreme pleasure, a pleasure denied to their present-day successors, of constructing large country houses for opulent clients. No particular style can be said to have predominated at this period, but houses were mostly firmly founded on traditional domestic buildings: they were solidly built and fairly conveniently planned replicas, which presupposed an adequate staff to run them. Few architects allowed their own personalities to obtrude so strongly as Norman Shaw and Edwin Lutyens; the majority remained content to keep carefully to precedent with the exteriors, and perhaps to indulge their fancies in the interior. In contrast to mid-Victorian houses, in which the rooms were often darkened by heavy mullions, there was a tendency to give the window-openings an exaggerated size; but at least plate-glass was no longer in favour and the windows were sub-divided by lead lights or wooden sash bars.

The higher-ranking architects cannot be held responsible for the astonishing examples of domestic building which were erected in great numbers along the southern and eastern coasts of England. Ever since railways had made travel to the coast easy, the seaside had been growing in popularity. Frith's picture of Ramsgate Sands, which had been hung at the Royal Academy of 1854 and had been bought by the Queen, shows a crowded holiday scene, and all through the Victorian era the summer crowds were becoming constantly greater. During the 'nineties the seaside had a tremendous vogue—a vogue

"Modern Dining-room panelled with Plain Oak" (c. 1900)

C. F. A. Voysey, Designer

which it has never lost—and many quiet little fishing villages found themselves converted during these years into noisy resorts. The local contractors, to whom much of the building was due, were free from all inhibitions and restraints: indeed the sea air seems to have given them that sense of licence which many Englishmen feel on leaving these grey shores for a holiday on the Continent.

Although there was much variety in detail, there was a general sameness in appearance about these monstrous buildings. The two essential ingredients were red brick and a great deal of white paint, paint on doors, windows, verandas, on balconies and gable barge-boards, in the interstices of sham timbering, and on projecting window-bays and corner turrets. It was assumed that buildings designed for enjoyment during the holiday season must be boisterously cheerful and bright, and this was the target at which the builders so disastrously aimed.

Between the designers of conventional houses and the perpetrators of seaside and kindred eyesores stood a number of architects and craftsmen of ability who remained apart from both groups. None of these achieved the fame of William Morris and his friends of earlier years, though their position was rather similar, except that they were not united as a band. One of the outstanding was C. F. A. Voysey, who was a designer both of houses and of furniture. The architectural style he favoured was a free rendering of the vernacular, with brick or rough-cast walls, lattice-windows, and plain gables and chimneys.

196

The effect was restrained and not unattractive. He liked to design the furniture for his houses, and it was here that he showed his strongest individuality. Though the rooms were generally low, the furniture was apt to be unexpectedly high. His chairs, for example, which were simple in type and soundly made in oak with rush seats, had very high backs, backs as high as Stuart chairs though in form they leaned rather to the late eighteenth century; while sideboards and such-like furniture would be flanked by tall tapering posts topped with flat caps, and bedsteads had similar characteristics. Though not to the taste of today, his furniture had both personality and merit.

Voysey's productions showed more invention than those of a group known as the Cotswold school, which consisted of Ernest Gimson, the Barnsley brothers, and one or two others. The firm which they formed was known as Kenton & Co. from the street in Bloomsbury where the workshops were first set up in 1890. Financially it was a failure, and three years later the three principal participants moved to Gloucestershire. Their designs were more traditional than those of Voysey, and were the epitome of solidity and good craftsmanship.

"Corner of a Modern Bedroom" (*c*. 1900). George Walton, Designer

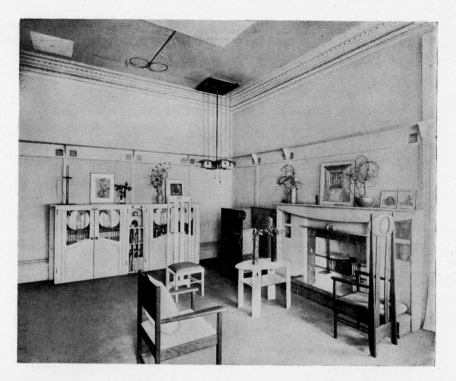

The Drawing-room of C. R. Mackintosh's own House in Glasgow (1900)

A more daring designer than any of the foregoing was George Walton who founded in Glasgow in 1888 a business known as "Ecclesiastical and House Decorators". The domestic furniture produced by this soberly-named firm was characterized by an extreme thinness, a thinness which was unusual even at a time when conventional furniture was excessively macilent. Walton seldom used oak, but preferred walnut, or birch stained black, ash or mahogany; beaten copper or forged iron was used for handles and decoration. These two materials he employed, too, for electric-light fittings, in which direction there was a new and open field; in the design of these he came near to the spirit of *art nouveau,* though he never indulged in the flowing, subaqueous line which the true spirit of the style demanded.

Though a native of Glasgow, Walton was not strictly a member of the Glasgow school of designers, in which Charles Rennie Mackintosh was the outstanding figure. The latter's furniture was in some ways a cross between that of Voysey and of Walton: it had the elongation of the former and the thinness and apparent frailty of the latter, but both characteristics he carried to extremes. Indeed much of his furniture appears as if seen in a distorting mirror, and there is little beauty in its grotesque and tortured lines.

FINALE

Much of the output of these various schools and craftsmen was far from satisfactory, yet the search for new forms and new materials indicated that there was an enquiring and enterprising spirit amongst many designers, who were determined to break away from the popular taste for the jejune variations on the Sheraton theme, and to produce work which was not solely derivative from traditional forms. The ultimate effect which these experiments had on the trend of design in furniture and decoration lies beyond the province of these pages, for it was not until the twentieth century that the influence of these schools spread beyond the narrow circles where their work was admired, and contributed to the formation of modern taste.

During the closing years of Queen Victoria's reign the whole tempo of life quickened: new ideas, new machinery, new measures of convenience and comfort were crowding forward. All that affected the life of the average citizen was gathering zest and speed. The previous decades in retrospect seemed positively torpid, so greatly enhanced were the vitality and pace of life. So much that had been accepted as immutable in former years was being overthrown, old conventions and fashions, and austere standards of conduct were being cast into limbo; indeed some might go so far as to whisper that the great Queen herself was something of an anachronism. However, she survived the opening of the new century by no more than a year and twenty-two days; and, after an intense display of mourning, the people of England turned with happy anticipation towards the new era which was opening so brilliantly before them.

INDEX

The numerals in **heavy** type denote the page numbers of illustrations.

Aberdeen, Marchioness of, *Frontispiece*, 168
Abrahams, Robert, 49
Achilles Statue, 165, 179
Adam brothers, 24, 43, 150, 151
Adam style, 151, **152**, 153, 163
Adelaide, Queen, 24
Aesthetes of 1880, **171**
Aesthetic Movement, 142, 170–172
Agriculture, *see* Farming
Albert Gate, Knightsbridge, 54, 121
Albert, Prince Consort, 24, 33, 34, 41, 54, **54**, 55, 62, 67, **71**, 77, 91
  as a leader in taste, 93
  gilt centre-piece designed by, 60
  model dwelling house, 69, **70**, 92
Albertian Hemlock, 191
Albert's yew, Prince, 191
Alexandra, Princess, 116
Algerine, 132
All the Year Round (Dickens), 72
Alton Towers, 27, **49**
Anglo-Catholicism, 111
Antiques
  growing interest in, 155
  lack of respect for, 115, 136
Apsley House, 61
Archer, Scott, 41
Archery, 139
Architecture, 1, 6, 14–39, **70**, 78, **79–81**, 82, 83, 92, **94**, 96, 100, **100**, 101, **101**, 102, **102**, 106, 125, **156**, 157, **157**, 182
  ecclesiastical, 77
  Palladian, 150, 151
  pattern books, 18, **32**, **33**, 37, **38**, **39**, 79, 91, 104
Architraves, 44
Armitage, Edward, paintings by, 160
"Art for Art's sake", 170, 171
Art Journal, 147
Art Nouveau, 198
Ascot, 166
Ashburton, Lord and Lady, 103, 104
Ashridge, 27
Aspidistra, 187
Assize Court, Manchester, 101

Atlantic, the (steamship), 89, **89**
Atlantic Cedar, 191
Austen, Jane, 9

Balfour, Eustace, 152
Balmoral, 92
  Queen's bedroom at, **94**
Barham, Rev. R. H., 40
Barnsley brothers, 197
Barry, Sir Charles, 17, 18, 35, 36, 50
  introduces the formal Italian garden, 192
Basements, 188
Basevi, George, 16, 17, 18, 35
Basket needlework, **145**
Bathrooms, 188
Battersea Park, 178
"Battle of the Styles", 18
Baudelaire, 142
Bayswater, 6, 16, 20, 30, 52, 56, 175
Beal, Miss, 168
Beards, 24
Bed, bedroom, 86, **94**, 103, **130**, **177**, 187, **190**, **197**
Bedford, Duke of, 1
Bedford Park, houses in, 148, **157**
Bedroom, Lily Langtry's, **188**
Beer Act (1834), 25
Beeton,
  Book of Household Management, 3
  Housewife's Treasury, 3, **5**, 133, **134**, 135, 136, **145**
Belgravia, **16**, 30, 50, 56
Belvedere (near Erith), 124
Bestwood, Notts, 103
Bethnal Green, 30
Bicycle, *see* Cycling
Birmingham Exposition of Arts and Manufactures (1849), 62
Blackburne, E. L., *Suburban and Rural Architecture*, 79, **79**
Blackmoor, Hants, 126–128, 157
Blackwell, Elizabeth, 108
Blenheim, 56
Blessington, Lady, 45, 46
Bloomer, Mrs., 58
Blore, Edward, 17, 18, 35, 68
Blue-and-white china, collecting, 141, 142, 148
Boehm (sculpt.), 24

Bonnardel, M., 69
Bookcase by Burgess, 103
Boudoir in Adam style, **152**
Bradford Temperance Society, 25
Bramston, Mr., M. P., 78
Brighton, 181
British Museum, 18, 35, 191
British Women's Review, 108
Brooks, S. H., *Designs for Cottage and Villa Architecture*, 37, **39**, 51
Brown, Capability, 192
Brown, Madox, 98
Buckingham Palace, 14, 25, 36, 55
Bulstrode, 103
Burden, Jane, 96
Burgess, William, 101, 102, 103
  house in Kensington, **102**, 103
Burne-Jones, Edward, 96, 98, 103, 158, 170, 171
Burton, Decimus, 18
Buss, Miss, 168
Butler, Samuel, 73
Butterfield, 144

Cabinet, oak, **69**
Cadogan Square, 158
Caldecott, Randolph, 161
Cambridge, undergraduate's room at, **131**
Cameron, Mrs. (photographer), 40
Camphine lamps, 48
Canford, 190
Cardiff Castle, 103
Cardigan, Lady, 74
Cardigan, Lord, 165
Carlton House, 42
Carlyle, Thomas and Jane, 46, **46**, 47, 55–57
  on country house life (quoted), 104
Carpets, 21, 42, 133
Carr, Jonathan, 157
Centre-piece designed by Prince Albert, 60
Chair, 21
  drawing-room, **23**, **149**
  easy, 115
  prie-dieu, **7**, 116
  Mackintosh, 198, **198**
  Victorian, early, 42
  Voysey, 197
  Walton, **197**, 198

Chambers, William, 144
Chandelier for summer-house, **90**
Chaperone, 176, 177, 178
Charity, 31, 71, 175
Chatsworth, 49
Chelsea
  Cheyne Row, 46, 99
  Old Swan House at, 159
Cheltenham College for Ladies, 168
Childhood, 73, 74, **75**, **126**
Children, employment of, 107
Chimney-pieces, 44, **45**, 83, 84, **86**, 151, **154**
Chimney-sweeping, 107
China, collecting oriental, 141, 142
Chinoiserie, 144
Chintz, 87
Cholera, 10
Church decoration, 62, **67**
Church parade, 165
Churches, 76, 94, 98
Churchill, Lord Randolph, 190
Classical style (archit.), 88
Clergy, position of the, 75
Clothes
  children's, **64**, **73**, **75**, **84**, **85**, **111**, **113**
  men's, 22, **43**, **46**, **71**, **84**, **111**, **114**, **134**, **139**, **140**, 141, **171**, **178**, 180, **180**
  women's, 22, **41**, **43**, **46**, **61**, **64**, **73**, **84**, **86**, 88, **111**, **113**
Cloverley Hall, Shropshire, **100**, 101
Clutton (architect), 103
Clyro Court, 140
Coaching Club, 165
Cobbett, William, *The English Gardener*, 192
Cobden, R., 57
Cockerell, Charles Robert, 17, 18, 35
Coke of Norfolk (Earl of Leicester), 35
Collecting
  art, 155
  bric-à-brac, 155
  oriental china, 141, 142, 156
Collinson, James, 61
Colour, 83, 85, 148, 151
Combe Abbey, 101
Comfort, increasing attention to, 187
Commerce, rising power of, 121
Compton Wynyates, 127, 150
Conservative Club, 35
Conservative Party, 123, 167, 176
Conservatories, 48, **49**, **161**
Conversation piece
  mid-century, **43**
  of late 'sixties, **114**
Cooking, 105
Copper, beaten, 198
Cornices, 44
Corn Laws, 54, 106, 120
Coromandel wood, 21

"Cosy corner", 186, **187**
Cotelan, 132
Cotman, John Sell, 43
Cotswold style furniture, 197
Cottage lodge in Old English style, **32**
Cottage residences, middle-class, **156**
Cottage Style
  gentleman's residence in, 37, **38**
  house in, **91**, **156**, **157**
Cottage, a Swiss, **12**
Cotterel, Mr., 60
Country life, 31, 124–125
Crace, 62, 67
Creevey, Thomas, 14, 26
Cretonne, 87, 132
Crimean War, 108
Crinoline, 88, 112, 114, **115**, 116
Croquet, 138, 139, 181
Crystal Palace, 62–69, 193
Cubitt, Mr., 16, 86
Cunard Line, 89, **89**
Curtains, 21, 42, 45, 84
Cycling, 178, **178**, 179, 180–1, **180**

Dado, 186
Daimler motor cars, 181
Daisies, diaper of (by L. F. Day), **146**
Damask, 45
Day, Lewis F., 131, 146
Dean and Woodward, Messrs., 82
Dean, G. A., *Selected Designs . . .*, 106, **107**
Death duties, 174
Decorated Gothic, 36
Decoration, 2, 3, 4, 131
Demidoff sale (1870), 156
De Morgan, William, 148
Department of Science and Art, 98
Deptford, 27
De Wint, 94
Dickens, Charles, 72
Dining-rooms, 105, **134**, **196**
Dinner party, **118**
  at Haddo. *Frontispiece*
Disraeli, Benjamin (Earl of Beaconsfield), 22, 105, 123
Dobson, Austin (on Kate Greenaway), 162
Domestic Gothic villa, **79**
Domestic service, 55, 57, **113**, 133, **134**, 188
Domestic Servants at Lacock Abbey, **41**
Door porter, cast-iron, **58**, **172**
Doors, four-panelled, 44
D'Orsay, Count, 45
Double-Cube room at Wilton, 98
Doulton, Messrs., 149
Doyle, Richard, 16, 118, 140
Drawers, chests of, 86
Drawing-rooms, 41, **84**, **87**, **161**, **186**, **189**, **198**

Drawl (affectation), 141
Drunkenness, 24
Ducie, Lord, 103
Du Maurier, George, 116, 122, **139**
Dunecht House, Aberdeenshire, 95
Dutch style, 158
Duveen, 155
Dyes, aniline, 83, 85

Eardley, Lord, 124
East India merchants, 122, 144
Eastlake, Charles, 41, 101, 102, 128–130, 144
  Hints on Household Taste, 3, 128, **129**, **130**
  History of the Gothic Revival, 80
Eatington Park, 81, 82
Eaton Hall, 78, 126, **127**, 157
Ecclesiastical architecture, 77, 78, 98
Ecclesiastical objects, 62, **67**
Eden, Miss Emily (quoted), 111
Edis, Robert, 3, 148, 153, **154**
  Decoration and Furniture of Town Houses, 148
Edison, 190
Education, 174
Education Act (1870), 174
Eglinton Castle, 28
Eglinton tournament, 27, 28
Electric light, 190
Electric fittings, 198
Elme, 18
Employer's Liability Act, 175
Employment of women and children, 107
Emslie, A. E. *Frontispiece*
Encaustic tiles, 129, 148, 149
Endsleigh, Duke of Bedford's house at, 1, **2**
Enfield and Edmonton Railway, 53
"Engaging the New Page", **113**
Escritoire, **149**
Etty, 44
Eugénie, Empress, 117
Exhibition
  Great (1851), 13, 41, 62–69, **64**–**69**, 91, 115, 146
  International (1862), 98
Exposition of Arts and Manufactures (1849), 62

Factory Acts (1891, 1895), 174
Family group of late 'sixties, **111**
Family prayers, 73, **73**, 111
Farming, 106
  decline of, 119
  drift of labour from, 106, 120
Fashions, *see* Clothes
Ferrey, 103
Feudal England, 174
Fielding, Copley, 44

INDEX

Fife, Duke and Duchess of, 181
Fitzwilliam Museum, 18, 35
Fonthill, 27, 36
Food, 55, 93
Footmen's liveries, 133
Ford Castle (Northumberland), 78
For Sale (painting), **61**
Fountain
　garden, **51**
　glass, at Great Exhibition, 68, **68**
　scent, **117**
Franco-Prussian War, 119
Freeman, Mrs., 137
Free trade, 119
French Gothic, 79, 80
"French Spring Mattress", 187
Fretwork, 136, 186
Friezes, 151
Frith, William P., 44, 195
Furniture, 6, 7, **8**, 42, **65**, 66, **66**, 67, 68, **69**, **84**, 86, **86**, 87–90, **90**, 96, **97**, 103, 105, **113**, **114**, 115, 128, 129, **129**, 130, **130**, 131, **132**, **134**, **135**, 144, 147, 148, **149**, 151, **152**, 156, **177**, **185**, **189**, 196, **197**, 198
　poor quality of, 115

Garden city (Bedford Park), **157**, 158
Gardens, 50, **51**, 191
Garrard, Messrs., 60
Gas Light and Coke Company, 47
Gas lighting, 47, **47**, **48**
Gaskell, Mrs., 72
George IV, 13, 22, 42
Gideon, Sampson, 123
Gillow and Co., 8, 66, 152
Gimson, Ernest, 197
Girton College, 167
Gladstone, Mr. W. E., *Frontispiece*, 111, 123, 124, 167, 174
Glasgow School of furniture designers, 198, **198**
Glass, 20
Gloom, modern ideas on Victorian, 9, 10
Goncourt, Edmond de, 142
Goodwood, 166
Gordon, General, death of, 167
Gore House, 45, 46
Gothic Style, 12, 13, 17, 18, 19, 36, 62, 68, 77, 78, 79, **79**, 82, 83, 88, 94, 95, **100**, 101, **101**
Grand Junction Railway, 27
Graphic, The, 193
Grates, 45, **45**, 84, 148
Greek mythology as inspiration for decoration, 153
"Green Dining-Room, The", 98
Greenaway, Kate, 161

Greenwich, 27
Greville, Charles, 53
Greville, Lady Violet, 193

Haddo, dinner party at, *Frontispiece*
Hair styles
　men's, 24
　women's, 22
Hamilton Palace, sale at, 156
Hampstead, 162
Hampton Court, 148
Harcourt, Sir William, 174
Hardman, Messrs., 62, 67
Hare, Augustus, 55, 73, 74, 76, 111
Harewood, 50
Hatfield House, 150
Hawksmoor, 13, 151
Haydon, Benjamin, 44, 56, 159
Heating, 39
Hedley, William, 26
Hennessy, James Pope-, *Flight of Youth*, 110
Hertford, Lord, 155
Hill, Octavious, 40
Hilton, J. and W., 65
Hobbies for women, 136
Holland, Henry, 19
Holland Park, 162
Horse racing, 165
Horse riding, 165, 179
Horsey, Miss Adeline de, 165
Hot-water systems, 39
House in "Cottage style", **91** **156**, **157**
House, Prince Albert's model, 69, **70**, 92
House of Lords, heating system of, 39
House party, the, 124–125
Household Words, 72
Housing, 69, **70**, 71
　rural, 106
Hudson, George, 53, 121
Humanitarianism, 176
"Hungry 'Forties", 34, 54, 120
Hunt, C., 126
Hyde Park, 65, 165

Illustrated London News (quoted), 66
Imperial Institute, S. Kensington, 181
Imp of Mischief (painting), **126**
Income tax, 35
Industry, rising power of, 121
Interior decoration, 2–4, **131**, **132**, **134**, **135**
Internal Combustion engine, 182
International Exhibition (1862), 98
Ionic Style, villa in, 38, **40**

Jackson, Sir Thomas, 173
Japanese art, craze for, 142, 172
Jeckell (architect), 142

Jekyll, Miss Gertrude, 194, 195
Jews, entry of, into English society, 123
Johnson, John (architect), 78
Jones, Inigo, 65
Jones, John, 155
Jones, Kennedy, 164
Jubilee (1887), 10

Kane-Pennington Motor Carriage, 181
Kauffmann, Angelica, 153
Kelmscott House, 99
Kelmscott Manor, 99
Kensington Palace, 14
Kensington, South, 6, 52, 162, 175
Kent, Duchess of, 14
Kent, William, 24
Kenton and Co., 197
Kerr, Robert, *The Gentleman's House*, 3, 104, 135
Kilburn, 28
Kilvert, Revs. Robert and R. F., 74, 139, 140
Kingsley, C., *The Water Babies*, 107
Kitchen equipment, 105
Kneller, Sir Godfrey, 159
Knightshayes, Devon, **101**, 102
Knole, 150

Labour, 54–57, 106, 119, 120, 174
Lace-making, 136
Lacock Abbey, 40, **41**
Lacquer work, 144
Ladies' Orchestra, Lady Folkestone's, 170
Lamps, 48
Lampstands, 186
Land, the drift from the, 106, 120
Landor, Walter Savage, 44
Landowners, 106, 120
Law courts, 36, 95
Lawn Tennis, 138, **139**
Lawrence, Sir Thomas, 44
Lawson's Cypress, 191
Leech, John, 161
Leighton, Frederick, Lord, 159, 162
　Daphnephoria, 160
Leopold, King of Belgians, 34
Leverton, Thomas, 19
Leverton, Mrs. Waldemar, 187
Leyland, Mr., 142
Liberal Party, 123
Liberty's, 143
Lifts, 188
Lincrusta, 151
Lindley, John, 157
Liverpool, 26, 27
Locomotive Act (1836), 181
Lodge, 52
　in Doric style, double, **33**
　in Old English style, Cottage, **32**

INDEX

London, 56, 77
  "Suggestions for the improvement of the Western part of", 29
Londonderry, Lady, 180
Long, Edwin, paintings by, 160, 162
  house in Hampstead, 162, **163**
Loudon, John, 50, 192
Loudon, Mrs., *Ladies' Companion to the flower garden*, 191
Lovelace, Mary, Lady, 178
Lutyens, Edwin, 194

Mackintosh, Charles Rennie, 198
  drawing-room of, **198**
Magazine of Art, 137, 149, 150
Mahogany, 21, 42, 87
Mamhead, Devon, 55
Manchester, 26
  Assize Court, 101
Manning, Cardinal, 111
Mansfield's new domestic gas light apparatus, 48
Marble, 44
Marble Arch, 14
Marjoribanks, Ishbel, 168
Marlborough Club permits smoking, 135
Marot, Daniel, 148
Married Woman's Property Act, 109
Martineau, R. B., 44, 161
Martyr's Memorial, Oxford, 78
Mediaeval Court (Exhibition), 62, 67, 78
Meiklejohn, Prof., 168
Melbourne, Lord, 14, 25
Melchet Court, 103
Messenger and Sons (Iron-founders), 62, **90**
"Midas, Sir Georgius", 122
Middle classes, 175
Mill, J. S., *Subjection of Women*, 109
Millais, Sir John E., 159, 162, 163
Milnes, Monckton, 110
Mirrors, 21, 84, **85**, 89, 186
Monopodium, 42
Montagu House, 35
Moore, Mr. and Mrs. (U.S.A.), 155
Moorland, nr. York, residence at, **107**
More, Hannah, 176
Morning-room, end view of, **185**
Morris, William, 8, 13, 28, 95–99, 115, 128, 142, 144, 158, 170, 172, 196
Morris, Marshall, Faulkner & Co., 97, 98, 103
Motor-car, The advent of the, 181, **182**
Moule's earth system, 189
Moustaches, 24

Municipal Reform Act (1835), 29
Munstead Wood, Miss Jekyll's house at, 195
Murdoch, William, 47
Music, 137
Myers, 67, 68, 69

Napoleon III, Emperor, 110
Nash, John, 14, 16, 17, 35, 38, 77
National Health Society, 108
Needlework pictures (Grospoint), 85
Nesfield, Eden, 100, 101
Nevill, Ralph, 164
New Oxford Street, 71
New rich, the, 122
New University Club, 88
Newnham College, 168
Nightingale, Florence, 108
  Cassandra (unpubl. novel), 108
North London Collegiate School for Girls, 168
Nottingham lace, 84
Novelists, 162
Nursing, 108

Oak settle, Morris's, 97, **97**
Ockwells, 102
Old Swan House, Chelsea, **159**
Orangeries, 49
Orchardleigh Park, Somerset, **80**, 81
Oriental art and pottery, public taste for, 142–145
Ornamentation, excessive, **58**, 59, **60**, 148, 149
Ornaments, 148
Osborne, 77, **86**, **87**, 92, 167
Osler, Messrs., 69
Ouida, 162
Overmantle, 186
Oxford
  college tutor's house, **173**
  Lady Margaret Hall, 168
  Martyr's Memorial at, 78
  Museum, 82
  Queen's College, 151
  Somerville College, 168
  undergraduate's sitting-room, 135
Oxford Street, 30

Pageant, 27, 28
Paget, H. M., 157
Painting, 91, 92, 137
  vogue for contemporary, 159
Palladian architecture, 150, 151
Pall Mall, 35, 178
Palmerston, Lady, 116
Palmerston, Lord, **71**, 72, 110
Palms, 186
Panton, Mrs. J. E., 3, **185**, 186
  A Gentlewoman's Home, 185

Papier mâché furniture, 21, 43
Paris fashions for March, **115**
Park, In a (painting), **166**
Parker, Louis Napoleon, 28
Parliament, Houses of, 18, 36
Parson, the poor, 76
Patterns, material, 133
Paxton, Joseph, 49, 63
Pears's Soap, 159
Pearson, J. L., 81, 82
Peel, Mrs. C. S., 3, 190
  The New Home, 191
Peel, Sir Robert, 55
Pelmets, 21, 42
Pentland, Lady, 168
Pentonville Prison, 35
Photograph album, the family, 112
Photography, 40, 83, 112
Pianoforte, 105, **189**
  Tadema "Byzantine", 163
Picnic, 140, **140**
Pictures, 43
Pier Glass, 21
Pimlico, 6
Pio IX, Pope, 110
Plague, the Great (1665), 30
Plaw, John, 19
Plumbing, 188
Plush, 132
Pokerwork, 136
Porcelain, 141–145, 155
Porden, William, 78, 126
Pottery, 142, 143
Poverty, 29, 54, 55, 175
Poynter, 103, 161
Pre-Raphaelites, 8, 10, 28, 95, 97, 99, 142, 170
Presentation Plate, 60
Preston Temperance Society, 25
Prince Imperial, 178
Prince's Gate, London (No. 49), 142, **143**
Prinsep, Val, 162, 166
Prior Park, Bath, 151
Problem Picture, the, 161
Proust, 82
Public houses, 25
"Puffing Billy", 26
Pugin, Augustus, 8, 18, 27, 36, 62, 67, 77, 78, 94, 97
  Contrasts, 77
Punch, 57, 88, 110, 122, 172

Quar Wood, Glos, 81, **81**
Queen's House, Chelsea, 99

Radicals, 176
Railway, 26, 52–54, **54**
Railway mania, 27, 52–54
Ramsgate Sands (Frith), 195
Raverat, Gwen, *Period Piece*, 116
Rectory in Old Decorated style of wooden architecture, **184**
"Red House, The" (Wm. Morris), 96, 97, 98, 157
Red Lion Square, 96, 97

Reform Bill, 34
Reform Club, 18, 35
Regency, 22, 33, 147, 177
Regency drawing-room, 42
Regent's Park, 38, 167, 178
Reid, Dr., 40
Religious revival, 72, **73**
Repton, Humphry, 49, 192
Richardson, C. J., *The Englishman's House*, 183, 184, 195
Riesener, furniture by, 156
Robinson, P. F., *Rural Architecture and Designs for Ornamental Villas*, 37, **38**, 106
Robinson, William, 193
"Rocket," the, 26
Roman Catholicism, 110
Romford, Church of St. Edward, 78
Rosewood, 21, 42, 87
Rossetti, D. G., 98, 99, 142, 170, 171
Rothschild Family, 124
Rothschild, Constance (quoted), 124
Rothschild, Lady de, 94
Rothschild, Baron Lionel, 124
Rothschild, Sir Nathaniel, 124
Rotten Row, 165
Rowdyism, upper-class, 25
Royal Academy, 44, 158
Royal Exchange, 35
Royal Horticultural Society, 193
Royal Photographic Society, 41
Royal railway carriage, **54**
Rural poor, the, 31
Ruskin, John, 76, 82, 111
   Stones of Venice, 82

St. Albans, Duke of, 103
St. George's Hall, Liverpool, 18
St. Giles, 71
St. James's, clubhouses of, 20, 88
St. James's Street, 35, 178
Salisbury, Lord, 167
Salivariums, 136
Salvin, Anthony, 18, 19, 55, 128
Sanitation, 30, 188
Scarisbrick Hall, 18
Scent fountain, **117**
Schefer, Ary, 156
School of Medicine for Women, 108
Schreiber, Lady Charlotte (quoted), 9, 153–156
Scotney Castle, 18, **19**
Scott, Gilbert, 18, 78, 94, 95, 98
Seamore Place, 45
Seaside, the, 195
Sefton, Lord, 26
Selborne, Lord, 127
Self-made man and society, the, 121

Sentimentality in art, 160–162
Servants, 55, **113**, 133, **134**, 188
   at Lacock Abbey, **41**
Settle, Morris's oak, 97, **97**
Sèvres vase, 156
Seymour, Lady, 28
Shannon, James, 162
Shaw, R. Norman, 156, 157, 158, 159, 163, 194
Sheraton, 151, 153, 186
Shrublands, 50
Sideboard, dining-room, **129**, 148, **149**
Silver ware, 87
Sitting-room
   corner of a cosy, **187**
   Princess Beatrice's, 86
   undergraduate's, **132**, **135**
Slums, 29, 30, 71
Smirke, Robert, 17, 18, 35
Smirke, Sydney, 29, 35
Smith, Cecil Woodham-, 108
Smith, Mr. (architect), 19
Smith, Dr. Protheroe, 72
Smoking, 135
Smoking-rooms, 135, 136
Snodhill Castle, 140
Soane, Sir John, 17, 44
"Société de Londres" (1885), 165
Society, 54, 120–125, 164, 165
Society for Improving the Dwellings of the Working Class, 70, 71
Society for the Preservation of Ancient Buildings, 98, 99
Sofa, 42
   sociable, **65**
   Wanstead, **66**
Solomon, Simeon, 103
Somerset, Duke of, 103
Spencer, Herbert, 139
Sphairistiké, 138, 141
Stafford House, 31
Stained deal panel, 184
Stanhope, Lady Elizabeth Spencer-, 74
State Party, A (1864), **118**
Stead's wooden paving blocks, 31
Steam carriages, 181
Steam-power, 59
Stephenson, George, 26
Stockton and Darlington Railway, 26
Stoke Rectory, 76
Stone, Marcus, **160**, 161, 162
Strachey, Lytton, 14
Stratfield Saye, 56
Strawberry Hill, 13, 18, 78
Street, George E., 36, 95
Street laying, 30
Stuart tartan, 93
Suffrage, 120
Sunday, the English, 111
Sunday school, 58
Sutherland, Duke of, 31
Sylvester's open grate, **45**
Syon House, 98, 150, 151

Table-cloths, 84, 88
Tables, 21, 42, 133
   console, 21
   dining-, 87
   library, **8**
Tadema, Alma, house of, 162, 163, **164**
Taine, Henri, 109, 116
Tait, Robert, 46, 47
Talbot, William Fox, 40, **41**
Taste
   changing, 4, 130, 147, 150, 151, 183–191
   decline in, 29, 59, 65
   sentimentality of popular, 161
Taylorian Institute, Oxford, 18, 35
Teaching for women, 168
Teetotalism, 25
Telegraph, 27
Temperance, 25
Tenniel, Sir John, 85
Teulon, 103
Tewkesbury Abbey, restoration of, 98
Tiles
   encaustic, 129, 148, 149
   hand-painted, 149
Times, The, 30, 34
Tite, Mr., 35
Toilet, The, **5**
"Tom and Jerryism", 26
Tortworth, Glos., 103
Toulmin, Camilla, *Landmarks of a literary life*, 45
Travellers' Club, 35
Trevelyan, Prof. G. M. (quoted), 29
Trousers for women, 88
Tudor Gothic, 79, 80, 103, 125, 127, **184**, 195
Turner, J. M. W., 44
Turner, Richard, 25
Twistleton, Mrs. Edward, 75

Umbrella stand, cast-iron, **60**

Vanbrugh, Sir John, 13
Varley, 44
Vases, 187
Vauxhall Gardens, 48
Veneers, 21
"Vicarage" Gothic, 83
Victoria (balloon), 48
Victoria Park, 31
Victoria, Queen, 13, 14, 24, 25, 33, 41, 54, **54**, 92, 117, 123, 124, 138, 146, 166, 172, 173
Victoria Street, 70
Victoria and Albert Museum, 98, 155
   Exhibition of furniture (1952), 8
Victoria and Albert pattern (chintz), 87
Volunteer Movement, 110, 118
Voysey, C. F. A., 196

Wages, 8, 106, 174, 175
Wales, Prince of, 123, 124, 135, 165, 166, 167
Wallace Collection, 155
Waller, Sidney, 161
Wall-papers, 99
Walpole, Horace, 12, 36
Walton, George, 197, 198
Ward, Mrs. Humphrey, 162
Wardrobes, 86
Water-closets, 189
Waterford, Lord and Lady, 26, 78
Waterhouse, Alfred, 6, 88, 100, 126, 127, 128, 157
Watts, G. F., 44, 162
Wax flowers, vase of, **11**
Webb, Sir Ashton, 36
Webb, Philip, 95, 98, 157
Week-end house-party, 124
Wellington, Duke of, 56, 60
Wellingtonia, 191
Wentworth Woodhouse, 56

Westmacott, 35
Westminster
    Duke of, 126
    Palace of, 36
What-not, Louis XV, **7**
Whippingham Parish Church, 77
Whiskers, 24
Whistler, J. M., 142, 143, 170
Whitechapel, 30, 31
Whyte-Melville, bust of, 24
Wilde, Oscar, 171
Wilkie, David, 44
Wilkins, William, 17
William IV, 13, 14, 22, 24
Wilton, Double-Cube room at, 98
Wimborne, Lord, 190
Winchester Guildhall, 101
Windows, 20
Windsor Castle, 25, 55, 94, 167, 172
Wines and spirits, 24

Women
    education of, 167, 168
    employment of, 107, 176
    hobbies for, 136
    position of, 107, 137, 167, 176
Women's Rights Campaign, 138
Wood-carving, 136
Wooden paving blocks, Stead's, 31
Working class, *see* Labour
Wornum, R. N., 65
Worsley Hall, 68
Wyatt, James, 18, 36
Wyatt, T. H., 80, 81
Wyatville, Sir Jeffrey, 2, 17
Wylam Colliery, 26

Yew, Prince Albert's, 191

Zola, 142